SABRE TO STEALTH

50 YEARS of the UNITED STATES AIR FORCE 1947–1997

Commemorating the 50th anniversary of
The United States Air Force

Compiled by PETER R MARCH

Publishing Director: PAUL A. BOWEN
Managing Editor: PETER R. MARCH
Assistant Editor: BEN DUNNELL
Editorial & Picture Research USA: KAREN PITTMAN, COL WAYNE PITTMAN USAF Ret'd
Research Editors UK: ROBBY ROBINSON, BRIAN STRICKLAND
Art Consultant: WILFRED HARDY GAvA
US Consultant: C. R 'BOB' DUTTON
Design: GRAHAM FINCH
RAFBFE Publishing Unit: CHERYL CLIFTON, CLAIRE LOCK, JULIET SMITH
Sponsorship Manager: CLIVE ELLIOTT
Consultant: MIKE BARNES

Cover Painting: *Fifty Years Have Flown* specially painted for 'Sabre to Stealth'
by WILFRED HARDY GAvA

Published by The Royal Air Force Benevolent Fund Enterprises
Building 15, RAF Fairford, Glos, GL7 4DL, England.

© The Royal Air Force Benevolent Fund Enterprises 1997

ISBN 1 899808 80 9
British Library Cataloguing in Publication Data.
A catalogue record for this book is available from the British Library

SOLD FOR THE BENEFIT OF
THE ROYAL AIR FORCE BENEVOLENT FUND

Produced in Hong Kong by Jade Productions

CONTENTS

The relationship between the Royal Air Force and the United States Air Force is as unique as it is strong. Nowhere else in the world do two armed services of two different countries cooperate as well or as extensively. Nowhere else could you find two such forces who have fought so valiantly and won so convincingly as the USAF and RAF.

This bond was formed during the great air battles that were instrumental to victory in World War II. American bombers and fighters rose from airfields across East Anglia and along with their RAF brothers, swept the skies over occupied Europe. This partnership continued during the long, dark days of the Cold War when our two Air Forces again joined forces to provide the deterrence to maintain world peace. This relationship also bore fruit in the Gulf War, where our Air Forces proved, yet again, the devastating power wielded from the air.

US Air Force pilots still fly from some of the same British airfields that saw their grandfathers and fathers launch into battle. This tradition continues even today in the skies over Bosnia and Iraq, where our crews serve in the same spirit of those who went before them to places like Berlin, Tripoli and Baghdad.

So it is truly fitting that the RAF Benevolent Fund publishes *Sabre to Stealth*. The book magnificently portrays the first 50 years of the US Air Force, a history greatly enriched by our close ties with the RAF. Together we have been, and will continue to be, victors in war and partners in peace.

Sheila E Widnall
Secretary of the Air Force

DEPARTMENT OF THE AIR FORCE
OFFICE OF THE CHIEF OF STAFF
UNITED STATES AIR FORCE
WASHINGTON DC 20330

It is a great honor to contribute a foreword to this magnificent volume on the rich history of the United States Air Force. Sabre to Stealth dramatically captures the development of our service over the past 50 years, in both word and picture.

The existence of the United States Air Force is inextricably linked to the Royal Air Force. We took our doctrinal bearings from the RAF's ground breaking efforts in World War I. We built our foundation upon the shared heritage of valor and sacrifice in battling the Axis powers during the Second World War. Our services combined to safeguard the Western world against communist tyranny and aggression during the Cold War. We fought side by side in the desert to liberate Kuwait and to occupy Iraq solely with airpower. Together again, we employed precision air strikes to compel the warring parties to sue for peace in the battered Balkans. We salute the memory of all those who have gone before us. Their devotion to duty serves as a tremendous example to all airmen.

Over the last half-century, the capabilities of military aviation have expanded enormously – from the era of the propeller-driven aircraft to the age of supersonic fighters, stealth bombers and earth-circling satellites. The dedicated efforts of visionary airmen and scientists from around the world have brought us to a new age of air and space power in which modern air forces will be the measure of great powers on the world scene.

The men and women of the United States Air Force stand ready to meet the challenges of the future with our comrades in arms from the Royal Air Force. We greatly appreciate the efforts of the Royal Air Force Benevolent Fund to prepare this extraordinary volume. It will serve as the benchmark historical work on the first 50 years of our service for decades to come. I wish you every success with it.

Ronald R Fogleman
General, USAF
Chief of Staff

MINISTRY OF DEFENCE
WHITEHALL LONDON SW1A 2HB

SECRETARY OF STATE

It is with very great pleasure that I take this opportunity to join others in a warm salute to the United States Air Force in the year of its fiftieth anniversary.

The United States Air Force has a special place in the development of post-war military aviation and this is vividly demonstrated by the fine work contained in this tribute. The United Kingdom has enjoyed a special relationship with the United States Air Force throughout its fifty years. The seeds were sown in the dark days of World War II when aviators of the United States Army Air Force, were first posted to the United Kingdom. The relationship flourished with the formation of the United States Air Force in 1947 and was strengthened during the long years of the Cold War. Today, this relationship endures in the coalition partnerships that have been forged from Iraq to Zaire and grows stronger as, together, we face the challenges of the new world order.

I know that this very special relationship owes much to the mutual respect of the men and women of each Air Force for the professionalism and dedication of their counterparts. As they admire each other's skills and commitment they draw inspiration to excel.

I send congratulations and best wishes to the United States Air Force. We look forward to coming decades of work together.

The Rt Hon Michael Portillo MP
The Secretary of State for Defence

MINISTRY OF DEFENCE
MAIN BUILDING WHITEHALL LONDON SW1A 2HB

CHIEF OF THE AIR STAFF

There will be many projects to mark the 50th Anniversary of the United States Air Force but few that will capture the history of this distinguished force with such vivid power. Many of the aircraft pictured in this book will, for those of my own generation, evoke childhood memories of the powerful partner who made such a contribution to NATO's deterrent posture during the Cold War. Others provide a reminder, if one were needed, of the crucial part played by the USAF more recently in maintaining the peace in the unstable world in which we now find ourselves. All, however, testify to the standards the USAF has demanded of its equipment and that commitment to technical excellence and innovation that has been both its own trademark and a benchmark for Air Forces around the world.

It gives me great pleasure to commend to readers, both specialised and general, 'Sabre to Stealth'. It provides a record by distinguished aviation artists of aircraft which have become legends in their own time, and it represents a fine tribute to a force which, through both its history and its current commitment to the pre-eminence of air and space power, remains the standard by which we must all be judged.

Sir Michael Graydon
Air Chief Marshal
Chief of the Air Staff

GOLDEN LEGACY

While 1947 marked the beginning of a US independent Air Force, the story of Army aviation in America goes back nearly 100 years. Back in 1898 the US Army first supported the development of a man-carrying aeroplane, making a $50,000 grant to Samuel P. Langley. In 1901 he flew a quarter-scale model successfully but his full size machine failed in two attempts to fly across the Potomac river in October and December 1903. This costly failure did not endear itself to Congress and the use of public funds was sharply criticised. This had an impact on the Army's attitude to the Wright Brother's achievement with their first sustained, controlled, powered flight, which was met with disbelief, scepticism, and disinterest. The governments of both Great Britain and France showed more interest in the Wright Brothers' accomplishments than did their own government.

It was not until the intervention of President Roosevelt that the War Department called for bids, late in December of 1907, for an aircraft that could carry two people at a speed of at least 40 mph for 125 miles. Three bids were submitted, but only the Wright aircraft was ever delivered. Meanwhile, the Army had already taken its first step toward building an Air Arm. On 1 August 1907, the Signal Corps had established an Aeronautical Division to 'take charge of all matters pertaining to military ballooning, air machines, and all kindred subjects'. Pending receipt of the first aeroplane, the Signal Corps simply expanded its balloon activity, experimenting with photography and radio reception from the air.

In the Autumn of 1908, the Wright brothers brought their machine to Fort Myer, VA, and on 3 September began a series of demonstration flights, that brought out thousands of spectators. The flights came to a tragic end with a crash on 17 September which severely injured Orville and killed his passenger, Lt Thomas Selfridge.

The brothers returned in June 1909 for the official tests, and after a month of practice flights, Orville, with Lt Frank Lahm as passenger, made the first official test flight on 27 July, establishing a world record for a two-man flight of 1hr 12min 40sec. The Army officially accepted the Wright's plane for service on 2 August.

As part of the Army contract, the Wrights agreed to train the first two Army aviators, Lts Frank Lahm and Frederic Humphreys. Both were officially announced pilots on 26 October 1909, but were immediately returned to their original duties in the Army. The only remaining aviation officer, Lt Benjamin Foulois, who had not yet soloed in the plane, was sent to winter the aircraft at Fort Sam Houston, TX. He was ordered to teach himself how to fly and experiment with possible military applications of the aeroplane. He began his efforts in February 1910. Until 1911, Foulois and his aircraft remained the sole asset of the Aviation Branch.

Despite a lack of enthusiasm amongst Army officers, and Congress as well, in March of that year, $125,000 was finally appropriated for Army Aeronautics. Five new airplanes were purchased and a handful of other officers now joined Foulois to begin training. A flying school was built at College Park near Washington DC, and the men and aircraft were moved there from Texas. Experiments were made in night flying and firing a gun from an aircraft. Record breaking altitude and distance flights were made. In the winter of 1912, the Army established its first permanent aviation school at San Diego, CA.

At the end of February 1913, some Army fliers were ordered to report to the 2nd Division at Texas City, TX, that had been formed due to strained relations with the Mexican government. This group was organized as the 1st Aero Squadron in order to operate more effectively with the 2nd division. As hostilities did not occur, the unit was not put to the test of

combat operations, but it did spend a good deal of time in the air mastering cross-country flying.

By 1914, the US had lost the aeronautical leadership gained by the achievements of the Wright bothers. It had fallen behind particularly in the area of military aviation. The most important difficulty facing the Army aviators was the lack of a clearly defined status and function within the service. Army aviation finally received statutory recognition with the creation, on 18 July 1914, of the Aviation Section of the Signal Corps, with an authorized strength of 60 officers and 240 enlisted men. Just a few weeks later, Europe plunged into the massive military struggle that became World War I. The Central Powers, primarily Germany, the Austro-Hungarian Empire, and the Ottoman Empire, fought the Allied Powers, led by Britain, France, Italy and Russia.

However, the first involvement of US Army aviation in a combat situation was in March 1916, when the 1st Aero Squadron was sent into Mexico with General Pershing's Punitive Expedition against the bandit Pancho Villa. The experiment was a near fiasco with 75% of the aircraft out of commission within the first month.

Technical assistance for American aeronautics had come with the establishment by Congress in March 1915 of the National Advisory Committee for Aeronautics, but this came too late for the American

Lt Benjamin D Foulois, a military balloonist, had been ordered to take the crated Wright Type A Biplane to the Army post at Ft Sam Houston, San Antonio, Texas, assemble it, and teach himself to fly. His first flight took place at 9.30am on the 2nd of March 1910. The historic flight, painted here in Gallant Beginning *by Keith Ferris, was the first by a US military trained aviator in a government owned machine. This painting is held by The National Bank of Fort Sam Houston, and is reproduced here by kind permission of the artist.*

These two pages generously supported by Messier-Dowty and Dowty Aerospace

Gallant Beginning by Keith Ferris ASAA

participation in World War I. The United States had to turn to her allies for planes to equip her squadrons and for the technical knowledge to produce her own.

Despite optimistic plans and ample funding, the United States proved unable to catch up to the European nations in aviation technology. Responding to criticism of the American aircraft effort, President Woodrow Wilson created the Army Air Service and placed it directly under the War Department on 24 May 1918. By the time of the armistice in November 1918, the Air Service had grown to more than 19,000 officers and 178,000 enlisted men, while American industry had turned out 11,754 aircraft (mostly trainers like the Curtiss JN-4 Jenny). The Air Service soon lost most of these people and planes in a rapid demobilization immediately after the war.

Although failing to deploy competitive combat aircraft, the United States had sent many fine airmen to Europe. Flying mostly French-built aircraft, they distinguished themselves both in allied units and as part of the American Expeditionary Forces (AEF) led by Gen John J Pershing. By the time Germany surrendered, Brig Gen Billy Mitchell had honed many of the AEF's aero squadrons and groups into a formidable striking force. While the outcome of the Great War was decided primarily by horrible attrition on the ground, and a strangling maritime blockade of Germany, air power had shown its potential for autonomous offensive operations as well as providing valuable support to surface forces. Great Britain had recognized the importance of air power by creating the Royal Air Force, that was independent of the British Army and Royal Navy, on 1 April 1918.

The Great War had left many US air leaders with the conviction that air power would be the dominant weapon of the future. Men like Billy Mitchell had seen the potential of air power, but did not have the weapons to prove their theories. The years 1919-1939 were hard for these early exponents of air warfare, but the time would come when technology would develop to the point where they could prove their ideas.

From the earliest days, there had been proponents of a separate Army Air Force. Many felt the time was not yet right for complete independence, but an important step was taken in the Army Reorganization Act of 1920. The Act made the Air Service a combatant arm of the Army with an authorized strength of 1515 officers and 16,000 enlisted men. The Air Service now had complete control of its own research and development, procurement and supply as well as personnel and training functions.

Billy Mitchell became an outspoken crusader against inadequacies in the Army and Navy. His continued advocacy of an independent air arm led to his eventual court martial and retirement from the Air Service in 1926. The concept did not die with Mitchell's absence, though his supporters temporarily left the spotlight.

Though sometimes overshadowed by the Mitchell campaign, the small core of Army fliers made some spectacular pioneering flights while continually pushing the limits of aeronautics. There were many altitude, speed, and endurance records set by such men as Jimmy Doolittle. The first of these highly publicised events was a 4,000 mile flight across the continent by four Curtiss JN-4 aircraft searching for possible air routes and landing fields – a necessary step toward improving aviation. The major efforts went into long distance and endurance flights. The first non-stop flight across the continent was made by Lts Oakley and Macready in May 1923. In June of the same year, the Air Service made the first successful in-flight refueling test, and two months later a new world record endurance flight remained airborne for over 37 hours. In 1924, the Air Service made the first round-the-world flight in 175 days in four specially built Douglas aircraft.

The next important organizational change came in 1926 when the Air Service became the Air Corps, which further strengthened the concept of military aviation as an offensive, striking air arm rather than an auxiliary service.

The history of the Army's air arm in the years preceding World War 2 is basically the struggle to develop the long-range bomber. The US Air Service in France had developed a doctrine of strategic bombardment as early as 1917. Steady improvement in aircraft performance in the 1920-30s gave impetus to those proponents of long-range bombing. As many earlier planes had been designed as multi-purpose aircraft, they were not as effective as those designed specifically for bombing. With the development of the Boeing B-9 and the Martin B-10, important steps had been taken toward the concept. Pursuit planes had been much superior to existing bombers before the B-9 and B-10, and had given the opponents of heavy bombing their best argument. The 8,290 mile round trip flight in 1934, by ten B-10 bombers, to Alaska from Washington, reinforced the concept of long-range flying.

During the winter and spring of 1934, the Army had also been called upon to take over the US mail routes. Due to obsolete planes and equipment, an improper ground organization, and lack of experience, the results of the experiment were disastrous. Nine fliers were killed in three weeks. The investigation resulting from the fiasco focused attention on the inadequacies in military aviation and clinched the argument for reorganization. Thus the development of the long-range bombers coincided with the establishment of the GHQ Air Force.

After September 1939, when Hitler launched World War 2 by invading Poland, the Air Corps began a steady growth from 26,000 personnel and fewer than

These two pages generously supported by the United States Air Force Museum

HH Arnold's career mirrored the development of American Air power from the earliest days and he is considered by most to be the father of the US Air Force. Arnold was one of a handful of early aviators who struggled throughout the years to develop the Army air arm and eventually establish the independent United States Air Force.

Henry Harley 'Hap' Arnold was born in Gladwyn PA on 25 June 1886. Following graduation from West Point in 1907, Arnold was appointed a second lieutenant and posted to the infantry. His first assignment was to the Philippines. He was next sent, in April 1911, to the Signal Corps where he learnt to fly at the Wright school in Dayton Ohio. He received the US Army's Pilots licence number 2 after about 15 hours of flying time.

Arnold was sent next to the Army's first regular flying field and flight school at College Park, Maryland. There he taught the new Chief of the Aeronautical Division, Captain Charles de F Chandler, to fly. The mission for these early Army aviators was broad and vague – simply to develop the aircraft into a military weapon. Following World War I, Arnold served a variety of commands, always fighting to keep the Air Service alive.

'Hap' Arnold found himself involved in many decisive events in the period leading up to World War II. At an early stage Arnold became one of the leading advocates of the strategic bomber concept. He led the 1934 Alaska flight of Martin B-10 bombers on a mission of over 7,000 miles, demonstrating the potential of long-range aviation. The B-10 was the first 'modern' bomber that the Air Corps had, leading eventually to the heavy bombers of World War II and after.

On 11 Feb 1935, Arnold was given command of the First Wing of the General Headquarters Air Force at March Field, CA. He continued to rise in the growing organization and as a major general become Chief of the Air Corps in 1938. At that time, the force consisted of some 20,000 personnel and a few hundred planes. Through Arnold's unrelenting drive to improve the service in the face of growing tension in Europe, by 1944 the organization had grown to over 2.4 million personnel and 80,000 aircraft.

Arnold became Chief of the Army Air Forces when the service was retitled in 1941 and Commanding General of the Army Air Forces following the War Department General Staff reorganization in March 1942. General Arnold was promoted in December 1944, to five-star rank as a 'General of the Army'.

'Hap' Arnold retired from active service in 1946 and three years later, on 7 May, 1949, the President of the United States signed a bill authorizing his title as 'General of the Air Force'. His decorations included the Distinguished Flying Cross, Distinguished Service Medal with two Oak Leaf Cluster and an Air Medal. He also received Brazil's Order of the Southern Cross, Morocco's Grand Cross, Yugoslavia's Pilot Diploma and France's Croix de la Legion d'Honneur among many others.

General Arnold died in 1959, at the age of 63.

General Henry 'Hap' Arnold by Rita Guzzi

2,000 aircraft. On 20 June 1941, the Department of War created the Army Air Forces (AAF) as its aviation element and shortly thereafter made it co-equal to the Army Ground Forces. The Air Corps remained as one of the Army's combat arms, like the infantry.

The fall of France in 1940 made national defense an immediate concern overnight and the Air Corps was presented with a blank cheque. The program to best achieve the necessary goals was drafted by a handful of brilliant young officers, resulting in the AWPD/1. This document proved to be a remarkably accurate forecast of AAF strategy and requirements for a simultaneous campaign in the Pacific and Europe. The plan established the strategic bombing campaign as the major contribution of the AAF.

Expansion of the AAF accelerated after the surprise Japanese attack on Pearl Harbor in December 1941 propelled the United States into the war. Under the leadership of Gen Henry H ('Hap') Arnold, the Army Air Forces oversaw mobilization of the nation's aviation industry and deployment of the largest air armada of all time. The AAF's inventory encompassed a wide range of training, transport, pursuit, attack, reconnaissance and bomber aircraft. These included the ubiquitous C-47 Skytrain, the splendid P-51 Mustang, the rugged B-17 Flying Fortress, and the mighty B-29 Superfortress. Drawing upon American industrial strength and human resources, the AAF reached a peak of 80,000 aircraft and 2.4 million personnel, organized into major commands, numbered air forces, air division, groups and squadrons.

Although initial defeats in the Pacific after the Japanese attack on Pearl Harbour overshadowed other efforts, America's participation increased in importance. A build up of forces in England prepared the way for the eventual invasion by Allied troops on the European continent. Air Forces were expanded, and in February 1942 Brig Gen Ira Eaker arrived in England to establish a Bomber Command headquarters. In June, Maj Gen Carl Spaatz arrived to take over command of the Eighth Air Force. US airmen concentrated on daytime precision bombing, counting on the growing firepower of the B-17, the accuracy of the Norden bombsight, and the eventual development of long-range escort fighters.

Following the invasion of North Africa and the subsequent conquest of Sicily and the Italian mainland, the Combined Bomber Offensive waged by the Eighth AF and the RAF, carried the strategic bombing campaign into the heartland of Germany. Finally, late in 1943, the problem of expanded range was solved and the P-38 Lightning, P-47 Thunderbolt and P-51 Mustang were available to escort the bombers to the enemy targets. By the time of the Normandy invasion in June 1944, the Allies were close to establishing air superiority over the skies of Germany.

Even as the US was fighting toward victory in Europe, the war in the Pacific forged ahead as well. Following the initial disasters resulting from Pearl Harbor, the AAF was finally able to take a stand and under the command of Lt Col Jimmy Doolittle, 16 B-25 Mitchell bombers were launched from the deck of the Navy carrier *Hornet* and carried out a bombing raid against Tokyo and other targets. The battles at Coral Sea and Midway following in 1942 proved to be the turning point in the Pacific war. The American effort now became one of island-hopping to control territory closer and closer to the Japanese homeland. The Fifth, Seventh, and Thirteenth Air Forces were heavily involved in the struggle for the Solomons, New Guinea, the Philippines and Okinawa. Simultaneously, a massive and difficult effort was carried on in the China-Burma-India Theater. Air Transport Command encountered tremendous odds in keeping open the only supply route 'over the hump' to China.

The Army Air Force engaged in long-range strategic bombing of Japan as the war progressed. With range always a problem, it was only with the eventual capture of the Mariana Islands in 1944 that the raids became really effective. The B-29 finally arrived at newly built bases on Saipan, Guam and Tinian, and incendiary raids were begun. Japan continued to fight on, but the dropping of atomic weapons on Hiroshima and Nagasaki by the *Enola Gay* and *Bockscar* in August 1945 finally brought the Japanese surrender.

The AAF made efforts to study the lessons of combat even before the war was over. One of the most successful was the US Strategic Bombing Survey. This and other studies following the war confirmed the AAF in its belief in the dominance of air in future warfare. With the end of hostilities, American aviation leaders were free to apply these lessons in the culmination of their long pursuit of an independent air arm with the establishment of the United States Air Force under the National Defence Act of 1947.

Much as it did a quarter century before, the United States immediately demobilised its armed forces after World War II. Based on the AAF's wartime achievements and after much debate, the United States Air Force was created as a separate armed service by the National Security Act of 1947. Appropriately enough, President Harry Truman signed the legislation while on board the Douglas C-54 presidential aircraft *Sacred Cow*. On 18 September 1947, the USAF achieved its independence as a full partner with the Army and the Navy. Stuart Symington became the first Secretary of the Air Force, and General Carl A Spaatz its first Chief of Staff. The scene was now set for the dramatic events that followed over the next 50 years.

Lawrence R Benson and Karen Pittman

The creation of an independent United States Air Force had been considered as far back as 1916 and several unsuccessful attempts were made to pass legislation to that effect. The wartime US Army Air Force (USAAF) was fundamentally an autonomous service in all but name and neither the Navy nor the Army challenged that position during hostilities. The conclusion of the Second World War provided an extra impetus for the creation of a separate Department of the Air Force. Wartime operations allowed the armed services to co-operate on an unprecedented scale that tested their resources and skills. However, the working agreement was scheduled to end six months after the war finished. This prompted detailed studies into the creation of a separate Department of the Air Force but with conflicting

General Carl A Spaatz

conclusions between the Army and Navy. The latter made a strong assertion that it would be placed in an inferior position compared with the Air Force and Army. A series of plans for three separate services backed by the Army, and counter plans from the Navy, were presented from March 1944.

In his message to Congress on 14 December 1945, President Harry S Truman put forward a plan to establish a single Department of Defense, with the Air Force being of equal status to the other services. It took a further 18 months to resolve continuing arguments between the Navy and Army, but on 25 July the new National Security Act 1947 became law, establishing a single civilian-controlled Department of Defense with Army, Navy and Air Force Departments. At the same time the National Security Council, Central Intelligence Agency (CIA) and the National Security Resources Board were set up.

Once the transfer of command from the Army to the new US Air Force had been completed, W Stuart Symington was sworn in as the first Secretary of the Air Force on 18 September 1947, now recognised as the official birthday of the United States Air Force. General Carl A Spaatz, who had replaced the renowned General 'Hap' Arnold as Commander, Army Air Forces on 15 February 1946, and remained in control of the USAF, had already introduced an organisational structure with three principal combat commands – Tactical Air Command, Strategic Air Command and Air Defense Command. Alongside these he established a new headquarters structure, five support commands and five overseas commands. The latter included the very large United States Air Forces in Europe (USAFE) and Far East Air Forces (FEAF) operating commands.

In the so-called 'Truman Doctrine' of 12 March, the President laid out plans for the USAF's build-up of a worldwide nuclear capability. Alongside this blueprint the service was preparing for the future in other significant ways. The advanced research work done by wartime

Lockheed P-80A Shooting Stars

German propulsion and aeronautical scientists had been brought to America and was paying great dividends in the development of swept-wing jet and rocket powered aircraft. In 1947 the North American XP-86, the first swept-wing jet fighter to see operational service and Boeing's swept-wing, six-turbojet engined XB-47 strategic bomber made their maiden flights.

Of possibly even greater long-term significance, Major Charles E 'Chuck' Yeager broke the sound barrier for the first time in the Bell XS-1, reaching Mach 1.06, after being released from the bomb-bay of its B-29 'mother ship' on 14 October. In executing this feat, Yeager not only made aviation history in the XS-1 but also helped America to move ahead of the rest of the world, the project effectively illustrating the potential for unrestricted high-speed and supersonic flight.

With a wide range of new aircraft types ready to enter operational service and even more advanced designs coming to fruition, the new US Air Force was firmly established as the world's leading air arm ready to reinforce the United States' position as a major superpower.

The pages for 1947 generously supported by Main Event Catering

1947

11 March: The first of six Boeing YC-97 transports, a military version of the Stratocruiser for the USAF, flew for the first time.

12 March: President Truman announced plans, that were key to the growth and expansion of US military air power. The 'Truman Doctrine' provided the forthcoming USAF with a blueprint for building a global nuclear force.

17 March: First flight of the North American XB-45 (later named Tornado), at Muroc, CA. It was the first US all-jet bomber to become operational, serving as an interim between the World War 2 designed piston-engined bombers and the swept-wing, jet powered Boeing B-47 Stratojet.

North American XB-45 Tornado

16 May: Mock air attacks were mounted on New York by the USAAF Strategic Air Command. It was planned that 101 B-29 Superfortresses should have simulated dropping bombs on targets in the city, but on the day 30 B-29s (23% of the force) were unserviceable and unable to take part in the exercise.

19 June: A Lockheed P-80R Shooting Star, piloted by Capt Albert Boyd – the chief USAAF test pilot – raised the world air speed record to 623.738 mph (1,003.6 km/h) at Muroc Dry Lake, CA.

25 June: The more powerful Boeing B-50 made its first flight.

Eventually 351 B-50s were delivered to the USAF and the bomber version served until 1955, with 136 subsequently converted to tankers and remaining in service until 1965.

25 July: The National Security Act of 1947 was signed, authorising the creation of the US Air Force.

28 August: The first of 22 production Convair B-36A Peacemakers, powered by six Pratt & Whitney R-4360-25 engines, was flown for the first time. This unarmed version was used principally for training and crew conversion by Strategic Air Command (SAC) at Carswell AFB, TX.

1 September: Stuart Symington was named as the first Secretary of the USAF.

18 September: The United States Air Force (USAF) was established under General Carl A. Spaatz. Though Commanding General of the USAAF from 9 February 1946, General Spaatz officially took up the new appointment on 26 September.

18 September: James V. Forrestal issued Order No 1, which approved transfer of military and civil personnel from the US Army Air Force to the Department of the Air Force and USAF.

22 September: Douglas C-54D-1-DC Skymaster (42-72461) of the USAF All-Weather Flying Center made the first automatic trans-Atlantic flight from Stephensville, Newfoundland to RAF Brize Norton, Oxfordshire.

October: 25 Lockheed P-80B Shooting Stars of the 94th *Hat in the Ring* Squadron were detached to Ladd Field, Alaska for six months of cold weather, Arctic, tests. This operation was intended to develop new packings and lubricants that would allow jet aircraft to operate in extreme low-temperature conditions and give air and ground crews valuable operational experience.

1 October: The North American XP-86 'Sabre' (45-59597), was first flown, piloted by George Welch. It became the world's first swept-wing jet fighter aircraft to enter operational service.

1 October: The first flight was made of the Grumman SA-16 (HU-16) Albatross rescue amphibian.

14 October: USAF Major Charles E. 'Chuck' Yeager, piloting Bell XS-1 (46-062), became the first person to break the sound barrier. After being dropped from the belly of a B-29 Superfortress at 20,000ft, Yeager fired all four XLR11-RM-3

North American XP-86 Sabre

rocket motors and climbed to 45,000ft, achieving Mach 1.06 (approximately 700 mph).

23 November: The first flight was made by the Convair XC-99 (43-52436), a transport version of the B-36 six-engined bomber. It had a new two-deck fuselage but retained the B-36's wings and tail unit. Only one example of this 400-seat troop carrier, then the world's largest land aircraft, was built. Delivered to the USAF in May 1949, it was used for special missions before being retired in 1957.

November: Fairchild C-82 Packet (45-57769), subsequently redesignated as the C-119A, was first flown with two 2,260-hp Pratt & Whitney R-4360-4 engines and a modified fuselage. It was later accepted by the USAF for production as the C-119B Flying Boxcar.

December: The first Republic P-84B Thunderjet unit reached initial operational capability (IOC) with the 14th Fighter Group at Dow Field.

17 December: The first of 2,032 Boeing B-47 Stratojet strategic bombers (XB-47 46-065) made its first flight from Moses Lake AFB to Seattle, WA. This was on the 40th anniversary of the Wright Brothers' historic first powered flight.

This new painting by Henry Godines shows the rocket-powered Bell XS-1 at Muroc Air Force Base, California being refuelled before its record-breaking first supersonic flight. It features team members, including the pilot, Major Charles 'Chuck' Yeager, going over last minute details before the historic flight on 14 October 1947.

Fueling the Orange Beast by Henry Godines ASAA

The new United States Air Force continued to expand its capabilities, with the original three operational Commands (Air Defense, Strategic and Tactical) augmented by the creation of the Military Air Transport Service (MATS). The need for an effective transport capability was clearly demonstrated in 1948. After the impact of Russian forces surrounding and isolating Berlin had been appreciated, the US military governor in Germany, General Lucius D Clay, requested the start of an airlift of supplies by the US Air Forces in Europe (USAFE) into the beleaguered city.

General Curtis LeMay, then Commander of USAFE, began operations with as many transport aircraft as were immediately available. This comprised a fleet of 102 Douglas C-47 Skytrains and just two Douglas C-54 Skymasters. The airlift commenced on 26 June with 80 tons of supplies arriving at Tempelhof, the airport in the American zone of Berlin. Control passed to the Airlift Task Force established by MATS on 29 July, and the arrival of 72 more Skymasters from the USA greatly enhanced its capability.

Alongside the MATS effort additional airlift support was provided by the Royal Air Force and British civilian operators, participating in what was now renamed the

Republic F-84B Thunderjets

General Curtis E LeMay

Joint Airlift Task Force. By the end of the year operations into the main 'airheads' at Tempelhof and Gatow from Fassberg, Celle and Rhein Main in West Germany were running smoothly and successfully, in all weathers. In October, the target of delivering 4,500 tons per day was raised to 5,620 tons. Use of an increasing number of the large, four-engined Skymasters instead of the smaller Skytrains offered much better operational efficiency. A total of more than 300 C-54s were ultimately allocated to the airlift.

It was not surprising that in the same year, the USAF's permanent presence in Europe was strengthened with the announcement that agreement had been reached with the

British Air Ministry to base fighter and bomber groups in the UK and Germany. The growing Russian threat to transports flying along the corridor to Berlin brought about additional deployments of Boeing B-29 Superfortresses and Lockheed F-80 Shooting Stars to Europe. The B-29s which arrived in Britain in July were the first American bombers to be based in the UK since the end of World War 2. These moves greatly strengthened the air power available in Europe, and paved the way for future enlargement of the USAF's assets across Europe, as the Cold War intensified.

The Lockheed TF-80C, a two-seat version of the F-80 Shooting Star, was first flown in 1948. Subsequently redesignated T-33, this advanced jet trainer was to play an important role with USAF training units for nearly 40 years.

Another significant development was the establishment of Strategic Air Command's first two Air Refueling Squadrons. They were equipped with Boeing KB-29M tankers converted from wartime Superfortress bombers that were in turn being replaced by the improved Boeing B-50, that first entered service in February 1948. The new air-to-air tanker aircraft considerably extended the USAF's operational effectiveness, as more front-line aircraft were deployed to bases abroad.

The increasing importance placed upon air-to-air refuelling capabilities and overseas deployments were key features of the initial re-organisation of Strategic Air Command under its new Commander, General Curtis LeMay. With the delivery of the first Convair B-36 to SAC, LeMay's bomber fleet was seen to be stepping up in size, range and capability, although it was to be short-lived as the turbojet bomber rapidly overhauled the last of the big piston-engined bombers.

Completed by the artist in 1973, this painting illustrates a typical winter's scene with Douglas C-54 Skymasters lined up on the apron. The painting is reproduced by kind permission of the artist and the McDonnell Douglas Aircraft Corporation.

The pages for 1948 generously supported by Aeroclub Sanicole

Berlin Airlift by Robert G Smith, ASAA

January: The last production Douglas C-54G Skymaster was delivered to the USAF from Santa Monica.

4 February: The airlift components of the USAF and US Navy were combined with the creation of MATS – the Military Air Transport Service.

16 February: SAC deployed B-29 Superfortresses to Germany from the US as part of an exercise in long-distance operations. A combined training exercise with the RAF involved interceptions over southern England.

20 February: The first Boeing B-50 (46-017) to enter service was delivered to the 43rd Bomb Wing.

5 March: First flight made by the Curtiss XP-87 all-weather interceptor, the last independent product from Curtiss. It was cancelled on 10 October 1948 in favour of the XF-89 Scorpion.

17 March: Headquarters Command was activated.

22 March: The first flight of the Lockheed TF-80C, the two-seat trainer prototype of the P-80 Shooting Star, was made. The designation was changed to T-33A in May 1949, and it was produced for the USAF until August 1959.

28 March: SAC completed a series of tanker aircraft trials with specially converted B-29 Superfortresses, with the designation KB-29M. A 2,300gal fuel tank was carried in the bomb bay and a hose and reel system was used for refuelling.

26 April: The sound barrier was broken for the first time by a turbojet powered aircraft. A North American XP-86 achieved a speed just in excess of Mach 1 when test pilot George Welch put the aircraft in a shallow dive.

May: The aviation engineering school at Francis E. Warren AFB, WY, was converted to a Technical School. It had been transferred to the Air Force in June 1947 under control of Air Training Command.

11 June: The USAF designation of fighters and reconnaissance aircraft was changed. Fighters, that had been given the prefix P since 1925, were assigned the letter F. Reconnaissance aircraft, that had been given the prefix F in 1930 changed to the letter R.

18 June: The USAF's first two Air Refueling Squadrons, the 43rd at Davis-Monthan AFB, AZ, and the 509th at Roswell AFB, NM, were activated. Both were equipped with Boeing KB-29Ms.

26 June: In Germany the Berlin Airlift commenced. USAFE, under General Curtis E LeMay, impressed Douglas C-47 Skytrains to lift supplies of milk, flour and medicine into the beleaguered city of Berlin after Soviet restrictions on road, rail and barge traffic were imposed.

26 June: The first Convair B-36 (44-92004) was delivered to an operational unit, the 7th Bomb Wing (Heavy), based just across the runway from the Convair factory at Fort Worth, TX. By the end of 1948 the unit was equipped with 35 of these heavy bombers.

8 July: The first fully operational B-36B made its first flight. With the introduction of the B-36, SAC changed the designation 'very heavy bomber' for its B-29s and B-50s to 'medium bombers', and designated the B-36 a 'heavy bomber'.

16 July: The US Defense Department and British Air Ministry announced plans to move USAF fighter and bomber groups to England and Germany. Under the guise of a long-term training programme, an informal agreement between the British and American governments reinforced strategic air power in Europe.

17 July: Arrival in Britain of the first USAF bombers – B-29 Superfortresses of the 28th and 307th Bombardment Groups – since the end of World War 2.

20 July: Sixteen F-80A Shooting Stars of the 56th Fighter Group landed in Scotland, en route to Fürstenfeldbruck, West Germany, on the first transatlantic deployment of a USAF jet fighter unit.

29 July: The Berlin Airlift Task Force, later renamed First Airlift Task Force, was formed with its headquarters at Wiesbaden, West Germany.

6 August: Two B-29 Superfortresses (*Gas Gobbler* and *Lucky Lady*) of the 43rd BG completed, in 15 days, a 20,000-mile round-the-world flight.

8 August: Completion of a non-stop, non-refuelled 9,400-mile round-trip flight by a B-36B Peacemaker between Fort Worth, TX and Hawaii.

16 August: First flight of the Northrop XF-89 Scorpion – the first two-seat all-weather turbojet interceptor.

23 August: The McDonnell XF-85 Goblin 'parasite' fighter, intended to be air-launched and recovered from a B-36, made its first free flight.

Convair B-36B Peacemaker

3 September: Operation *Dagger*, the first major air defence exercise involving RAF aircraft and USAF B-29s, took place.

15 September: Major Richard L Johnson, flying F-86A Sabre (47-611) at Muroc Dry Lake, set a new world air speed record, flying at an average speed of 670.981 mph (1,079.61 km/h).

18 September: First flight of the Consolidated Vultee XF-92A delta wing experimental aircraft.

19 October: General Curtis E LeMay was appointed commander of USAF Strategic Air Command.

20 October: The McDonnell XF-88 was first flown. Cancelled in 1950, it led to the development of the bigger F-101 Voodoo.

November: The 47th Bombardment Wing at Barksdale AFB, LA received the first B-45 Tornado to be delivered to an operational unit. It was the first jet bomber to fly with the USAF.

5 November: The marking 'USAF' was officially approved for all US warplanes except those operated by MATS. The US Navy, Marine Corps, Army and National Guard retained their own markings.

1 December: Continental Air Command was activated.

2 December: The first Beech YT-34 Mentor two-seat military trainer had its maiden flight.

9 December: A Convair B-36 and a Boeing B-50A completed a non-stop round trip flight from Carswell AFB, TX to Hawaii. The B-36 flew more than 8,000 unrefuelled miles in 35.5 hours, whilst the B-50A was refuelled in flight three times by KB-29M tankers.

As the Cold War escalated, the blockade of Berlin continued into the New Year, much to the concern of the West. Such increasing aggression by the Soviet Union required firm mutual action, and on 4 April the leaders of Belgium, Canada, Denmark, France, Iceland, Italy, Luxembourg, the Netherlands, Norway, Portugal, the UK and the USA met in Washington DC to sign the North Atlantic Treaty, declaring that the members of the newly-formed North Atlantic Treaty Organisation (NATO) would stand together if any of them was attacked. The US Air Force's huge air power assets formed a formidable part of the alliance's defensive capabilities from the outset.

In the meanwhile, the Berlin Airlift, otherwise known as Operation *Vittles*, remained very busy, with cargoes continuing to increase as the number of aircraft on the daily flights to the besieged city increased. To help alleviate the air traffic control problems another airport was brought into use, the French-controlled airfield at Tegel. The so-called 'Easter Parade', of 16 April, saw almost 13,000 tons of cargo being delivered in over 1,300 sorties – a record day of operations. Soon afterwards, with the airlift achieving its objective and with the formation of NATO, it became clear to the Russians that the blockade of Berlin could not continue. On 9 May 1949, the USSR's military governor of Berlin announced that the blockade would be lifted at one minute after midnight on 12 May. The Russians had backed down. They had used harassment, had flown in close formation and even buzzed

North American F-86A Sabre – 1st Fighter Group

the airlift aircraft in the corridor from the West into Berlin, but had not used force. Had the USAF's presence in England and with B-29s and F-80s close at hand in Germany helped to avert a major conflict? Undoubtedly the growing NATO airpower with its potential to deliver nuclear weapons had influenced Soviet thinking.

USAF flights to the city continued, for over four months, only finishing with the last C-54 departure back to Rhein-Main on 30 September. 2,325,000 tons of supplies had been airlifted to Berlin since the previous June, 1,783,000 tons by the USAF.

There were many advances within Strategic Air Command's bomber force, with the turbojet/pusher, piston-powered Convair B-36D entering service, and the Boeing B-50A provided a demonstration of the air power available to the Command by making the first non-stop round-the-world flight, including four air-to-air refuellings from KB-29s. The USAF's newest bomber type, the XB-47

Stratojet, also impressed by making a non-stop flight from Moses Lake, Washington to Andrews AFB, MD, breaking the existing transcontinental record. There could be no better way to demonstrate to the Russians the long-range capabilities of the new line of jet bombers that were destined for Strategic Air Command.

Another of the year's milestones was the delivery of the first F-86A Sabre to an operational unit. The new swept-wing North American design represented a major step forward from the current front-line F-80 Shooting Stars and F-84 Thunderjets, and would soon prove its worth in combat. Another important technical development came with the first flight of the Sikorsky S-55 single main-rotor helicopter with its nose-mounted engine providing a cabin large enough to accommodate troops or equipment. The S-55 and the larger S-58 that followed it into production were to play an important part in the use of helicopters by the US air arms for many years to come.

North American F-82E Twin Mustang

The pages for 1949 generously supported by The Royal Air Force Benevolent Fund

3 January: The USA introduced a Bill to speed up the development of guided missiles.

5 January: Major Charles 'Chuck' Yeager set an unofficial climbing speed record of over 13,000ft per minute in the Bell X-1. This was also the first standard take-off of a rocket-propelled research aircraft.

25 January: The slate blue uniform was adopted for the Air Force to replace the previous Army olive buff.

February: The first F-86A Sabre was delivered to an operational unit, the 1st Fighter Group at March AFB, CA.

8 February: The Boeing XB-47 completed a non-stop flight from Moses Lake airfield, Washington to Andrews AFB, MD in 3hr 45min. The 2,289 mile distance was covered at an average speed of 607.2 mph – half the time of the then existing trans-continental records.

9 February: The USAF established a Department of Aviation Medicine at its School of Aviation Medicine, Randolph AFB, TX.

2 March: The first non-stop flight around the world by B-50A Superfortress (46-010) *Lucky Lady II* was completed. Six KB-29M tankers were used during the 23,452 mile (37742 km) flight, that commenced on 26 February and was completed in 94hr 1min.

26 March: First flight was made by the Convair B-36D powered by four J47-GE-19 turbojets mounted in pairs under the outer wing sections in addition to the six pusher engines.

Boeing B-50Ds

This boosted its maximum speed to 439 mph and raised the bomb load it could carry to 84,000lb.

30 March: A Bill was authorised for the establishment of a permanent radar defence network.

4 April: The North Atlantic Treaty Organization (NATO) was established under the North Atlantic Treaty that came into effect on 24 August.

16 April: First flight of a radar-equipped version of the two-seat Lockheed TF-80C. This was a forerunner of the YF-94 Starfire all-weather interceptor fighter.

16 April: The maximum day's effort of the Berlin Airlift was achieved when 12,940 tons of life-sustaining cargo was delivered on 1,398 sorties.

12 May: The Soviet Union ended its blockade of Berlin, although the airlift continued for nearly five more months.

4 June: First flight of the Lockheed XF-90 prototype was made. In competition with the McDonnell XF-88, it lost out to that aircraft in its development as the F-101 Voodoo.

1 July: The Lockheed YF-94 Starfire all-weather interceptor fighter (48-356), with nose mounted radar and engine afterburner, had its maiden flight. It was converted from the prototype TF-80C/T-33.

22 September: The Convair T-29, a navigator/bombardier trainer version of the Convair 240 airliner, was first flown at San Diego.

26 September: The North American XT-28 Trojan (48-1371) was flown for the first time. This new trainer was to replace the T-6 Texan as a combined primary and basic trainer.

30 September: The Berlin Airlift officially ended, when the last USAF C-54 Skymaster departed Berlin for Rhein-Main. During Operation *Vittles*, USAF, US Navy, RAF and Commonwealth air forces and British independent airlines, carried some 2,325 million tons of food, fuel and equipment to the people of Berlin.

15 October: The first of 50 Boeing C-97As was delivered to MATS.

7 November: First flight of the single-rotor Sikorsky S-55 was made. This set a trend that influenced future helicopter design. It was the first helicopter to have a cabin unrestricted by the engine, which was mounted in the nose.

Lockheed XF-90

18 November: A Douglas C-74A Globemaster flew from Mobile, AL to RAF Marham, Norfolk with 103 passengers and crew. It was the first flight to carry more than 100 people across the Atlantic.

27 November: First flight of the Douglas YC-124 Globemaster II. The type went into service with SAC, MATS, Tactical Air Command, Air Materiel Command and the Far East Air Force.

5 December: The USAF announced that it was to build a radar network in Alaska and Greenland, to warn of the approach of hostile aircraft up to 300 miles away.

December: Deliveries began of the Northrop C-125A Raider short-field light transport.

22 December: The North American YF-86D all-weather interceptor was first flown. The 'Sabre Dog' had a re-contoured nose to carry radar above a lip intake and the gun armament was dropped in favour of a retractable tray carrying 24 x 2.75-in air rockets.

In this painting, the late Bob Cunningham captures 'the immense power and grace of the B-36 that allowed it to soar along at 50-60,000 feet above the earth in the silent brightness of those altitudes'. The painting is reproduced by kind permission of Lockheed Martin Tactical Aircraft Systems, Fort Worth.

The High and Mighty by Robert E Cunningham ASAA

Since the end of World War Two, conflict had been simmering in Korea. North of the 38th Parallel, the Soviet Union had been responsible for disarming Japanese forces, with the USA having that responsibility in the South. Once this had been completed, it had been hoped that Korea would again be unified, but the establishment of a Communist regime in the North prevented this from taking place. From early in 1948 there followed two years of skirmishes on the border between the Democratic People's Republic of Korea in the North and the Republic of Korea in the South. While most Western nations recognised the latter, the North had the support of the Soviet Union and its Communist allies. The full strength of the forces massing in North Korea was seriously underestimated by the South Korean and the US governments.

American troops had been withdrawn from the Republic of Korea in 1949, such was the belief that no major conflict would occur there. This proved to be a tactical mistake, as it led the North Koreans to believe that the South was a soft target. Early on 25 June 1950, the North Korean army launched a massive attack against the south. The following day, an evacuation of American citizens including all military personnel was launched, air cover for the ships involved being provided by F-82 Twin

Mustangs. A flight of these was 'bounced' by a North Korean Yak-9 fighter whilst patrolling Inchon harbour – the first Communist aircraft to be encountered. An airlift of refugees was implemented a day later, again escorted by fighters from the 68th Fighter (All-Weather) Squadron. During a series of encounters with North Korean aircraft an F-82G flown by Lieutenant William Hudson shot down a Yak-11, to make the first 'kill' of the Korean War.

On the same day, 27 June 1950, the United Nations called on its member countries to support the military action being taken against the invasion. The US responded immediately with the first USAF offensive missions being launched from Andersen AFB, Guam. Boeing B-29 Superfortresses and B-26 Invaders bombed North Korean forces near Seoul and combat patrols were carried out by F-80 Shooting Stars.

Support for UN ground operations was provided initially by F-51D Mustang and F-80 units, acting against armour and supply lines, with F-84 Thunderstreaks being deployed to the theatre later in the year. Alongside these, two Groups equipped with B-26 Invaders flew in the night interdiction role, particularly against supply columns and rail links. Four more Wings of B-29 Superfortresses were deployed by Strategic Air Command and were primarily used against troop and tank

Lockheed F-94A Starfires

concentrations and supply dumps until August. After that the B-29s began to strike manufacturing centres and transportation links in the North, supporting the Allied invasion at Inchon.

The advances made by UN forces came to a halt in November, as they began encountering Chinese troops who had now become openly involved in the conflict. A new danger also developed overhead, as the first Chinese MiG-15 jet fighters appeared over North Korea in the same month. One was shot down by a USAF F-80C Shooting Star in the first jet-to-jet combat in history, but the faster Soviet type provided the first serious opposition to UN air superiority. However, the situation was rectified by deployment of the F-86A Sabre to the theatre in December, which proved more than a match for the MiGs in spite of some early teething troubles. By the end of 1950, the UN's position in the skies above Korea was once again looking more secure, although operations on the ground saw Communist troops making important gains at the Allies' expense.

The specially commissioned painting Bolt from the Blue *by Anthony Cowland shows Lt William Hudson's F-82G Twin Mustang after he had successfully shot down a Yak-11, recording the first aerial 'kill' of the Korean War.*

North American F-51D Mustang – 67 FBS

Boeing B-29 Superfortress – 19 BG

The pages for 1950 generously supported by the SSVC Group

Bolt from the Blue by Anthony R G Cowland GAvA

15 January: Death of General of the Air Force, Henry H 'Hap' Arnold.

18 January: The first flight of the Lockheed YF-94C prototype (50-955) was made. Developed from the F-94B, with a modified nose and larger wing tip tanks, it was the Air Force's first rocket-armed jet interceptor when it entered service in March 1953. A total of 387 was produced.

23 January: USAF Research and Development Command (renamed Air Research and Development Command on 16 September) was established, separating the research and development functions from those of procurement and logistics, which remained with Air Materiel Command.

30 January: President Truman announced the decision to proceed with development of a thermonuclear, or hydrogen, bomb as the first step in acquiring weapons many thousands of times more powerful than the atomic bomb.

1 February: The USAF's Continental Air Command was directed to establish a civil Air Raid Warning system.

22 March: The Atlantic Pact arms aid agreement that had been signed in January and made provision for the supply of 88 Boeing B-29s to the Royal Air Force, resulted in the first delivery on this date of a B-29 to RAF Marham, Norfolk.

18 April: The planned procurement of 1,250 new aircraft for the USAF, at a cost of $1,203 million, was announced.

May: The Douglas C-124 Globemaster II entered Air Force service, with strategic support squadrons of Strategic Air Command.

1 June: The USAF was authorised to organise a Ground Observer Corps.

3 June: First flight of the YF-96A Thunderstreak (49-2430) was made. This was Republic's first swept-wing aircraft, a fighter-bomber based on the F-84 Thunderjet. The designation was changed to YF-84F on 8 September 1950.

25 June: Communist forces of North Korea invaded the Republic of Korea (ROK), south of the 38th Parallel. US Far East Air Force (FEAF) elements based in Japan, Okinawa and the Philippines were put on alert.

26 June: A flight of F-82 Twin Mustangs, of the 68th and 339th Fighter (All-weather) Squadrons, Fifth Air Force, made the first encounter with a Communist aircraft whilst providing air cover for evacuation ships in the harbour at Inchon.

27 June: The first aerial 'kill' of the Korean War was credited to Lt William Hudson (pilot) and Lt Carl Frasee (navigator), the crew of an F-82G Twin Mustang from the 68th Fighter (All-weather) Squadron, who downed a North Korean Yakovlev Yak-11.

27 June: B-29s of the 19th Bombardment Group attempted the first bombing operations against North Korean forces south of the 38th Parallel, under authorisation of a United Nations resolution calling for a military response to the aggression. Owing to adverse weather the two missions on this day failed.

28 June: A force of 12 Douglas B-26 Invader light bombers of the 8th Bomber Squadron, 3rd Bomb Group, successfully attacked railway installations at Munsan, just below the 38th parallel. On the same day B-29s of the 19th BG made bombing raids along road and rail lines between Seoul and Kapyong and between Seoul and Uijongbu.

29 June: The first US bomber strike into North Korea was made by B-26s of the 3rd BG, against the airfield at Pyongyang.

29 June: First delivery of the Lockheed F-94A Starfire all-weather jet fighter to the 319th Fighter (All-weather) Squadron, Air Defense Command.

11 August: First flight of the Fairchild XC-120 Packplane (48-330). This comprised a C-119B Flying Boxcar wing and tail unit, with a flight deck in an upper fuselage component. The lower component was a detachable cargo-carrying pod.

26 August: Delivery of the first RB-45C Tornado reconnaissance variant to SAC's 91st Strategic Reconnaissance Wing at Barksdale AFB, LA.

4 September: The first emergency rescue of a pilot from behind enemy lines by helicopter in Korea was accomplished by a Sikorsky H-5 of the 3rd Air Rescue Squadron, flown by Lt Paul W van Boven.

9 September: FEAF Bomber Command commenced intensive B-29 operations against railheads and marshalling yards, in support of the impending Inchon landings to push Communist North Korean forces from South Korea.

18 September: A mass ferry flight of 89 F-84E Thunderjets from the 27th Fighter-Escort Wing, on delivery to the 36th Fighter Bomber Wing, concluded at Furstenfeldbruck AB, West Germany having departed Bergstrom AFB, TX on the 15th. 91 more fighters were delivered in mid-October, to the 86th FBW at Neubiberg AB, West Germany.

22 September: In the first non-stop crossing of the North Atlantic by a turbojet aircraft, a Republic EF-84E, modified for in-flight refuelling by Flight Refuelling Ltd in the UK, flew from RAF Manston, Kent to Limehouse, ME in ten hours.

27 September: All strategic air operations against targets in the far north of Korea were halted by the US Joint Chiefs of Staff.

9 October: General MacArthur authorised air operations to be directed against communist infiltration from China and directly resulted in air-to-air combat with Chinese pilots.

20/21 October: In support of the Wonsan invasion on the northeast coast of Korea, Douglas C-47 Skytrains and Fairchild C-119 Boxcars of the 314th Troop Carrier Group delivered paratroops and supplies.

November: Tactical Air Command commenced development of a nuclear role for fighter bombers in Europe. This resulted in the adaptation of the F-84G Thunderjet to carry the weapon.

8 November: The first all-jet battle took place when F-80 Shooting Stars of the 16th Fighter Interceptor Squadron attacked Chinese MiG-15s. A MiG-15 was shot down by Lt Russell Brown, being the first occasion that one jet fighter was destroyed in combat by another.

23 November: The FEAF in Korea began a major air offensive to support the push by the Eighth Army against communist forces in North Korea.

6 December: F-84 Thunderjets of the 27th Fighter Escort Wing flew their first combat missions over Korea, flying from Itazuki in Japan.

17 December: The commander of the 336th Fighter Interceptor Squadron became the first pilot in the conflict to attack and shoot down a Chinese MiG-15 while flying an F-86A Sabre.

On New Year's Day the North Korean offensive recommenced, with the Communist forces taking Seoul within just three days. In the air, the arrival of the F-86A Sabre in the theatre of operations had already greatly enhanced the Allied air combat capability, but ever-increasing numbers of Chinese MiG-15s resulted in the Far East Air Force's air superiority gradually being diminished. On the positive side the USAF's heavy bomber capability was being put to good effect. From early January through to mid-April, B-29 Superfortresses dropped the massive 12,000lb Tarzon bombs on important transportation routes including roads, bridges and railways, disrupting the North Korean army's supply lines.

By mid-March, the UN's position on the ground had temporarily improved. The South Korean capital Seoul was retaken and the Communists were pushed back across the 38th Parallel, but a spring offensive by the Chinese saw the front line move back to a position just north of the city. The USAF Fifth Air Force launched a huge attack on the Communist airfield at Sinuiju, destroying many aircraft and support facilities, which it was believed were to be used for an imminent counter-offensive.

Alongside the successful strikes on airfields, the start of Operation *Strangle* (as the name implies, an attempt to 'strangle' the North Korean transport system) led to B-26 Invaders destroying 1,245 vehicles in two months. The operation was later extended to railways, causing great damage to the Communist army's support system, reducing ammunition, fuel and food supplies to the front-line. This campaign continued until other targets became available.

By the end of the first year of operations in Korea, the Far East Air Force had lost a total of 247 aircraft compared with 391 Communist aircraft believed to have been destroyed. The air war continued as no formal settlement was reached with the Chinese after their declaration that they would discuss peace terms. Talks did come to fruition but broke down on 23 August, heralding a new Communist offensive which seriously threatened

Cessna LC-126A

UN ground forces. The Chinese MiG-15 strength had by now grown still further, with a number of the fighters being flown by Soviet instructors. This became increasingly evident as the numbers of 'enemy' combat kills dropped, and by October the FEAF was beginning to struggle in the face of the Red offensive. A new danger also materialised, as North Korean night 'nuisance raids' on airfields by the so-called Bedcheck Charlies (Po-2 biplanes and Yak-18s) caused a disproportionate amount of damage while being almost impossible for Allied fighters to counter.

The first month of renewed full-scale aerial combat saw one of the Korean conflict's fiercest air battles. During a B-29 attack on Namsi airfield, south of the Yalu river, six MiG-15s were destroyed by FEAF aircraft while three USAF bombers were lost and four more badly damaged. Ground-attack missions against supply routes were by then having more limited results, and the UN aircraft were suffering increasing losses. As air superiority began to move towards the Communists, calls by the end of the month for an increased UN fighter strength were refused, which, coupled with the increasing numbers and success of the Chinese MiGs (among which were now the latest MiG-15bis variants) made the situation in the skies over Korea appear more finely-balanced for the first time.

Douglas B-26C Invader

The pages for 1951 generously supported by the Rolls-Royce Aerospace Group

1951

13 January: A B-29 of the 19th Bomb Group made the first use of the new 12,000lb Tarzon bomb, which had radio-controlled tail-fins, dropping it on a vital railway bridge at Kanggye in North Korea.

14 January: The 5th Air Division was activated in French Morocco.

16 January: The first six Convair B-36D Peacemakers of the 7th Bombardment Wing landed at RAF Lakenheath, Suffolk after flying from Carswell AFB, TX. They were the first of these SAC bombers in Europe.

23 January: The Far East Air Force started to lose its advantage over enemy aircraft in Korea because of increasing numbers of Chinese-operated Soviet jet fighters.

23 January: The North Korean airfield of Sinuiju was heavily attacked by 33 F-84E Thunderjets.

5 February: The USA and Canada announced jointly their intention of setting up a DEW (Distant Early Warning) radar system for North America.

6 March: Air Materiel Command implemented the production of the English Electric Canberra jet bomber by the Glenn L Martin Company as the B-57. It was the first aircraft of non-US design to be accepted for service with the USAF.

20 March: SAC's 7th Air Division was activated in England, with its headquarters at South Ruislip, near London.

2 April: The USAF Air Research and Development Command (ARDC) became operational.

14 April: By this date, B-29 Superfortresses had destroyed 48 out of 60 bridges and 27 out of 39 marshalling yards – strategic targets assigned to them in North Korea – at a cost of eight bombers destroyed.

21 April: The Fairchild XC-123A Avitruc was flown for the first time. It was fitted with four J47 turbojets in paired pods under the wing and as such was the first US-developed jet transport.

9 May: A massive Fifth Air Force air attack was made on the Communist-held airfield garrison of Sinuiju in North Korea.

20 May: Captain James A. Jabara flying an F-86A Sabre of the 4th Fighter Interceptor Wing shot down his fifth and sixth enemy aircraft in Korea, becoming the first jet air 'ace'. He had a final total of 15 victories.

31 May: Initiation of Operation *Strangle* with the objective of paralysing the enemy transportation network in North Korea.

June: The Air Force Flight Test Center (AFFTC) was formally established at Edwards AFB, CA.

1 June: The first of 18 Northrop F-89A Scorpions was delivered to an operational unit, the 84th FIS at Hamilton AFB, CA.

20 June: F-51 Mustangs of the 18th Fighter Bomber Group, FEAF attacked, for the first time, Ilyushin Il-10s (second generation Sturmoviks) over Korea. An escorting Yak-9 was also destroyed.

20 June: A Martin B-61 Matador missile, later the TM-61, was launched for the first time – the USAF's first tactical guided missile.

20 June: First flight of the Bell X-5 research aircraft, based on the unflown Messerschmitt P1101, which was the first aircraft with a variable wing sweep, adjustable in flight.

6 July: The first air-to-air refuelling over enemy territory was made between a Boeing KB-29M of the 91st Strategic Reconnaissance Wing operating out of Yokota AB, Japan, and three Lockheed RF-80As from the forward operating base K-2 at Taegu. It was the culmination of Project Collins initiated by the Wright Air Development Center in response to an urgent operational requirement from FEAF in 1950 to extend the endurance of its jet aircraft.

14 July: First delivery of a Boeing KC-97E (51-183) aerial tanker to an operational unit, the 306th ARS at MacDill AFB, FL. The type could fly fast enough to match the minimum speed of the B-47 Stratojet.

5 August: Action during the Korean War resulted in the posthumous award of the first Medal of Honor to a member of the Air Force, going to Major Louis J Sebille, an F-51 Mustang pilot.

17 August: The 100km closed circuit speed record was broken by Colonel Fred J Ascani in an F-86E Sabre, at a speed of 635.686mph.

25 August: Thirty-five B-29 Superfortresses, escorted by 23 F9F Panthers and F2H Banshees from the USS *Essex*, dropped 291 tons of bombs on Rashin, close to the Siberian border, obliterating the town's marshalling yards. No aircraft were lost.

5 September: A contract was awarded to modify a B-36 Peacemaker to carry a nuclear reactor for tests on airframe, instruments and electronics. This provided vital research to ascertain whether an atomic-powered bomber was feasible.

23 October: Deliveries of the B-47B Stratojet began, with the first unit equipped being the 306th Bomb Wing (Medium) – comprising the 367th, 368th and 369th Bomb Squadrons at MacDill AFB, FL, with a total of 45 aircraft.

23 October: In the Korean War's biggest air battle to date, ten B-29 Superfortresses escorted by 89 fighters (mostly F-86s) were intercepted by about 150 MiG-15s while attacking Namsi airfield, south of the Yalu river. Three B-29s were shot down and four made emergency landings in South Korea, while six MiGs were destroyed.

24 October: A daylight raid was made against a road/rail bridge at Sunchon by B-29s – one bomber was lost. Final daylight raids were made on 27-28 October against road/rail bridges, without loss.

31 October: In the first month of renewed aerial combat, following the breakdown of peace talks in the Korean War, the FEAF claimed 32 MiG-15 destroyed for the loss of 15 US aircraft.

30 November: Twelve Tupolev Tu-2s, escorted by 16 La-9s and 16 MiG-15s, were intercepted by 31 F-86 Sabres of the 4th Fighter Interceptor Group. Eight Tu-2s, three La-9s and a MiG were shot down - the biggest air combat success so far for the UN air forces.

1 December: F-86 Sabres of the 51st Fighter Interceptor Wing began operations in Korea. This brought the total number of Sabres in the theatre to 127, with 40 more in reserve in Japan.

The USAF's first jet fighter, the Lockheed P-80 Shooting Star, saw combat service in the Korean War, used initially as an interceptor and then for ground attack. The untitled painting by Chuck Hodgson, depicting a 'contact' with two enemy MiG-15s, is reproduced by kind permission of the Lockheed Martin Skunk Works.

Lockheed P-80 Shooting Star by Chuck Hodgson

Since Operation *Strangle* had focused its attention to attacks on railways as well as roads in North Korea, it had met its objectives. However, early in 1952 this effort was further stepped-up with the introduction of Operation *Saturate*, a three-month around-the-clock series of interdiction missions against major rail links. FEAF losses, though, were heavy from operations during these campaigns.

During the spring, Chinese MiG-15 activity also reached new heights. It was during this upsurge in enemy operations that 83 Communist MiGs were 'downed' compared to only six FEAF losses. A new tactic by the enemy MiG pilots – arriving over the border from Manchuria at a lower height than previously – led to a change in strategy by the Allies, who now met the intruders at lower level while continuing higher-altitude cover. The ever-increasing number of sorties flown by the FEAF reached a new peak in May, with 5,190 patrols being achieved, during which 32 Communist aircraft were destroyed for the loss of only nine Allied aircraft.

By the summer, the enemy air forces had over 1,000 jet

Republic F-84E Thunderjet

fighters on strength and 5,360 Soviet units were deployed to the region. Communist tactics had improved, and the increased numbers of MiG-15s now appearing over the Yalu River posed a potentially more serious threat to FEAF pilots. Despite being outnumbered the F-86s and their more experienced crews were able to gain the upper hand over their opponents. It was decided to increase the intensity of aerial operations against the enemy in order to push forward peace talks. As an indication of this Operation *Pressure Pump* utilised every available UN air

unit deployed to the theatre including Fifth Air Force F-51D Mustangs and F-84 Thunderjets, for a strike on 30 targets in Pyongyang on 11 July. A repeat of this raid took place on 29 August, but still the talks faltered.

September proved to be an especially heavy month of air combat, but again the still inferior tactics of the Communist pilots meant that the FEAF Sabres, some now the latest F-86E and F variants, were able to inflict heavy losses on the MiG-15s. Strikes on important North Korean industrial and supply targets continued, the emphasis being turned towards the power system with attacks on hydro-electric plants by F-84s, F-80s and F-51s, while B-29s executed strikes on bridges, important industrial centres, ports and railheads. In spite of these successful attacks, ceasefire negotiations remained at a standstill. As the end of 1952 approached, the air war over Korea continued to meet the UN's objectives, but peace still appeared only a distant possibility.

Away from Korea, 1952 saw the first flight of the YB-52 Stratofortress from Boeing Field, Seattle, in mid-April. It had been ordered into full scale production in February 1951, with the contract for the first 13 B-52As finalised on 7 November 1952. It was clear that the big jet-bomber was to be a focus of SAC's future development to meet the objectives laid down for the USAF in the 'Truman Doctrine' of 1947, in building up a global nuclear force. As a deterrent, the Stratofortress was immediately a powerful symbol of US foreign policy worldwide. On a smaller scale, formation of the Air Force's first tactical helicopter squadron on 16 December provided a precursor to the future expansion of its rotary-wing capability, as helicopters would become ever more important in battlefield support and troop mobility.

Another painting by the late Bob Cunningham, 'Gabby' Scores Again shows top-scoring Korean War ace, Col Frances Gabreski, scoring another kill. It is reproduced by kind permission of Lockheed Martin Tactical Aircraft Systems, Fort Worth.

Sikorsky SH-19A Chickasaws

The pages for 1952 generously supported by Boeing Defense and Space Group

'Gabby' Scores Again by Robert E Cunningham

1952

3 March: Operation *Saturate* was initiated, during which an around-the-clock interdiction effort would be maintained against key railways in North Korea. This replaced Operation *Strangle*.

14 March: Responding to the national emergency announced in December 1950, as a result of the Korean War, plans were made to expand the production of nuclear and thermonuclear weapons.

18 March: Two F-84 Thunderjets landed after the longest sustained jet flight, when they covered 2,000 miles from the USA to Neubiberg in Germany in 4 hours 48 minutes, without refuelling.

19 March: Developed under the impetus of the Korean War, the improved North American F-86F-25 Sabre was flown for the first time. It had a new wing leading edge to improve the fighter's manoeuvrability at high altitudes, where it had been at a disadvantage in combat with MiG-15s.

20 March: A plan for a Civil Reserve Air Fleet was signed, implementing a December 1951 agreement between the Department of Defense and the Department of Commerce. In the following months the airlines were briefed and agreement was reached on their obligation to provide supplementary airlift to MATS in the event of an emergency.

15 April: The prototype eight-turbojet Boeing YB-52 Stratofortress (49-231) was flown. It was designed to carry nuclear weapons to any target in the world.

23 April: A Convair RB-36F Peacemaker made a successful first flight with a retractable trapeze below its modified bomb

Boeing YB-52 Stratofortress

bay. It was in preparation for the development of a retrieval and launch sequence of a Republic F-84F Thunderflash in the fighter conveyor programme (FICON).

May: Following service trials, two squadrons of the 374th Troop Carrier Wing re-equipped with the C-124A Globemaster II for long-range operations between the US, Japan and Korea.

3 May: A USAF Douglas C-47 Skytrain, fitted with a wheel/ski landing gear, made the first successful landing at the North Pole.

29 May: Full-scale use was made of air-to-air refuelling in support of a ground-attack mission over enemy territory. Boeing KB-29 tankers refuelled 12 F-84E Thunderjet fighter bombers of the 159th Fighter Bomber Group, that had taken off from Japan, and were en route to attack targets in Sariwon in North Korea.

23/24 June: The largest single air effort since World War 2 was made when 1,200 USAF, USN and USMC sorties virtually destroyed North Korea's electrical power potential.

2 July: The existence of the Lockheed F-94C Starfire interceptor was revealed. This was the first fighter to have no guns – the two-seater jet carried 48 Mighty Mouse rockets.

10 July: The commanding FEAF General issued a directive allocating priority to stepping up air pressure on the Communist forces in an effort to press peace terms at the negotiating table.

11 July: Operation *Pressure Pump* mobilised every available UN air unit in the Korean War for a mass assault on 30 targets in the Pyongyang area.

17 July: In Operation *Fox Peter One*, 58 F-84G Thunderjets of the 31st Fighter Wing at Turner AFB deployed to Misawa and Chitose Air Bases in Japan. This was the first large-scale deployment of escort fighters with in-flight refuelling being used for crossing the Pacific Ocean.

19 July: The USAF announced that, for periods of over three days, it had successfully flown free balloons at controlled, constant altitudes in the stratosphere.

29 July: An RB-45C Tornado (48-042) made the first non-stop jet flight across the Pacific Ocean – from Elmendorf AFB, Alaska to Yokota AB in Japan – which involved two in-flight refuellings from Boeing KB-29s.

Boeing B-47B Stratojet

31 July: The first trans-Atlantic flight was made by helicopters, when two Sikorsky H-19s (51-3893 and 51-3894) flew from Westover AFB to Prestwick in Scotland. Landings were made en route in Labrador, Greenland, Iceland and the Hebrides.

13 August: It was announced that the Boeing B-52 had been ordered into full-scale production. The first contract for 13 B-52As was finalised on 7 November.

18 September: The US and Denmark announced the completion of a huge Arctic air base at Thule, Greenland.

30 September: First launch of the Bell GAM-63 Rascal air-to-surface missile was made.

23 October: First flight of the USAF's experimental Hughes XH-17 heavy cargo helicopter, which incorporated four long legs that straddled a cargo container secured to the fuselage underside.

1 November: The world's first thermonuclear explosion took place on the Eniwetok atoll in the Pacific.

3 November: First flight of a Convair B-36 fully adapted to carry a thermonuclear bomb. A total of 36 Peacemakers was subsequently modified for this role.

19 November: Captain J Slade Nash broke the world absolute air speed record when he achieved 698.505 mph in an F-86D.

3 December: A C-47 Skytrain was forced down by Soviet fighters over Hungary and was impounded.

16 December: The USAF Tactical Air Force Command's first helicopter squadron was activated. It was equipped with Sikorsky H-19As.

Concern was expressed at the start of the year regarding the large number of jet aircraft being supplied to Communist forces by the Soviet Union. The Chinese Air Force now operated 950 MiG-15s and 100 new Ilyushin Il-28 medium bombers alongside its older, conventional types. Nevertheless, the UN air forces continued their concentrated strikes on Communist targets, and in February the Chinese indicated that they would consider resuming ceasefire negotiations. In March, the USAF retired its last F-80C Shooting Star from service in Korea, as the new F-86F Sabres re-equipped the 8th Fighter Bomber Group at Suwon. By June, attacks by FEAF F-84G Thunderjets had breached two important irrigation dams, and on the 15th Communist forces came under the largest one-day UN assault yet, in response to an enemy offensive that had begun five days earlier. That same month saw a record number of MiG-15 'kills', 129 being taken out of action by F-86s of the FEAF. No better illustration could have been provided of the Sabre's air combat capabilities.

Through into July, North Korean airfields came under heavy attack from F-86Fs, while UN ground forces stabilised the front line prior to another all-out strike against enemy troops from 13 July, countering another brief Red offensive. Within six days, the Communists had agreed to an armistice, and after the terms had been accepted by South Korea's President Rhee, this was signed on 27 July.

Since hostilities had commenced in June 1950, a total of 720,980 sorties had been flown by the FEAF over Korea, delivering around 476,000 tons of ordnance against enemy targets. American fighter pilots claimed 810 Communist aircraft destroyed in combat, of which the very great majority were MiG-15s. Often unsung, the FEAF's 315th Air Division, operating C-46 Commandos, C-47 Skytrains, C-54 Skymasters, C-119 Flying Boxcars and C-124 Globemasters, flew 210,343 transport sorties during the war, carrying 2,065,591 passengers and 39,763

Lockheed F-94C Starfire

tons of freight. Overall, UN air power, primarily that of the FEAF and the Fifth Air Force, had triumphed over the Communists – air superiority had been gained from an early stage, strikes on diverse ground targets had been successful and met their objectives by shutting off supply lines and destroying industry, while the air transport and Army support operations had progressed smoothly and efficiently.

1953 also saw a number of new aircraft types which would play their parts in future conflicts make their first flights. The first of the 'Century Series' of USAF fighters, the North American YF-100A, took to the air from Edwards AFB in May flown by George Welch. Originally known as the Sabre 45, as it was developed from the F-86 Sabre, with a new low-set, 45-degree swept wing, it also featured a slab tailplane. In October the first production F-100A was flown and the YF-100A established a new World Air Speed Record of 755.149 mph. When it entered service the following year, the Super Sabre was the first operational fighter in the world able to reach supersonic speed in level flight.

The first Martin-built B-57A, one of eight modelled on the English Electric Canberra B2, was airborne at Baltimore on 20 July. A further 67 similar RB-57As followed from the production line. The B-57 was not only the first foreign-designed military aircraft to be procured by the USAF since World War I, but it was also a major step forward for the Air Force as a replacement in the medium bomber role for the wartime B-26 Invader that was still in service. The B-57 went on to be extensively modified for various new tasks in a long service career.

Curtiss C-46A Commando

The pages for 1953 generously supported by Pat, Kevin, Kim, Cindy and Chris Ryan and dedicated to their father Col William J 'Pat' Ryan, United States Air Force 93BS/19BW

30 January: First flight made of the Boeing B-47E Stratojet. This version was the major production type, of which 1,341 were eventually delivered to SAC, together with 255 RB-47Es.

12 February: Convair received a contract for the detailed design and assembly of a prototype supersonic bomber. This led to the B-58 design which incorporated a delta wing with four podded engines, area-rule fuselage and large-scale use of honeycomb sandwich skin panels for the wing and fuselage.

10 March: Communist fighters made the first attack on aircraft flying in West European airspace, when two MiG-15s of the Czechoslovak Air Force attacked a pair of USAF F-84 Thunderjets. One F-84 was shot down but the pilot ejected safely.

21 March: Operation *Spring Thaw*, a short intensive aerial interdiction effort in North Korea, was started.

27 March: A classified design study was issued, calling for a special reconnaissance aircraft able to operate at over 70,000ft. This ultimately led to Lockheed's U-2 'spyplane'.

31 March: The last Lockheed F-80C Shooting Star first-generation jet fighter-bomber was retired from front-line service in Korea.

25 April: The first Boeing RB-47B Stratojet conversion (51-2194) was delivered to the 91st Strategic Reconnaissance Wing at Lockbourne AFB, OH. It carried eight cameras and

Piasecki YH-16 Transporter

equipment in a special bomb-bay container. The 24 RB-47Bs were mainly used for crew-training.

13 May: Four waves of 59 FEAF F-84G Thunderjets of the 58th Fighter Bomber Wing attacked and breached the Toksan dam, north of Pyongyang.

16 May: Ninety F-84Gs attacked and destroyed the Chasan Dam.

18 May: Captain Joseph McConnell of the USAF's 39th FIS downed three North Korean MiG-15s to become the top scoring fighter ace of the Korean War, with 16 enemy aircraft to his credit.

25 May: Maiden flight of the North American YF-100A (52-5754) was made at Edwards AFB. It was the first of the 'Century Series' of USAF fighters.

1 June: The new US Air Force Demonstration Team, the *Thunderbirds*, was formed at Luke AFB, AZ, flying F-84G Thunderjets.

3 June: Strategic Air Command introduced mobility training by regularly rotating the B-47 Stratojet Wings through overseas stations in the Pacific, North Africa and England. Each of the wings was deployed overseas for 90 days at a time.

5 June: The first SAC B-47 Stratojet wing completed its deployment from MacDill AFB, FL to RAF Fairford, Gloucestershire.

15 June: Communist forces in Korea came under attack in the largest one-day air assault mounted by UN forces – in response to a Communist offensive that had begun on 10 June. 2,143 sorties were flown by FEAF.

16 July: Lieutenant Colonel W F Barnes set a new absolute world air speed record of 715.6 mph flying an F-86D Sabre.

20 July: The first Martin B-57A – the American-built version of the English Electric Canberra bomber – made its maiden flight at Baltimore.

22 July: F-86F Sabres of the 51st Wing encountered MiG-15s for the last time in the Korean War, shooting one down.

27 July: The Armistice, bringing an end to hostilities between Communist forces of North Korea and the Allied forces of the UN, came into effect.

29 July: A Boeing RB-50 of the 55th Strategic Reconnaissance Wing, operating out of Yokota AB, Japan, was shot down by

Soviet MiG-15s after straying over Russian waters off Vladivostok. Of the 17 crewmen, only one survived.

20 August: The first mass flight by jet fighters over the Atlantic under Operation *Longstride* commenced, when eight F-84 Thunderjets of the 31st Strategic Fighter Wing flew from Turner AFB, GA to Nouasseur AB, French Morocco followed by 20 F-84s flying to RAF Lakenheath, Suffolk.

25 August: First successful air-launch and recovery of an RF-84F by a modified RB-36F, using the FICON (FIghter CONveyer) system, which was intended to provide the Thunderflash with an improved strategic capability.

1 September: The first jet-to-jet aircraft in-flight refuelling was announced when a Boeing YB-47F was refuelled by a KB-47G using the British hose and drogue system.

11 September: Announcement of the first successful interception by the Sidewinder air-to-air missile, which hit and destroyed a Grumman F6F Hellcat pilotless target.

October: The first of ten Lockheed RC-121C Super Constellations was delivered to the 552nd AEW & C Wing of Air Defense Command.

12 October: The US signed an agreement in Athens that allowed the USAF conditional use of Greek air bases.

23 October: Piasecki flew the first of two YH-16 Transporter twin-rotor helicopters.

24 October: Convair's experimental YF-102 flew for the first time at Edwards AFB, CA. It was destroyed eight days later when its engine failed on take-off.

29 October: The absolute world speed record was broken by Lieutenant Colonel Frank K Everest, USAF, who flew a YF-100A Super Sabre at 755.149 mph.

12 December: Major 'Chuck' Yeager flew the air-launched Bell X-1A at a speed of Mach 2.435 (1,650 mph; 2,655 km/h) and an altitude of 70,000ft (21,430m).

Hugh Polder's painting Mission Inn *shows a B-29 Superfortress of the 22nd Bomb Group based at Kadena, being escorted by an F-86F Sabre of the Osan-based 12th FBS, on a mission over Korea in 1953. It is reproduced here by kind permission of the artist.*

Mission Inn by Hugh Polder

It was announced in mid-year that a new 12-month record had been set for post-World War 2 aircraft procurement. Since 30 June 1953, the start of Fiscal Year 1954, some 5,662 aircraft had been accepted into service by the USAF. The latest front-line fighter and bomber aircraft types, such as the F-100 Super Sabre and B-47 Stratojet were being delivered in increasing numbers.

There were also several important new types that flew for the first time in 1954. The Lockheed XF-104 Starfighter, with its revolutionary 'missile with a man in it' design concept, set the USAF fighter trend for the next decade. Powered by a General Electric J65 turbojet (with the more powerful J79 in production F-104s), and the aerodynamic combination of a highly streamlined fuselage and thin, short-span wings, this tactical day fighter had a startling performance. When in service it was the first production interceptor capable of sustaining speeds of over Mach 2.

Another very significant Lockheed designed aircraft, the YC-130 Hercules, also made its first flight in August, in the hands of Stan Betz and Roy Wimmer. The Korean conflict had identified a requirement for a versatile tactical transport capable of hauling freight and dropping paratroops as well as being able to be adapted for a host of other battlefield tasks. Lockheed produced the four-engined

C-130 that remained in production for the next four decades, proving to be one of the most successful aircraft ever built and serving with air arms throughout the world.

In contrast, a different type – the Cessna XT-37 – that was also to remain in USAF service for many years, had its first flight in October. Later known as the 'Tweety', the Cessna T-37 became the Air Force's first basic jet-powered trainer and was also developed as an armed close support aircraft. The twin-engined Fairchild YC-123 Provider tactical transport was another new type to fly for the first time during 1954. Two further, and very different fighters took to the air. The McDonnell YF-101 Voodoo, the biggest and heaviest fighter aircraft of the time, was developed into a potent interceptor and tactical strike platform, while the Convair YF-102A was the first delta-wing fighter and forerunner of the production F-102 Delta Dagger. The latter displayed for the first time the pinched 'coke-bottle' fuselage waist configuration developed via NACA designer Richard Whitcomb's area-rule concept to find the optimum shape for transonic aircraft.

The USAF also formed its first Airborne Early Warning and Control Division, initially using ten Lockheed RC-121C derivatives of the civilian Super Constellation. Originally intended for the US Navy but diverted to the

Convair YF-102A Delta Dagger

Air Force, these early models were soon replaced by RC-121Ds (subsequently redesignated EC-121Ds). Dedication of this pioneering unit followed another important step forward in providing radar early warning of any attack on the North American continent, namely approval of construction of a Distant Early Warning (DEW) defence line across Alaska, Canada and Greenland.

The conclusion of the top secret Strategic Missiles Evaluation Committee that intercontinental ballistic missiles were feasible, saw worries within SAC that provision for its bombers' survivability may be threatened. This led to a new requirement for a future strategic aircraft, the B-70 supersonic bomber. Design studies were put in hand by Boeing and North American, while the former was just commencing production of the B-52A Stratofortress. Following demands from General LeMay, side-by-side cockpit seating was adopted for production B-52s, as opposed to the tandem arrangement used on the prototype and the earlier B-47. Thus equipped, three B-52As were built for test and evaluation purposes with the B-model following as the first definitive production variant. An older Boeing bomber, the B-29 Superfortress, was finally retired from USAF service in November as the 307th BG relinquished its last B-29A.

The Northrop F-89D Scorpion, shown in this untitled painting by Jack Young, was a twin-engined jet interceptor fighter that entered service in 1954. This painting is from the Air Force Art Collection.

Lockheed RC-121D Constellation

The pages for 1954 generously supported by Aerosystems International

Northrop F-89D Scorpion by Jack Young

January: The first swept-wing Republic F-84F Thunderstreaks were received by the 506th Strategic Fighter Wing at Dow AFB, ME. The aircraft was assigned to Strategic Air Command as a fighter escort.

24 February: Approval was given for the construction of the Distant Early Warning (DEW) radar line covering Alaska, Canada and Greenland.

4 March: First 'full' flight made by the Lockheed XF-104 Starfighter at Edwards AFB, CA, piloted by Tony Le Vier. The aircraft had 'hopped' off the ground during taxying trials on 28 February.

March: The USAF's highly classified Strategic Missiles Evaluation Committee chaired by John von Neumann concluded that intercontinental ballistic missiles (ICBMs) were a feasible proposition, resulting in demands from SAC under General Curtis LeMay for improved bomber technology.

1 April: The USAF Academy was inaugurated. It was required to 'provide instruction and experience to all cadets so they graduate with the knowledge and character essential to leadership and the instruction to become career officers in the US Air Force'.

1 April: MATS received the first of 26 Convair C-131A twin-piston transports, a military derivative of the Convair 240 airliner.

1 May: The USAF's first Early Warning and Control Division was formed, equipped with ten Lockheed RC-121Cs diverted from the US Navy.

May: Incirlik AB, Turkey, was activated under the control of the 39th Tactical Group.

Republic F-84F Thunderstreak

18 June: First flight was made by the Martin B-57B, the interdictor-bomber variant of the earlier B-57A/RB-57A.

21 June: Three B-47 Stratojets of the 22nd Bomb Wing, led by Major General Walter C Sweeney Jr, Commander of the US 15th Air Force, completed a non-stop 6,700-mile flight from March AFB, CA to Yokota AB, Japan, in less than 15 hours. It included two in-flight refuelling sessions with KC-97s.

24 June: Colorado Springs, CO was named as the location for the new US Air Force Academy.

28 June: The USAF's first Douglas RB-66A Destroyer made its maiden flight from Long Beach, CA to Edwards AFB, CA.

30 June: A record total was set for post-WW2 USAF aircraft procurement in one year on this date, as 5,662 aircraft had been accepted in the previous 12 months.

1 July: The Western Development Division was established, this later developing into the USAF's Ballistic Missile Program.

15 July: 'Tex' Johnson made the first flight of the Boeing 367-80 prototype, which became known as the civil Boeing 707 airliner. It was evaluated by the USAF and was ordered as the KC-135A Stratotanker in September 1954.

5 August: The maiden flight was made by the first production B-52A Stratofortress (52-001). It differed from the prototypes in having a new cockpit seating the two pilots side-by-side, rather than in tandem, as in the B-47.

6 August: Operation *Leap Frog*, whereby B-47s on intercontinental bombing missions flew a bombing mission and went on to land at a friendly airfield further along, instead of forward-basing and returning to the point of departure.

23 August: The prototype Lockheed YC-130 Hercules (53-3397) flew for the first time.

26 August: Major Arthur Murray, USAF, set a new manned altitude record of 90,443ft flying an air-launched Bell X-1.

1 September: First flight of the Fairchild C-123B Provider transport was made.

1 September: USAF Continental Air Defense Command established.

27 September: The F-100A Super Sabre reached operational status with Tactical Air Command's 479th Fighter Day Wing at

North American F-100A Super Sabre

George AFB, CA, having received its first aircraft the previous November.

29 September: First flight of the McDonnell YF-101 Voodoo (53-2418), successor to the earlier XF-88/A testbeds. Test pilot Bob Little (uniquely, at the time) took the new aircraft past Mach 1 on this first flight.

12 October: The prototype Cessna XT-37 (54-0716), the USAF's first basic jet trainer, made its maiden flight at Wichita.

October: The USAF formulated a requirement for its B-70 supersonic bomber, which stipulated an aircraft able to strike targets at a distance of 3,500 miles and fly unrefuelled in both directions at Mach 3, carrying a wide range of nuclear weapons.

4 November: Final flight of the USAF's last B-29 Superfortress, the aircraft (42-94032, a B-29A) being retired as a bomber from the 307th BW and flying to Davis-Monthan AFB, AZ for storage.

7 November: Plans announced by USAF for the construction of a special laboratory for the detailed design and manufacture of atomic engines for large aircraft.

17-19 November: Colonel David A Burchinal, USAF, flying a B-47 Stratojet, broke all endurance records for jet aircraft with a 47hr 35min flight of some 21,000 miles (including nine in-flight refuelling links) between Sidi Slimane in French Morocco and RAF Fairford, England, when bad weather prevented him landing.

20 December: First flight of the revised prototype Convair YF-102A (Model 8-90), the definitive pre-production configuration for the Delta Dagger. The F-102A was the first USAF fighter to become operational armed only with guided missiles and unguided rockets.

The 93rd Heavy Bombardment Wing located at Castle AFB, CA, started a new era for SAC and the USAF's strategic bomber force as it took delivery of the first B-52 Stratofortress (an RB-52B reconnaissance-configured variant) to be allocated to an operational unit. A total of 50 B-models were produced, of which 23 were basic B-52Bs and the remainder dual reconnaissance-bombers 'RBs'. The RB-52B was unique in having a large, cylindrical pressurised capsule fitted into the greater part of the bomb-bay. Two crewmen could operate photo and electronic reconnaissance or electronic countermeasures (ECM) equipment from this capsule. Almost all of the 50 aircraft went to the Castle-based Wing.

Shortly after the B-52 entered service, one of its long-serving predecessors was retired – the last Boeing B-50D being withdrawn from the 97th Bombardment Wing. The era of the Boeing Superfortress bomber family had come to an end, although KB-50 aerial refuelling tankers (subsequently replaced by the KC-135 Stratotanker, for which Boeing received its first major production contract in 1955) and WB-50 weather reconnaissance aircraft, remained operational until the late 1960s.

The first flight of the Lockheed U-2 from the secure Groom Lake airfield, NV, clearly did not attract the same attention. It had been secretly transported to the flight test facility inside an Air Force C-124 Globemaster II. The unmarked high-altitude reconnaissance aircraft became airborne for nearly a quarter of a mile during taxy trials in the hands of Tony Le Vier on 1 August. Its first planned 20-minute flight took place on 4 August. In spite of demands from General Curtis LeMay that the new spyplane should be assigned to the Air Force's Strategic Air Command, operational management was handed to the Central Intelligence Agency (CIA). Pilot training did remain with the Air Force and almost all of the early U-2 pilots came from SAC.

The Lockheed U-2 was to become one of the most politically and internationally controversial aircraft ever to be operated by the US. It was essentially a very high flying jet powered glider. It used a basic Lockheed F-104 fuselage

North American F-86D 'Sabre Dog'

with very high aspect ratio wings to carry various packages of photographic and electronic cameras and sensors over long ranges at very high altitude. The U-2 was designed to fly above the maximum height that it was thought Soviet interceptor fighters could reach.

Another, rather less classified, first flight during the year was that of the Republic YF-105A Thunderchief, which, like the YF-101 before it, broke the sound barrier whilst in the air for the first time. This single-seat fighter-bomber was designed as an F-84 replacement. Also on the fighter front, the first Convair F-102A Delta Dagger was handed over to the USAF on 1 June, the early aircraft going to Edwards AFB for evaluation before deliveries for squadron use commenced a year later.

Earlier USAF fighters were also 'in the headlines', with two new records being established. In May, the first dawn-to-dusk round-trip transcontinental flight was made by an F-86 Sabre of the Air National Guard, flying between Los Angeles and New York and back in 11hr 26min. Then in August, the world absolute air speed record was broken by Colonel H A Haines, flying an F-100C Super Sabre. This was a new fighter-bomber version of the original F-100, which raised the record set by the YF-100 prototype in 1953 by almost 70 mph.

Lockheed XF-104 Starfighter

The pages for 1955 generously supported by the Society of British Aerospace Companies

4 January: Air Research and Development Command called for an unmanned reconnaissance aircraft with a range of 3,450 miles capable of operating at 100,000ft.

20 January: The South Vietnamese Government reached an agreement with the US whereby it (together with Britain and France) would supply equipment for the modernisation of its air forces.

25 January: First flight made by the Boeing RB-52B, the reconnaissance version of the Stratofortress.

1 March: The 551st Early Warning and Control Wing at Otis AFB, Falmouth, MA, the first modernised early warning unit covering the east coast of Continental US, began operating the Lockheed RC-121D Constellation airborne early warning (AEW) platform.

2 March: The Boeing Company demonstrated its Model 367-80 airliner to the USAF fitted with an improved flying boom for in-flight refuelling as an aerial tanker.

10 March: The first production C-130A Hercules (53-3129) was rolled-out at the Lockheed plant at Marietta, GA. Its first flight took place four weeks later, but it was badly damaged by an engine fire on its third flight. However, repairs were effected, the C-130 flew again and was later modified as an AC-130A gunship, serving until early 1995 with the Air Force Reserve.

10 May: Douglas delivered the last of 448 C-124 Globemaster

Douglas C-124C Globemaster II

Douglas SC-54D Skymaster

II transports, affectionately known as 'Old Shaky', to the USAF.

15 May: The US and Canada reached agreement on the final details of the construction of the Defense Early Warning (DEW) radar line, aiming to protect the North American continent from unexpected hostile air attack from the Soviet Union.

21 May: The first dawn-to-dusk, round-trip, transcontinental flight was made by an Air National Guard F-86A Sabre (49-1046), flying from Los Angeles to New York and back in 11hr 26min.

1 June: The first Convair F-102A Delta Dagger all-weather interceptor was handed over to the USAF. Deliveries to squadrons began a year later.

29 June: The first Boeing B-52 Stratofortress (an RB-52B, 52-8711) was delivered to an operational unit – the 93rd Bombardment Wing at Castle AFB, CA.

July: The 1502nd Air Transport Wing was formed at Hickam AFB, HI, operating the C-124 Globemaster II.

11 July: The USAF Academy was dedicated at its temporary location at Lowry AFB, CO. The first 306 cadets were sworn in on the same day.

1 August: Initial USAF research into zero-gravity commenced, with Lockheed F-80s and T-33s providing aerial simulation platforms.

4 August: The first Lockheed U-2 spyplane had its 'official' maiden flight at Groom Lake, a secure airfield in the Nevada desert. It had made a quarter-mile 'hop' during taxy trials three days earlier.

20 August: The world absolute air speed record was broken by Colonel H A Haines flying an F-100C Super Sabre. He reached an average speed of 822.135 mph (1,323.03 km/h).

27 September: Maiden flight of the first production Cessna T-37A (54-2729) was made. 534 were ultimately to be produced for the USAF as basic jet trainers and light attack aircraft.

30 September: The design and manufacture of three X-15 (Project 1226) hypersonic research aircraft was awarded to North American Aviation Inc. A letter of contract was issued on 6 December and the final go-ahead to commence building in June 1956.

5 October: After successful demonstrations of the prototype Model 367-80, Boeing received an initial production order for 29 KC-135A tanker/transport aircraft for the USAF. The company eventually went on to build a total of 732 KC-135s and a further 88 similar variants.

20 October: Strategic Air Command's last B-50 Superfortress, a 'D' model (49-330) was withdrawn from service with the 97th Bombardment Wing, Biggs AFB, TX.

22 October: First flight made of the Republic YF-105A Thunderchief (54-0098), affectionately known as the *Thud*. It exceeded the speed of sound on this flight.

11 November: Boeing and North American were awarded with competitive preliminary design contracts for the USAF's supersonic intercontinental bomber programme, Weapon System 110A.

18 November: The Bell X-2 (46-674) made its first powered flight when a Boeing EB-50A released the aircraft at altitude. It achieved a speed of Mach 0.95 (627 mph).

10 December: The Ryan X-13 Vertijet prototype (54-1619) VTOL research aircraft was flown for the first time. This vertijet, tail-sitting experimental fighter made its first conventional flight using a temporary tricycle landing gear.

Robert T McCall captures the icy wind of the Canadian winter in DEW Line Helicopters at Goose Bay. *An Air Force Sikorsky H-19A Chickasaw helicopter gives valuable assistance to the construction project. This painting is from the Air Force Art Collection.*

DEW Line Helicopters at Goose Bay by Robert T McCall ASAA

The USAF's transport fleet was further modernised this year, with delivery in December of the first C-130A Hercules to an operational unit, the 463rd Troop Carrier Wing at Ardmore AFB. The first crews to fly the type immediately found its manoeuvrability and power a major improvement over the existing Fairchild C-119, and in flight trials the Hercules exceeded all the performance goals laid down in the USAF's original requirement.

The first production Douglas C-133A Cargomaster heavy strategic freighter made its first flight in April, just over three years after detailed design had commenced. Unusually, this type went directly from the drawing board into production, without a prototype being flown. A total of 35 C-133As, powered by four 6,500hp Pratt & Whitney T34-P-7WA turboprops, was built before production switched to the improved C-133B. The Cargomaster was the USAF's first transport aircraft capable of airlifting ballistic missiles.

Another 'heavy' aircraft to fly for the first time during the year was the KC-135A Stratotanker, the military tanker/transport development of Boeing's Model 367-80 (707) airliner. This aircraft was delivered to the USAF early the following year, and in operational service replaced the earlier KB-50 and KC-97. SAC also started to receive improved versions of the Boeing B-52C and 'D

Martin B-57E

McDonnell F-101A Voodoo

Stratofortresses in 1956. The former was a dual bomber-reconnaissance variant of which 35 were built, while the B-52D was a dedicated bomber, production totalling 170 – making it the second most numerous Stratofortress model built. Boeing delivered the last production B-47 Stratojet to the USAF during 1956 as well, the fleet being heavily utilised during the year as SAC undertook Operations *Power House* and *Road Block* which saw over 1,000 B-47s and KC-97s involved in a two-week mass exercise.

The USAF's first supersonic bomber, the Convair XB-58 Hustler, made its initial flight towards the end of the year. The delta-winged machine, powered by four General Electric J79-GE-5A turbojets, was capable of speeds in excess of Mach 2 at altitude, although its range was limited to 4,400 miles. Early flight tests showed the aircraft to be over 200 mph faster than the USAF's then-current front-line fighters. Meanwhile, the first flight of the Convair F-106 Delta Dart took place at the end of December. This development of the F-102, with a more powerful Pratt & Whitney J75 turbojet and improved flight controls, used a re-evaluation of the 'area rule' concept to produce a more aerodynamically-efficient

fuselage. A total of 340 of these supersonic all-weather interceptors was produced.

The entry into service of the Lockheed U-2 commenced in 1956, with the formation of the CIA's first unit, covertly titled Weather Reconnaissance Squadron Provisional (WRSP) 1. It was first deployed in April to the USAF base at RAF Lakenheath, but moved to Wiesbaden AB in West Germany for the first overflights of the Soviet Union, which began on 4 July. The U-2's first tactical use came later in the year, when missions over the UK, France and Israel were executed in order to photograph movements of weapons from storage dumps – this provided the US with its first confirmation that preparations were being made for military action in response to the Suez Crisis. Additionally, naval movements in Mediterranean ports were observed by U-2s. Following these missions, deployment of USAF aircraft took place as a precaution against the possible expansion of hostilities.

Before production ended in 1957 over 2,000 B-47 Stratojets were built for the USAF. John Young's painting Cold War Warriors *shows the 1950s backbone of Strategic Air Command. This painting is reproduced courtesy of Aerodrome Press Inc, Seattle, WA.*

The pages for 1956 generously supported by Boeing Defense and Space Group

Cold War Warriors by John Young GAvA, VP ASAA

1956

1 January: The 1,000th B-47 Stratojet entered service with Strategic Air Command (SAC).

10 January: First launches of the 50ft-diameter Moby Dick balloon with the WS-119L camera system were made from Incirlik, Turkey and from West Germany, for strategic reconnaissance operations over Russia.

17 February: Initial flight made by the first production Lockheed F-104A Starfighter, the single-seat air superiority fighter.

20 February: Following reports on prospects for building a hydrogen-fuelled test engine, Lockheed was contracted for six CL-400 hydrogen-burning reconnaissance aircraft, under a project named Suntan.

9 March: First flight made by the multi-mission B-52C Stratofortress. Delivery of 35 to SAC began on 14 June. It had a higher all-up weight and larger underwing tanks.

April: The Convair F-102A Delta Dagger entered service with the 327th Fighter Interceptor Squadron at George AFB, CA.

April: The CIA's first Lockheed U-2 unit, Weather Reconnaissance Squadron Provisional (WRSP) 1, was deployed to RAF Lakenheath. It moved to Wiesbaden AB, West Germany following security fears by the British Government.

2 April: The USAF launched a Snark guided missile. Its experimental flight covered 1,500 miles.

23 April: Maiden flight of the Douglas C-133A Cargomaster was made. 50 examples of the high-wing transport (35 C-133A and 15 C-133B) were delivered to the USAF from late 1957. Uniquely, the type entered production immediately, with no prototypes.

21 May: Operation Redwing - the first hydrogen bomb was dropped from an aircraft, a B-52B of the 93rd Bombardment Wing, during a series of tests carried out in the vicinity of Bikini Atoll, in the Pacific.

31 May: The first Martin RB-57D reconnaissance aircraft (with increased wingspan for high-altitude operations) was delivered to the 4080th Strategic Reconnaissance Wing at Turner AFB, GA.

4 June: The first of 170 Boeing B-52Ds (55-049), had its maiden flight at Wichita. Service delivery to SAC commenced on 1 December. The B-52D was similar to the B-52C but equipped solely as a long-range bomber.

22 June: Operation *Sixteen Ton*, the first sustained operational mission by the Air Force Reserve, involving cargo airlift to the Caribbean was started.

4 July: The first CIA U-2 spyflight by WRSP-1, to penetrate Soviet territory, took off from and returned to Wiesbaden AB. The mission took the U-2 over Minsk, Leningrad and the Baltic States.

15 July: The Sixteenth Air Force was activated at Torrejon AB, Spain, directly under the control of Headquarters USAF. It monitored construction of bases in Spain for use by deployed bombers and tankers of SAC.

18 July: The 592nd and last Boeing KC-97G was rolled out from the Boeing factory at Renton.

19 July: A Northrop F-89J Scorpion fired a Douglas MB-1 Genie, the first nuclear-armed air-to-air missile to be launched.

31 August: First flight of the Boeing KC-135A Stratotanker (55-3118), of which 731 more examples would follow before production ended in 1965. It was delivered to the USAF on 31 January 1957.

7 September: A new altitude record for manned flight of 126,200ft was achieved by Captain Iven Kincheloe, in a Bell X-2.

10 September: First flight of the Lockheed YF-107A, a developed version of the F-100 Super Sabre, with a split intake above the fuselage was made. Tactical Air Command selected the F-105 Thunderchief instead – thus the F-100 became the last production fighter built by North American.

27 September: The last surviving Bell X-2 and its pilot, Captain Milburn Apt, were lost. After release from its EB-50D 'mother ship' at 31,800ft it descended in a shallow dive, reaching Mach 3.196 (2,094mph) before control was lost.

24 October: Boeing delivered the last production version of the B-47 Stratojet. A total of 2,041 new-built B-47s were accepted by the Air Force, comprising two XB-47s, 10 B-47As, 397 B-47Bs, one YB-47C (later redesignated XB-56), 1,341 B-47Es, 255 RB-47Es and 35 RB-47Hs.

31 October: Britain and France began military operations against Egypt after President Nasser nationalised the Suez Canal.

November: The first operational tactical reconnaissance flights by US Lockheed U-2s were made over Britain, France and Israel, monitoring military activity as the Suez conflict developed. Some deployments of USAF aircraft were made in readiness for a possible expansion of hostilities.

6 November: The Air Research and Development Command formally organised its manned glide rocket system design work into Project HYWARDS – Hypersonic Weapons Research and Development System.

11 November: First flight of the Convair XB-58 Hustler (55-0660) was made at Fort Worth, TX. It was the USAF's first supersonic nuclear bomber. Subsequently 30 pre-production aircraft were used for extensive flight testing at Carswell AFB, variously designated YR/RB-58/58A.

24 November: Operation *Quick Kick*, a two-day exercise, when four B-52Bs from the 93rd Bomb Wing together with four from the 42nd Bomb Wing, made a non-stop flight around the perimeter of the US, being refuelled in the air four times during the 31hr 30min flight.

28 November: The Ryan X-13 Vertijet made the world's first jet vertical take-off and landing (VTOL) transition from vertical to horizontal flight at Edwards AFB, CA.

9 December: The first C-130A Hercules to be assigned to an operational unit were delivered to Tactical Air Command's 463rd Troop Carrier Wing at Ardmore AFB, OK.

11 December: Operations *Power House* and *Road Block*, a two-week mass exercise involving over 1,000 B-47 Stratojets and Boeing KC-97 tankers of SAC, were completed.

23 December: The first of five flights was made by a modified Martin B-57, with one of its two engines using a hydrogen fuel system, and the other a conventional JP-4 fuelled unit.

26 December: The first Convair YF-106 Delta Dart was flown from Edwards AFB, CA. A total of 340 examples of this supersonic, all-weather interceptor were eventually delivered. The aircraft had originally been designed as a second-stage F-102 with a more advanced engine and control system and refined area rule fuselage.

The man who, more than any other, had shaped Strategic Air Command for the Cold War, General Curtis E LeMay, was replaced after nine years as Commander-in-Chief on 1 July by General Thomas S Power. He had been LeMay's deputy for three years, and his arrival coincided with delivery of two new significant types of aircraft to SAC. Both would significantly affect the Command's strategy and improve its operational effectiveness in the future. The first Lockheed U-2A to be assigned to the USAF went to the 4080th Strategic Reconnaissance Wing at Laughlin AFB, TX. SAC now had its own 'spyplanes' rather than depending on information supplied by the CIA. The KC-135A Stratotanker, first delivered to the 93rd Air Refueling Squadron at Castle AFB, CA from June onwards, played a very important part in the development of SAC's global capabilities. As a 'force multiplier' the Stratotanker extended the range and potential of the bomber fleet and its supporting fighter escorts.

This new potential was well demonstrated by a round-the-world flight by some of SAC's latest bombers. Under Operation *Power Flite* three B-52Bs of the 93rd Bomb Wing completed the first non-stop circumnavigation of the globe by turbojet aircraft. Activation of the USAF's first Strategic Missile Wing, the 704th SMW, provided a further offensive capability. It was equipped with the Northrop SM-62 Snark, an air-breathing intercontinental missile with a range of 6,325 miles, a maximum speed of 650 mph and a nuclear warhead of around 20 megatons in yield. Further Wings would become operational in due course. By the end of the year, SAC aircraft at several bases had been placed on One-Third Ground Alert, with the aim of achieving take-off within 15 minutes in the event of an ICBM attack on the USA.

Introduction of the B-52 and, earlier, the B-47 Stratojet, led to a change in SAC's operational procedures as these fast jet types replaced the Convair B-36. The Command had, up until April, held seven Tactical Fighter

Douglas C-133A Cargomaster

Wings in its inventory (each operating F-84F Thunderjets) for the purpose of escorting the B-36s, but with the advent of jet bombers they were considered unnecessary. During 1957, the first of these were either transferred to Tactical Air Command or inactivated, as numbers of B-36s in service steadily dwindled – by April, only 76 remained on strength. A deployment of B-47 Stratojets to Sidi Slimane in French Morocco was used to initiate the *Reflex Action* alert programme, replacing the 90-day rotational training concept for forward-based SAC aircraft. This was then adopted at all other Forward Operating Locations.

Air Defense Command meanwhile was awaiting delivery of its first two-seat McDonnell F-101B Voodoo, which made its first flight in March. The primary role of this long-range interceptor was the attack of massed formations of enemy bombers, using nuclear missiles – a new operational concept. A further addition to the US air defence organisation, the Distant Early Warning radar line, was declared operational in July, with Air Defense Command and the Royal Canadian Air Force implementing a co-operative programme which had as one of its primary deterrents the deployment of nuclear-armed fighters such as the new F-101B.

The first Convair F-106A Delta Dart

The pages for 1957 generously supported by Lockheed Martin Corporation

4 January: Operation *Safe Haven* was completed, having begun five and a half weeks earlier, following the Soviet repression of the uprising in Hungary that began on 16 October. 10,000 refugees had been flown from Hungary to the USA.

16 January: Start of Operation *Power Flite*, the first non-stop round-the-world flight by turbojet aircraft, by three Boeing B-52Bs of the 93rd Bombardment Wing. They made the 24,325 mile flight in 45hr 19min.

February: The USAF's last F-51D Mustang (44-74936) from the 167th Fighter Squadron, West Virginia ANG, was flown to the USAF Museum at Wright-Patterson AFB on its retirement, for eventual exhibition.

17 February: The experimental Bell X-14 was successfully flown. This was the first ascent and hover by a vertical take-off and landing (VTOL) 'flat-riser'- configured aircraft.

1 March: First test flight was made of the SM-78 (later re-designated the PGM-19) Jupiter C liquid-fuelled intermediate-range ballistic missile (IRBM) with a nuclear warhead in the one-megaton range. Originally an Army project, it came into Air Force hands in 1959 following the decision to assign all weapons with more than 200 miles' range to the service.

27 March: The McDonnell F-101B Voodoo was first flown. It was developed to the WS-217A long-range interceptor specification for Air Defense Command. A total of 480 of these two-seat Voodoos was acquired by the USAF.

1 April: The first of SAC's seven tactical fighter wings operating Republic F-84F Thunderstreaks was transferred to Tactical Air Command. The transfer of the remaining SAC fighter wings was completed by July.

11 April: The Ryan X-13 VTOL 'vertijet' research aircraft completed a full transition. This involved a vertical take-off followed by a conversion to horizontal flight, then the reverse procedure to accomplish a successful tail-sitting landing.

2 May: The McDonnell F-101A and F-101C Voodoos both entered operational service with the 27th Fighter Bomber Wing at Bergstrom AFB, TX.

30 May: A development of the Hughes Falcon air-to-air guided missile armed with a nuclear warhead, was disclosed.

11 June: The first Lockheed U-2 (56-6696) was delivered to the 4080th Strategic Reconnaissance Wing at Laughlin AFB, TX. While the CIA's aircraft were painted all-black, Air Force U-2s retained an overall aluminium finish at first.

28 June: The first Boeing KC-135A Stratotanker (55-3127) was delivered to the 93rd Air Refueling Squadron at Castle AFB, CA.

28 June: An unmanned 200ft diameter balloon with a capacity of 3.75m cu ft, lifted two tons of equipment to a height of 104,000ft.

July: The last F-51D Mustang in service, flown to the USAF Museum in February, was finally retired from flying – it had been kept airworthy for final airshow appearances.

1 July: General Thomas S Power replaced General Curtis LeMay as Commander-in-Chief of USAF Strategic Air Command.

1 July: The Sixteenth Air Force in Spain was transferred to SAC control.

1 July: Twenty B-47 Stratojets of the 2nd Air Force were deployed to Sidi Slimane, initiating *Reflex Action*, an alert status which replaced the 90-day unit rotational training concept for forward-based SAC aircraft.

1 July: The first Strategic Missile Wing (704th SMW), equipped with the Northrop Snark, was activated.

1 July: Far East Air Force (FEAF) was renamed Pacific Air Command (PACAF). Its headquarters was moved to Hickam AFB, HI.

13 July: President Eisenhower became the first US president to fly in a helicopter when he was flown from The White House to an unnamed military post in a USAF Bell UH-13J.

19 July: The first live-firing of a nuclear-tipped Douglas Genie air-to-air missile was made from an F-89J Scorpion at 15,000ft over Yucca Flat, NV.

31 July: The North American DEW line was declared fully operational. It was aimed at protecting the continent from surprise attack.

1 August: A joint US-Canada North American Air Defense Command (NORAD) was activated informally.

13 August: The first conventional flight was made by the Boeing Vertol VZ-2A (Model 76) tilt-wing research aircraft.

19-20 August: Major David G Simmons established a new world altitude record for balloon ascent in the craft *Man High I*, reaching 101,516ft at the peak of his ascent from Crosby, MN.

September: The first deployment of C-130 Hercules to Europe was made, when USAFE's 317th Troop Carrier Wing at Evreux AB, France received its first aircraft.

4 September: First flight of the Lockheed CL-329 Jetstar utility transport was made. It eventually entered service with MATS Airway and Air Communications as the C-140.

19 September: Funding for the Project Suntan hydrogen-fuelled aircraft programme was cut by two-thirds.

20 September: The Chief of Staff announced the development of a radar system with the capability of detecting ICBMs at a range of 3,000 miles (4,830 km).

1 October: General Power ordered a 'One-Third Ground Alert' condition at several bases in the US and overseas, preparing for the possibility of a future attack on SAC by intercontinental ballistic missiles.

1 October: An Air Force crew launched an intercontinental missile, a Northrop Snark, for the first time from Cape Canaveral.

10 October: Scheduled to follow on from the X-15, Air Research Development Command brought together the earlier ROBO, HYWARDS and Brass Bell programmes to publish its development plan for the Dyna-Soar (dynamic soaring) hypersonic project.

10 December: A Directorate of Aeronautics was established by the USAF.

12 December: Major Adrian Drew set a new world speed record in F-101A Voodoo (53-3426) of 1,207.34 mph (1,943.03 km/h) at Edwards AFB, CA.

23 December: North American Aviation was awarded a contract to develop the B-70, an intercontinental Mach 3 strategic bomber.

Charles Thompson captures the graceful lines of Lockheed's VC-121A in this specially commissioned painting entitled A Real Honey. *The Air Force ordered ten examples of the L-749 Constellation for service with MATS, examples of which were used by President Eisenhower and General MacArthur.*

A Real Honey by Charles J Thompson GAvA, ASAA, GMA

After a delay of two years, the Lockheed F-104A Starfighter finally entered service with the 83rd Fighter Interceptor Squadron at Hamilton AFB, CA, in January. However, problems with the early General Electric J79 turbojet in production F-104As (which caused a number of accidents) led to a grounding order in April to await a new version of the powerplant to be fitted. These first Starfighters, of which 155 were built, were equipped with a 20-mm M61 Vulcan multi-barrel cannon and provision for two AIM-9B Sidewinders. It was the first fighter in the world to use a downward-firing ejector seat. The Lockheed interceptor was soon breaking aviation world records, notably a world altitude record for ground-launched aircraft of 91,243ft and a new absolute speed record. These flights were made by pilots from the 83rd FIS.

Another type to enter service during 1958, three years later than planned, was the F-105B Thunderchief, with which the 335th Tactical Fighter Squadron became fully operational in August at Eglin AFB, FL. Thus equipped, it became the first unit in the world with a Mach 2 strike capability – a major advance compared to the F-84F which the Thud, as the F-105 became known, replaced. Production aircraft had been delayed by the addition of various modifications over pre-production machines, including the APN-105 all-weather navigation system and

Convair YB-58 Hustler

provision for tactical nuclear armament. Meanwhile, the initial flight of the McDonnell XF4H-1, first prototype of the F4H Phantom ordered by the US Navy, was another of the year's significant events, although it would not be ordered for the USAF for another four years.

Long-distance flights by KC-135A Stratotankers of SAC underlined the fact that the new air-to-air refuelling platform would be a major asset to the Command in its role as a global deterrent. One aircraft flew non-stop between California and New Zealand, this being followed by a record-breaking 5hr 53min flight between London and New York by two KC-135s. Boeing flew its latest B-52G Stratofortress variant in October, of which 193 were built between 1958 and 1961 at the Wichita plant. It was the first Stratofortress model to possess a stand-off capability, provided by the GAM-77/AGM-28 Hound Dog air-to-surface missile. The B-52G also had major structural changes, with integral wing fuel tanks, a shorter and wider fin and rudder and a remotely controlled rear gun turret.

Looking to the future, SAC gave the name Valkyrie to its forthcoming North American B-70 strategic bomber, at the time scheduled to fly in production form in December

Boeing B-52F Stratofortress

1961 and become fully operational in 1964. The contract, from the Weapon System 110A requirement to replace the B-52, had been awarded to North American the previous December, with the programme dates having been moved forward due to fears of increasing Soviet aggression.

A further indication of increasing tension in the Cold War came in September, with another US aircraft shot down by Soviet fighters. An electronic intelligence-gathering (ELINT) C-130A-II Hercules of the Rhein-Main-based 7406th Combat Support Squadron, operating out of Adana in Turkey, was attacked by a flight of MiGs over the border between Russia and Turkey, and crashed near the village of Sassnaken, near Yerevan in Armenia. With the Soviet threat ever-growing at this time, the frequency of overflights of the region and ELINT missions by a variety of aircraft was increasing, in spite of a number of earlier 'casualties', falling both to fighters and anti-aircraft artillery (AAA).

Eventually equipped with 135 Atlas ICBMs at eleven bases, SAC was to place considerable dependence on this deterrent. The late Ralph Iligan depicts the enormous power of the missile in Launching an Atlas ICBM, *a painting from the Air Force Art Collection.*

The pages for 1958 generously supported by GEC-Marconi Avionics

Launching an Atlas ICBM by Ralph Iligan

1958

26 January: Deliveries of the Lockheed F-104A commenced (two years behind schedule) to the 83rd Fighter Interceptor Squadron at Hamilton AFB, CA. Pilots from this squadron were later responsible for the first speed and altitude record flights by the Starfighter.

31 January: The first US satellite, Explorer I, was launched into orbit from Cape Canaveral, using a Jupiter C rocket.

1 February: The 706th Strategic Missile Wing was activated at Francis E. Warren AFB, WY, as the USAF's first Atlas Strategic Missile Wing.

18 February: The USAF disclosed that an airflow speed of approximately 52,140 km/h (32,400 mph) had been attained briefly in the test section of a wind tunnel at Arnold Research and Development Center, Tullahoma, TN.

26 March: A North American F-100D, propelled by an Astrodyne rocket motor, was flown from a zero-length launcher. These were designed for use in shelters being planned for the protection of TAC aircraft on exposed airfields against a nuclear attack.

27 March: A KC-135 Stratotanker completed a non-stop flight from California to New Zealand.

May: C-130 Hercules deployed US Army paratroops and equipment to Puerto Rico, after violence in Caracas during Vice-President Nixon's visit to the Venezuelan capital.

7 May: Major Howard C Johnson achieved a new world

Convair TF-102A Delta Dagger

altitude record when he reached a height of 91,243ft in an F-104A Starfighter.

12 May: North American Air Defense Command (NORAD), formally established with headquarters at Colorado Springs. With an international command of US and Canadian forces, NORAD had the responsibility for protecting the North American continent from attack through early warning and active defence.

16 May: Captain Walter W Irvin, flying an F-104A Starfighter, increased the world absolute air speed record to 1,403.79 mph (2,259.18 km/h).

24 May: The Bell X-14 made its first full transition from hovering to horizontal flight. It moved from vertical lift-off to forward motion in less than 30 seconds.

27 May: The first operational Republic F-105B Thunderchief fighters were accepted by the 335th Tactical Fighter Squadron, based at Eglin AFB, FL.

27 May: First flight of the McDonnell YF4H-1, prototype of the F-4 Phantom II was made. It subsequently became the USAF's most significant fighter of the '60s and '70s.

29 June: A record 5hr 53 min flight between London and New York was made by two Boeing KC-135As from SAC's 99th Air Refueling Squadron.

July: The 4228th Strategic Wing was formed at Columbus AFB, MS, flying the B-52F Stratofortress and KC-135A Stratotanker.

July: A USAFE airlift moved 2,000 troops from Germany to the Middle East in response to the Lebanese crisis.

3 July: The name Valkyrie was chosen by SAC from over 20,000 suggestions, for the new B-70 strategic bomber.

15 July: TAC deployed its Composite Air Strike Force Bravo to Lebanon and SAC was placed on increased alert, following a request from the Lebanese President who felt that a Soviet invasion of his country was imminent.

August: Three years later than planned, the F-105B became fully operational with the 335th Tactical Fighter Squadron at Eglin AFB, FL.

August: C-124 Globemaster IIs were used to airlift Pacific Air

Force F-104A Starfighters and their support equipment to Ching Chuan Kang AB on Formosa (now Taiwan), after China, supported by Russia, had partitioned two Formosan islands and threatened to occupy them.

23 August: Forces of the People's Republic of China launched artillery and air attacks on Nationalist Chinese across the Formosa Straits, leading to deployment of a TAC Composite Air Strike Force to bases in Taiwan, Okinawa, Japan and the Philippines, supported by C-130s.

2 September: A USAF Lockheed C-130A-II of the 7406th Combat Support Squadron, on an electronic intelligence gathering (ELINT) mission along the Turkish-Soviet border, was shot down near Yerevan in Armenia by five Soviet MiGs.

9 September: The Lockheed X-7, a pilotless test vehicle for ramjet engines and missile components, achieved a speed of Mach 4, following air-launch from a Boeing EB-50.

15 September: The first test of Operation *Head Start I*, an airborne alert concept for B-52s, was conducted by the 42nd Bombardment Wing at Loring AFB, ME.

16 September: First flight of the North American NA-246 six-seat jet transport (N4060K), subsequently developed into the T-39 Sabreliner liaison and training aircraft.

19 September: The first of 18 Kaman H-43A Huskie piston-engined helicopters for the USAF was flown. It was purchased for the airborne fire-fighting and crash rescue role at Tactical Air Command bases.

26 October: First flight of Boeing's latest Stratofortress variant, the B-52G, which remained in service until early 1994. It could carry two North American AGM-28 Hound Dog (WS131B) air-to-surface missiles, one under each wing.

1 November: The first Lycoming T53-L-1A shaft turbine engined Kaman H-43B (58-1841) for the USAF was flown. A total of 203 was eventually delivered for use at bases of all flying Commands throughout the Continental US and overseas as detachments of the MATS Air Rescue Service. The designation was changed to HH-43B in mid-1962.

18 December: The USAF placed in Earth orbit a small communications relay satellite.

The new missile threat from the Soviet Union led to a re-evaluation of the USAF's offensive missile capability, to the detriment of the manned bomber force. The first merger between the missile and aircraft forces was on 1 January, when Strategic Air Command's Eighth Air Force took control of the 702nd Strategic Missile Wing at Presque Isle AFB, ME. Later, the USAF's first intercontinental ballistic missile, an Atlas D, was placed on alert status at Vandenberg AFB, CA. The primary casualty of the increasing reliance on such weapons was the North American B-70 Valkyrie bomber programme. The concept of using boron-fuelled General Electric YJ93-GE-5 engines in the type was also abandoned in favour of the GE-3 version using refined jet petroleum fuel, thus effectively cutting the Valkyrie's range by 10%.

North American was also instructed to halt the development of the B-70's projected escort fighter, the advanced design F-108 Rapier. This was a Mach 3 interceptor, similar in configuration to the giant bomber. However, the final nail in the B-70's coffin came in December, with the announcement that plans for production of the bomber for SAC had been abandoned. Budgetary difficulties and the new strategic importance of

Douglas C-47A Skytrain

Boeing B-47 Stratojet

ballistic weapons saw to it that SAC would not receive what, at the time, was the world's most advanced bomber. Work on only one XB-70 prototype was to proceed, and subsequent research work was to be only on a relatively small scale.

However, the year did see Strategic Air Command receive its first Boeing B-52G Stratofortress, when it was delivered to the 5th Bomb Wing at Travis AFB, CA. Whilst the new version included several major improvements over earlier variants, the first 55 examples built were not yet able to carry the new North American GAM-77/AGM-28 Hound Dog missile which was first live-fired from a B-52D in April. With its Pratt & Whitney J52-6 turbojet engine and a one-megaton nuclear warhead, this stand-off weapon was essentially an early cruise missile. B-52Gs and Hs were all eventually equipped with the Hound Dog, the earlier 'G' models being modified to carry it. After service entry, this weapon remained in operational use with SAC until 1976.

With the B-70's cancellation the year became somewhat controversial as SAC said goodbye to an earlier era with

Lockheed C-130D Hercules

the retirement of its last Convair B-36J Peacemaker, that had served with the 95th Bomb Wing at Biggs AFB, TX. This left SAC, for the first time, with a bomber force consisting entirely of jet aircraft – a little way behind the RAF, whose last Boeing B-50 Washingtons had left the inventory in 1958 following the introduction into service of the Canberra.

There were several record-breaking flights during the year, notably on 15 December when the absolute world air speed record was raised to 2,455.74 km/h (1,525.93 mph) by Major Joseph W Rogers, flying a Convair F-106A Delta Dart. Never again would an operational fighter break this record. 1959 saw an indication of progress being made by the USAF and NACA/NASA in building ever faster aircraft, as the North American X-15A made its first powered flight after release from a B-52. It attained a speed of Mach 2.11 (1,393 mph) using a Reaction Motors XLR-11 rocket powerplant in place of the XLR-99 which was not as yet fully ready for use. This engine was not actually declared operationally ready until late the following year.

The pages for 1959 generously supported by Lockheed Martin Skunk Works

1 January: The 702nd Strategic Missile Wing was activated and assigned to the Eighth Air Force. This was the first time that missile and bomber forces had been integrated in this way.

February: The last Lockheed F-94C Starfires were retired from Air National Guard squadrons.

6 February: The first successful launch of the SM-68 (later redesignated LGM-25) Titan ICBM.

12 February: The last Convair B-36 Peacemaker (52-2827) was retired from SAC. This B-36J of the 95th Bombardment Wing at Biggs AFB, TX was flown to Amon Carter Field, Fort Worth, where it was displayed as a memorial to the type.

13 February: The first Boeing B-52G (57-6478), that became the most widely used variant of the Stratofortress, was delivered to the 5th Bomb Wing at Travis AFB, CA.

28 February: *Discoverer I* was placed in orbit by the USAF.

10 March: A Bell X-15 rocket-powered research aircraft made its first captive-inactive flight suspended by a pylon beneath the starboard wing of a modified Boeing B-52 carrier-plane. One B-52A and one B-52B had been modified for this project.

9 April: The 405th Tactical Fighter Wing was activated at Clark AB in the Philippines, to replace the 6200th Air Base Wing flying the F-100D Super Sabre and F-102A Delta Dagger.

10 April: First flight of the Northrop YT-38 Talon (58-1191) was made from Edwards AFB. It was a derivative of the company's N-156 lightweight fighter and went into service as the USAF's first supersonic trainer.

23 April: The first successful live firing of the GAM-77 Hound Dog strategic air-to-surface missile, was made from a B-52D. The first of these missiles entered service with the 4135th Strategic Wing at Eglin AFB, FL.

May: Deliveries of the Convair F-106A Delta Dart began to Air Defense Command, the type entering service with the 498th Fighter Interceptor Squadron at Geiger AFB, WA.

12 May: USAF operation of the Boeing 707 series began, when the first of three 707-153s (designated VC-137As) was delivered to the 1298th Air Transport Squadron, that was later to become the 89th Military Airlift Wing.

27 May: Delivery of the first Northrop Snark missile was made to the 702nd Strategic Missile Wing at Presque Isle AFB, ME. The Snark was placed on alert on 18 March 1960 and the Wing was declared operationally alert on 28 February 1961. It was short-lived as the force was deactivated on 25 June 1961 as ICBMs entered service.

3 June: The first class of 207 cadets graduated from the new purpose-built Air Force Academy at Colorado Springs. The Academy had moved from its temporary base at Denver in August 1958.

8 June: The Bell X-15 rocket research aircraft made its first unpowered drop from a B-52 flying at 37,500ft. It reached a speed of Mach 0.79 during the gliding descent.

12 June: The first of 123 Lockheed C-130B Hercules was delivered to the 463rd Troop Carrier Wing's 774th Squadron at Sewart AFB, TE.

July: Following President de Gaulle's refusal to grant the US atomic weapon storage rights in France, the 48th, 49th and 50th Tactical Fighter Wings were withdrawn from their French bases under Project *Red Richard*, and were relocated to bases in England.

30 July: First flight of the Northrop N-156F, that was later adopted as the F-5 Freedom Fighter. It exceeded a speed of Mach 1 during this initial flight test.

11 August: It was announced that the Boron-fuel concept for the General Electric YJ93-GE-5 after-burning engines in the supersonic B-70 Valkyrie programme was to be abandoned.

29 August: The contract was awarded to Lockheed for a high-altitude, high-speed CIA reconnaissance aircraft, designated A-12. Known as Project *Oxcart*, it was to be managed by the USAF.

9 September: An Air Force crew carried out the first service launch of an Atlas ICBM from Vandenberg AFB, CA. It flew for some 4,300 miles, reaching 16,000 mph.

17 September: The North American X-15A research aircraft made its first powered drop from a B-52 in the hands of Scott Crossfield. It attained a speed of Mach 2.11 (1,393 mph) and a height of 53,341ft.

23 September: North American's advanced F-108 Rapier supersonic interceptor, designed as a miniature version of the XB-70 Valkyrie, was cancelled after two years of development.

15 October: Only a month after its initial flight, the first production Convair B-58A Hustler made a 1,680-mile flight in 1hr 10min, with one refuelling, and maintained a cruising speed in excess of Mach 2 for over one hour.

31 October: The Douglas C-133B was flown for the first time. It was a developed version of MATS' basic Cargomaster.

31 October: First Intercontinental Ballistic Missile (ICBM), an Atlas D, was placed on alert.

3 November: Initial airlift delivery of an Atlas ICBM was made by a C-133 Cargomaster, the first USAF transport capable of accommodating such a missile.

9 November: The USAF selected Boeing for a contract to build the Dyna-Soar hypersonic boost-glide vehicle, designated Weapon System 620A. Project control was moved to the Wright Air Development Division at Wright-Patterson AFB, OH.

3 December: Funding for the XB-70 Valkyrie programme was cut back to a single prototype.

9 December: At Bloomfield, CT, a Kaman H-43B rescue helicopter set a rotary-wing altitude record of 29,846ft.

14 December: A Lockheed F-104C Starfighter reached a new record altitude of 103,389ft (31,502-m). It was the first Air Force pilot (Captain Joseph B Jordan) and the first USAF aircraft to exceed 100,000ft.

15 December: A new absolute world air speed record was achieved by Major Joseph W Rogers, flying a Convair F-106A Delta Dart (56-467) at Edwards AFB, CA, with an average speed of 2,455.74 km/h (1,525.93 mph) – the last world speed record set by a single-engined, operational service fighter.

23 December: The first Hound Dog nuclear-armed air-to-surface missile was delivered to the 4135th Strategic Wing at Eglin AFB, FL.

By 1959, the Lockheed F-104 Starfighter was established in USAF service and consistently breaking speed and altitude records. This untitled painting by Chuck Hodgson is reproduced by kind permission of the Lockheed Martin Skunk Works.

Lockheed F-104 Starfighter by Chuck Hodgson

Reconnaissance flights by the USAF over and around the Soviet Union continued, as did those by the CIA using its Lockheed U-2s. They had uncovered disturbing evidence that the Russians were making significantly faster progress with the development of inter-continental ballistic missiles than had been previously thought. Around 30 such overflights by the type had been made since 1956, when on 1 May Francis Gary Powers took off from Peshawar in Pakistan, to photograph the missile test sites at Plesetsk and in Kazakhstan. Unfortunately, the Soviet defences were alerted to the spyplane's presence and a salvo of SA-2 surface to air missiles apparently caused a structural failure which brought the U-2 down near Sverdlovsk, with Powers managing to eject.

Although direct overflights of the USSR were halted, the USAF continued to make reconnaissance flights close to Soviet borders. Losses continued, and in July, exactly two months after Powers' shootdown, an ERB-47H Stratojet of the 55th SRW operating from RAF Brize Norton was 'downed' by a Soviet MiG-17 in international airspace over the Barents Sea. Four crew members were killed, but the pilot, Captain John McKone and navigator Lieutenant Bruce Olmstead were rescued by the Soviets. They were initially held for spying but were released seven months later. The attacking MiG pilot, Lieutenant Vasili Polyakov, reported that he believed the Stratojet to be heading towards a top secret Soviet nuclear submarine base, but this was disputed by the USAF. Quite clearly a worsening in the Cold War was now happening.

Further Cold War measures were evident by the start of operational trials of the airborne command post and communications centre concepts, using a specially-configured Boeing KC-97 and five modified 34th Air Refueling Squadron KC-135As. Commencing in July, the programme proved the concept's viability within six months, paving the way towards full operational status the following year.

SAC received its first B-58A Hustlers during the first quarter of the year, the 43rd Bombardment Wing at Carswell AFB, TX being the initial unit to become fully operational on the type. The introduction of such an advanced new bomber, capable of speeds over Mach 2, required special training. A unique feature of the B-58 was

Douglas RB-66C Destroyer

its jettisonable under-fuselage pod which could carry nuclear or conventional bombs, fuel or reconnaissance equipment. A total of 108 production Hustlers was delivered to SAC (in addition to the two prototypes and eleven B-58s used for development and trials work). The type set numerous speed and altitude records during its relatively short service career.

Flying still faster through 1960 was the North American X-15A, whose XLR-99 rocket powerplant was used for the first time in November. Prior to that, USAF Captain Robert M White had set an unofficial height record flying the X-15 fitted with the earlier XLR-11 motor. Five USAF test pilots would fly the X-15 during its flight test lifetime, White being joined by Major Robert Rushworth, Captain William Knight, Major Michael Adams and Captain Joseph Engle. Between them, they amassed 89 flights out of the total of 199 made by the aircraft. Major Rushworth himself flew it 34 times – the highest total of any of the aircraft's pilots.

The three North American X-15 rocket powered hypersonic research aircraft flew faster and higher than any other 'conventional' machine. Air-launched from a B-52, the X-15 was accompanied by other aircraft that monitored its return from The Edge of Space, brought together here in Wilf Hardy's painting.

Douglas C-133B Cargomaster

The pages for 1960 generously supported by Flight International

The Edge of Space by Wilfred Hardy GAvA

15 March: Having moved from Davis-Monthan, the 43rd Bombardment Wing of SAC was formed at Carswell AFB, TX as the first unit to operate the B-58A Hustler.

April: The results of the *Phase Alpha* review of the Dyna-Soar programme were released, confirming Boeing as the prime contractor.

1 April: The first US weather satellite, TIROS 1, was placed in orbit.

1 May: CIA pilot Francis Gary Powers was shot down in a Lockheed U-2C over Sverdlovsk, Russia. This event put a stop to further overflights of the Soviet Union by U-2s.

4 May: Specific Operational Requirement 182 was issued. It defined the tasks to be assigned a new strategic military jet transport for the Military Air Transport Service (MATS).

12 May: A record test parachute drop of 35,000lb (15,876kg) mass was made from a C-130 Hercules whilst in flight. This was increased to 40,500lb (18,370kg) on 20 July.

21 May: The last B-25 Mitchell (a TB-25) was retired from USAF service after use as a staff transport at Eglin AFB, FL.

24 May: The first early warning satellite, MIDAS II, was placed in earth orbit.

1 July: SAC established a major presence in Alaska, when the 4157th Combat Support Group (later Strategic Wing) was formed at Eielson AFB.

1 July: An ERB-47H Stratojet of the 55th Strategic Reconnaissance Wing was shot down by a Soviet MiG-17, while operating in international airspace over the Barents Sea. Of the six-man crew, four were killed, but the pilot and navigator were held by the Russians as spies.

1 July: SAC began operational testing with an airborne tactical command post and communications centre – one of five specially converted KC-135s of the 34th Air Refueling Squadron, operating from Offutt AFB, NE. The aircraft were kept on ground alert and ready to take-off within 15 minutes of an attack warning being received.

14 July: Specific Operational Requirement 183 was issued. It called for a Tactical Fighter Experimental (TFX) to replace the F-105 Thunderchief.

Douglas C-118A

14 July: The Congo airlift, Operation *Safari*, commenced. It involved some 130 C-130 Hercules and C-124 Globemaster IIs which transported almost 38,000 UN troops across Africa.

1 August: The first B-58 Hustler unit, the 43rd Bomb Wing, was declared operational.

10 August: Launch of *Discoverer XIII*, the first successful Corona spy satellite mission, which concluded with the capsule being safely recovered. This was the first man-made object returned intact from space.

12 August: The North American X-15 reached a new unofficial record height of 136,500ft when flown by a USAF test pilot, Captain Robert M White.

16 August: Captain Joseph W Kittinger Jr parachuted from a balloon at a height of 102,800ft, a new altitude record for unpowered flight, free falling 84,700ft – with a top speed of 614 mph in 4min 38sec – the longest delayed parachute jump ever to be made.

18 August: The first successful in-flight retrieval of an orbited capsule. It was recovered after ejection from the *Discoverer XIV* satellite, at an altitude of 8,000ft by a Fairchild C-119 transport using a specially-developed 'snatch' technique.

30 August: The first ICBM squadron, the 564th Strategic Missile Squadron with six Atlas missiles, became operational at Francis E Warren AFB, WY.

18 September: A B-58A Hustler (58-1015) was flown from Fort Worth, TX to Bakersfield, CA at a height of between 100ft and 500ft and at a speed that did not drop below 690 mph, to demonstrate the low-altitude mission capabilities of the normally high-flying supersonic bomber.

21 September: TAC formally accepted its first Republic F-105D Thunderchief supersonic tactical fighter-bomber in a ceremony at Nellis AFB, NV.

October: It was announced that the USAF had been conducting studies on an aerospace-aircraft capable of operating between the outer atmosphere and space by ingesting large quantities of air at hypersonic speed.

24-31 October: A combined US Army/USAF exercise, named Operation *South Wind*, and involving MATS and TAC, was held to test their capability to deploy over 10,000 Strategic Army Command troops to a distant base.

31 October: Funding for the North American XB-70 programme was increased to allow for the construction of two prototypes and a structural test airframe.

4 November: It was announced that a converted Boeing KC-97 was being operated as an airborne tactical command post and communications centre in addition to the KC-135s.

12 November: A restartable rocket engine was used for the first time when *Discoverer XVII* was launched from Vandenberg AFB.

14 December: A B-52G Stratofortress of the 5th Bombardment Wing at Travis AFB, CA completed a record unrefuelled flight of 10,078.84 miles in 19hr 44min.

Northrop YT-38A

In response to the Russian build-up of its missile forces, the USAF announced that Strategic Air Command had been trialing continuous airborne alert operations with B-52 Stratofortresses during the previous two years. Over 6,000 sorties had proved the feasibility of maintaining a nuclear-armed airborne presence. Later in the year, SAC's alert status was increased to 50% – half the B-52 force being ready to take off within 15 minutes of a warning of impending attack being received. Among these B-52s (nicknamed by their crews 'BUFFs' or 'Big Ugly Fat Fellows' would soon be the latest B-52Hs, powered by the cleaner Pratt & Whitney TF33 turbofan engine, the first of which were delivered to the 379th Bomb Wing at Wurtsmith AFB, MI in May.

Early in the year it was announced that production of the B-70 Valkyrie was to be restricted to just two XB-70 prototypes and one YB-70. Originally planned to be the B-52's replacement in SAC, the Valkyrie would now be restricted to high-speed aerodynamic research. Record-breaking flights by B-58A Hustlers continued, including a point-to-point record between New York and Paris. Such flights early in an advanced new aircraft's operational life contributed much to systems development and the accumulation of performance data.

Lockheed U-2A

The first elements of the Ballistic Missile Early Warning System (BMEWS) at Thule AB, Greenland, were also declared operational – these radar installations (with three more stations to follow) being able to detect and track conventional and nuclear ballistic missiles and thereby alert air defence systems in the US and overseas.

A potential crisis was indeed to develop during the year when the Russians pressed hard for a resolution to arguments which had been continuing for three years. The Soviet Union had continued to make access to Berlin difficult, and (afraid of the prospect of a unified Germany) had suggested that it be handed over as a demilitarised city in exchange for concessions. This had been rejected by the West, and in 1961 the possibility of a bilateral agreement between the USSR and East Germany (combined with an increase in the Soviet defence budget) led to President Kennedy to request that Reserve and National Guard units be mobilised, along with regular forces.

Construction of the Berlin Wall in August and closure of many entry points to the city hastened the US action, with 18,500 Air National Guard personnel reporting for duty on 1 October. USAF Europe's own assets were augmented by several ANG units through Operation *Stairstep*, with C-97s and C-124s of MATS supporting the deployment. Four squadrons of F-84F Thunderstreaks were stationed at French bases from October, along with a wing of F-86H Sabres and a reconnaissance squadron of RF-84F Thunderflashes, with a wing of F-104A Starfighters arriving the following month. However, diplomatic negotiations succeeded and the ANG units soon started to return to the US, the process being completed by the following August.

Tension in Europe had lessened, but was building in Southeast Asia, as it had been doing since the late 1950s. Following the defeat of the French at Dien Bien Phu, Vietnam had been partitioned, the South being supported by the US. However, civil war broke out in 1957 as Communists in the South carried out various attacks.

Convair F-106A Delta Darts

These armed elements, later known as the Viet Cong were supported by the North under its leader Ho Chi Minh. The situation developed, with North Vietnamese Army (NVA) troops establishing supply lines into Laos (where civil war had also broken out). The deteriorating situation was of much concern to the US and support for the South was increased, initially with equipment and advisers, but ultimately by covert military operations. A flight of RF-101C Voodoos from the 15th TRS was deployed to Tan Son Nhut AB in October, following wider NVA movements. It was soon to become clear that a larger US military response was necessary for this escalating conflict.

The pages for 1961 generously supported by Boeing Defense and Space Group

1961

12 January: The first of a series of 14 world speed and altitude records were set by a Convair B-58 Hustler.

18 January: It was announced that SAC had been running trials of continuous airborne alert operations for two years using B-52 Stratofortresses.

25 January: The two crew members held prisoner by the Soviets following the shootdown of their RB-47 Stratojet the previous July, were released.

1 February: SAC announced that the first elements of BMEWS were operational at Thule AB, Greenland. This provided the Command with sufficient warning time to launch its aircraft before enemy missiles reached US bases.

1 February: Launch of the first LGM-130 Minuteman ICBM, which would eventually provide half the total weaponry supporting the US nuclear war plan – a maximum of some 1,000 missiles on alert at any one time.

3 February: Under Operation *Looking Glass*, SAC began round-the-clock flights using a limited number of KC-135s (later designated EC-135s) as continuously manned airborne command posts.

9 February: Responsibility for space surveillance functions were transferred from the Air Research and Development Centre to the Air Defense Command, marking the establishment of the USAF's SPADATS (Space Detection and Tracking System).

6 March: The first of 102 B-52H Stratofortresses (60-0006) flew at Wichita. This version was originally developed to carry the Douglas GAM-87A Skybolt air-to-surface missile. It was powered by eight TF-33-P-3 turbofan engines.

7 March: The McDonnell GAM-72A Quail decoy was declared operational with SAC. The first test drop was made from a B-52G from the 4135th Strategic Wing on 8 June 1960.

17 March: The first Northrop T-38A Talon was delivered to Randolph AFB, TX, where it went into service (replacing the T-28 Trojan) with the 3510th Flying Training Wing of Air Training Command.

28 March: The upgrade of SAC's alert posture to 50% was announced, and was completed in July.

1 April: Air Materiel Command was redesignated Air Force Logistics Command (AFLC). Air Research and Development Command was redesignated Air Force System Command (AFSC).

21 April: A North American X-15 became the first aircraft to travel faster than 3,000 mph, when Captain Robert M White achieved Mach 4.62 (3,074 mph) at a height of 70,000ft before climbing to 105,000ft.

3 May: First silo launch of a Titan ICBM was made.

9 May: The first Boeing B-52H Stratofortress (60-001) was delivered to SAC at Wurtsmith AFB, MI, for the 379th BW.

19 May: The first of 15 C-135A Stratolifters, cargo versions of the Boeing KC-135A, made its first flight. Deliveries to MATS began on 9 June.

26 May: A B-58A Hustler flew non-stop from Carswell AFB, TX to Paris, a distance of 5,183 miles to commemorate the 34th anniversary of Lindbergh's crossing.

June: Announcement of the merger between the USAF Tactical Fighter Experimental (TFX) programme and the US Navy's Fleet Air Defense Fighter requirement.

3 June: The B-58A that flew to Le Bourget for the Paris Air Show crashed after taking off during the air show and its crew of three was killed.

23 June: The North American X-15, piloted by Captain Robert M White, became the first manned aircraft to exceed Mach 5, when he flew it to 107,700ft and a speed of Mach 5.27 (3,603 mph).

30 June: USAFE received its first F-105 Thunderchiefs.

1 July: The Air Force Communications Service, responsible for communications and air traffic control, was activated.

10 July: A TAC pilot flew a Republic F-105D Thunderchief for more than 1,500 miles (2,410km) without any external reference, in a test to ensure that the instrumentation and radar system of the F-105 was adequate for a squadron pilot to make long-range IFR low-level missions.

25 July: President Kennedy requested a build-up of regular US forces plus Reserve and National Guard units, following a Soviet threat of a bilateral solution with Communist East

Germany regarding access to the divided city of Berlin and an increase in the Soviet defence budget.

12/13 August: The Berlin Wall was constructed and almost all entry points to the city were closed by the Russians, hastening US military preparations for deployment to Germany to counter any Soviet aggression.

25 August: The first Lockheed C-130E Hercules flew.

1 October: 18,500 Air National Guard personnel reported for duty in response to the Berlin Wall crisis, as several ANG units were to deploy to Europe to support USAFE Wings as Operation *Stairstep*.

6 October: First placing of an ICBM (a Titan) was made in a hardened silo installation.

11 October: The North American X-15 became the first manned aircraft to reach 200,000ft when Captain Robert M White attained an altitude of 217,000ft and reached a speed of Mach 5.21 (3,647mph).

18 October: A USAF Kaman H-43B Huskie helicopter attained an altitude of 32,840ft (10,010-m).

20 October: RF-101C Voodoo detachments began flying photo-reconnaissance missions over Vietnam as a result of increased activity by the North Vietnamese Army.

9 November: Another milestone was reached by Captain Robert M White flying the North American X-15, when he became the first pilot to fly at Mach 6.04 (4,093 mph).

16 November: The *Farm Gate* Detachment (Air Commandos) became operationally ready in Vietnam, using AT-28 Trojans, Douglas SC-47s and B-26 Invaders.

1 December: It was announced that a powered derivative of the Titan ICBM had been selected to fire the Dyna-Soar winged space vehicle into orbit, following initial air-launched drops from a B-52 carrier-aircraft.

As thunder clouds retreat beyond the hills, a North American F-100D prepares for a practice bombing mission from Nellis Air Force Base, NV. Appropriately titled Soon Distant Thunder, *this painting by John Young GAvA, VP ASAA is reproduced courtesy of Aerodrome Press Inc, Seattle, WA.*

Soon Distant Thunder by John Young GAvA, VP ASAA

Before the start of the year, US instructors had been training South Vietnamese pilots under Project *Farm Gate*. The 4400th Combat Crew Training Squadron was established at Bien Hoa with piston-engined aircraft including T-28 Trojans and B-26 Invaders (jet types were forbidden under the Geneva Accord). These provided the Vietnamese Air Force with a major boost to its offensive capability whilst the USAF continued to build up in Southeast Asia. This included Fairchild UC-123Bs of the Special Aerial Spray Flight which, under Project *Ranch Hand*, operated out of Tan Son Nhut on missions to defoliate areas of the tree canopy under which Viet Cong troops were operating. The crash of one of these aircraft killing the three-man crew on 2 February was the first loss of a USAF marked aircraft and the first official USAF fatalities in Southeast Asia.

Air defence provision was made by the *Water Glass* deployment of F-102A Delta Daggers from the 509th FIS based in the Philippines, sharing this role with the US Navy from March onwards – this was further extended the following year. A single Douglas EC-54 electronic surveillance aircraft began operations to locate Viet Cong radio transmitters. At the end of 1962, there were no signs that this increase in the USAF's involvement in Vietnam would tail off, as the need to prepare for possible offensive operations became more pressing.

In addition to the situation in Southeast Asia, the USAF's ability to react to crises was heavily tested by another potentially very dangerous 'flashpoint' that emerged during the year. After the Bay of Pigs débâcle the year before, where a US-encouraged and supplied invasion of Cuba by exiles had failed as actual American military support was not forthcoming, the Soviet Union started a flow of arms to Fidel Castro. An overflight by a CIA Lockheed U-2 in late August revealed a major Soviet military build-up on the island, where the presence of intermediate-range ballistic missiles presented a considerable danger to the continental USA. This was confirmed

Douglas B-26B Invader

photographically by a U-2E of the 4080th SRW on 14 October (the Air Force having taken over the Cuba reconnaissance missions earlier in the month from the CIA).

USAF bomber, reconnaissance and fighter units were deployed to bases in Florida and put at maximum readiness, should the need for attacks on Cuba have arisen, while SAC missile crews went to full alert status. U-2 flights were stepped-up, and McDonnell RF-101C Voodoos carried out low-level missions. The risks were high – one U-2 was shot down by a Soviet SA-2 SAM and its pilot, Major Rudolph Anderson, was killed. Ultimately it was the threat of a US invasion of Cuba that forced the Soviets to remove their offensive weapons. It was an RF-101 that provided the photographic evidence of a withdrawal of Soviet missiles on 29 October. The arms quarantine that had been imposed on the island was lifted a month later. This confrontation between the two major superpowers had been the most serious so far in the Cold War. Once again the USAF had played a major part in ending the possibility of military action.

Evaluation by the Air Force of the US Navy's latest carrier-borne fighter, the McDonnell F4H/F-4 Phantom, would soon prove significant, as it would become the first Navy combat aircraft to be adopted by the USAF. Twenty-nine F-4Bs were 'borrowed' for trials purposes and the USAF realised the aircraft's potential when it was compared in a fly-off (Operation *Highspeed*) against the then-current F-106 Delta Dart. It was ordered in March, initially designated F-110A Spectre, though this was soon changed to F-4C Phantom. Alterations for USAF service included the adoption of Pratt & Whitney J79-15 engines and the installation of APQ-100 radar. The F-4C entered service the following year. SAC received its last B-52 Stratofortress, a B-52H, in October along with the last three B-58A Hustlers. No new strategic bombers were in the production pipeline for the USAF, but Defense Secretary McNamara requested that plans should be drawn up for a B-52 replacement.

Secretly flown for the first time in 1955, the Lockheed U-2 was used by the CIA and the Air Force as a high flying reconnaissance aircraft. The black-painted U-2C in this painting by Otto Kuhni was operated over Southeast Asia throughout the sixties. It is reproduced here by kind permission of the Lockheed Martin Skunk Works.

The pages for 1962 generously supported by Lockheed Martin Skunk Works

Lockheed U-2C by Otto Kuhni

January: USAFE's official aerobatic team, the *Skyblazers*, was officially disbanded. Formed in 1948 with F-80 Shooting Stars, it had been the USAF's first jet display team and went on to use F-84s, F-86s and finally F-100s.

1 January: A detachment of US advisers began training Vietnamese pilots to fly T-28 Trojan ground-attack aircraft supplied by the US to the VNAF 2nd Fighter Squadron. The US training commitment was code-named *Farm Gate*.

13 January: First full-scale Operation *Ranch Hand* (defoliation) mission in Vietnam. It was aimed at defoliating the jungle canopy in areas occupied by Viet Cong troops.

24 January: The first two (of a batch of 29) US Navy McDonnell F4H/F-4B Phantoms were delivered to Tactical Air Command at Langley AFB, VA for test and evaluation.

2 February: A USAF Fairchild UC-123B Provider transport crashed during a low level training flight near Bien Hoa, killing the crew of three. This was the first USAF aircraft and crew 'officially' lost in Vietnam.

28 February: The first live ejection was made from a Convair B-58A's escape-pod system while the aircraft was flying at 565 mph, at 20,000ft over Edwards AFB, CA.

5 March: The Bendix Trophy was awarded to Captain Robert G Sowers for a record round trip in a Convair B-58A (59-2458) between New York and Los Angeles in 4hr 41min 11.3sec.

22 March: Four Convair F-102 interceptors were deployed from Clark AFB in the Philippines to Tan Son Nhut. They began operations over South Vietnam, following reports that unidentified low-flying aircraft had been sighted over the Central Highlands.

30 March: The USAF ordered a new version of the US Navy F4H/F-4B Phantom for close air support, designating it F-110A Spectre. This was soon changed to F-4C Phantom.

19 April: The first live firing of a Douglas XGAM-87 Skybolt air-launched ballistic missile was made from a B-52G flying from Elgin AFB, FL.

20 April: The first Titan I ICBM was put on alert at Lowry AFB, CO.

26 April: First flight of the top-secret Lockheed A-12 single-seat spyplane (60-6924) from the Groom Lake research facility in Nevada.

27 April: The Special Air Warfare Center was established at Eglin AFB, FL.

19 June: The Dyna-Soar winged re-entry vehicle was given the experimental classification X-20.

7 July: First flight of the Lockheed VZ-10 Hummingbird VTOL research aircraft. The Hummingbird carried out flight research until it was destroyed in an accident in March 1969.

17 July: A manned aircraft reached a height in excess of 300,000ft for the first time, when Major Robert M White flew the X-15 to a height of 314,750ft and a speed of Mach 5.45 (3,832 mph). For this flight the pilot was awarded astronauts' wings.

30 August: A USAF Lockheed U-2E 'strayed' over the Soviet-occupied island of Sakhalin in the north west Pacific. This followed the discovery by a CIA U-2 of Soviet military movements on Cuba. The flight provoked sharp complaints from the Soviet authorities.

9 October: The Air Force received its first Boeing VC-137C (62-6000), specially fitted out for Presidential transport duties with the 89th Airlift Wing. It was allocated the special radio call-sign Air Force One.

14 October: A USAF Lockheed U-2E of the 4080th Strategic Reconnaissance Wing obtained the first photographic evidence of the Soviet deployment of offensive missiles to Cuba.

17-22 October: Seven U-2 flights were made each day over Cuba to monitor the build-up of Soviet intermediate-range ballistic missiles. Low-altitude overflights were also made by McDonnell RF-101Cs, which confirmed about 40 bombers at Holguin and San Julian.

22 October: President John F Kennedy announced an arms quarantine against Russian shipments destined for Cuba and demanded the removal of the missiles already there.

22 October: SAC battle staffs were placed on 24-hour alert duties. The B-47 Stratojet force was dispersed and the B-52 force went on actual airborne alert. All bombers and missiles were armed with nuclear weapons.

Convair B-58A Hustler

25 October: With the arms quarantine in effect SAC RB-47 Stratojets and KC-97 tankers joined other forces in the massive air-sea search for ships bound for Cuba.

26 October: SAC received its last Boeing B-52, an -H model (61-040) and the last three B-58A Hustler supersonic bombers (67-2078/2080).

27 October: A Lockheed U-2, flown by Major Rudolph Anderson, was shot down over Cuba by a Soviet SA-2 Guideline SAM, one of a large number deployed to the island to protect the Soviet intermediate-range SS-4 Sandal missiles.

28 October: The Soviets agreed to remove their offensive missiles from Cuba.

29 October: Confirmation of the dismantling of the offensive missile sites on Cuba was received from photos taken by an RF-101 Voodoo.

24 November: The Defense Department awarded General Dynamics the TFX contract to build the F-111A for the USAF.

27 December: The first production batch of six Lockheed SR-71 reconnaissance aircraft were ordered. The SR-71 was developed from the experimental Lockheed A-12, which first flew in April.

USAF operations over Vietnam continued to increase with the number of advisers and air support growing all the time. The air defence task was taken up by the *Candy Machine* deployment of F-102A Delta Daggers from the 509th Fighter Interceptor Squadron, based at Tan Son Nhut and Da Nang. For ground support work, the 1st Air Commando Squadron was formed at Bien Hoa, receiving Douglas A-1E/H Skyraiders to supplement its existing B-26 Invaders and T-28 Trojans. Among the unit's roles was the provision of air support for helicopter operations, which became an ever more important aspect of its tasking, as the US Army's rotary-wing activities grew appreciably. The year had started with a strike by Bien Hoa-based units on Viet Cong targets in the Tay Ninh area which also saw Army Piasecki CH-21B helicopters carrying out troop transport duties. Tactical transport operations also assumed greater importance, with three more squadrons of Fairchild C-123B Providers being sent to the region.

The first use of the Lockheed U-2 in the theatre took place in December when the 4080th SRW set up an

Boeing C-135B

Douglas A-1E Spad

operational detachment at Bien Hoa. The Douglas EC-54 previously used to track down Viet Cong transmitters was replaced in February by a Boeing EC-97G. Further intelligence-gathering was carried out by a new detachment of Martin RB-57Es, also based at Tan Son Nhut. By the year's end (the final year before formal American involvement), 117 USAF aircraft were deployed to Vietnam, and 6,929 sorties had been flown in the preceding 12 months.

Back in the USA there were a number of notable first flights during the year, including the Lockheed C-141A StarLifter – the first jet-powered strategic transport for MATS. Other transport elements of the Air Force began to follow their front-line counterparts, by replacing older piston-engined types with turboprop and turbojet powered aircraft. The USAF's important multi-role fighter, the F-4C Phantom, was airborne for the first time in May. It entered service in November with the 4453rd Combat Crew Training Squadron at MacDill AFB, FL,

and subsequently became operational with the 12th TFW. Although the Cuban missile crisis had, following evaluation of the F-4, focused much attention on getting the type into service quickly, it was in Southeast Asia where the Phantom would make its initial impact. The same was true of the two-seat F-105F Thunderchief, intended as a mission trainer but which was modified for the *Wild Weasel* anti-radar role – in which guise the 'Thud' (as it became known) served well in Vietnam. One new aircraft not destined to serve at all was the Lockheed YF-12A, that got airborne from the top-secret Groom Lake facility in August. This version of the CIA's A-12 reconnaissance aircraft was intended to replace the cancelled F-108 Rapier as an advanced long-range interceptor, and three A-12 prototypes were converted. Congress agreed to $90 million of funding for the project, but Defense Secretary McNamara refused to allow production to proceed. Two of the three YF-12s were used for a flight test programme until 1979.

The pages for 1963 generously supported by the McDonnell Douglas Corporation

2 January: The entire USAF and VNAF force at Bien Hoa was committed to Operation *Burning Arrow*, an hour-long air strike against Viet Cong targets in the Ap Bac/Tay Ninh areas. The strike was followed by air drops and a trooplift by Piasecki H-21 helicopters.

February: The 4039th Strategic Wing, operating B-52Gs, was re-numbered the 416th Bombardment Wing. It was one of 26 units with four-digit designations that were subsequently replaced by three-digit numbers with historical or notable lineages.

28 February: The first Minuteman ICBM squadron (10th SMS) became operational at Malmstrom AFB, MT.

1 April: United States Air Force Europe received its first rotational TAC squadron of F-105 Thunderchiefs with the arrival of the 344th Tactical Fighter Squadron at Moron AB, Spain. SAC KC-135 Stratotankers were used in support of the deployment.

11 April: The North American X-15 rocket research aircraft, piloted by Major Robert A Rushworth, reached Mach 4.25 (2.864 mph) and a height of 74,000ft in the first of a new series of scientific and research flights. This was raised to Mach 5.2 (3,600 mph) and 95,600ft on 14 May.

18 April: The Northrop X-21A (basically a converted Douglas WB-66D) made its maiden flight, to commence a research programme aimed at the evaluation of boundary layer control techniques.

7 May: One of two RB-57E reconnaissance aircraft allocated to Project *Patricia Lynn* in Vietnam, flew its first operational sortie.

8 May: It was announced that two squadrons of A-1E/H Skyraiders would be added to the 1st Air Commando Group at Hurlburt AFB, FL. The intention was that 75 Skyraiders would be sent to Vietnam as replacements for B-26 and T-28 aircraft, which were suffering combat and attrition losses.

27 May: First flight of the McDonnell Douglas F-4C was made at St Louis. Production of this version totalled 583 for TAC, of which 36 were adapted for the *Wild Weasel* defence suppression role in Vietnam, taking the unofficial designation EF-4C.

8 June: The first Titan II Squadron (570th SMS) became operational.

11 June: The Republic F-105F two-seat mission trainer version of the Thunderchief was flown for the first time. Service introduction followed in December with the 4520th Combat Crew Training Wing at Nellis and the 4th TFW at Seymour-Johnson. The 'F' was used extensively in Vietnam for *Wild Weasel* missions.

17 June: The Sikorsky CH-3C heavy transport helicopter, of which 75 were built, was flown for the first time. It was developed from the civil S-61 and featured a hydraulically-operated rear ramp.

25 July: A Partial Test Ban Treaty, banning the testing of nuclear weapons in the atmosphere, outer space or under water, was signed.

31 July: The first single-seat Northrop YF-5A was flown. The aircraft was selected by the Defense Department as the 'Freedom Fighter' for participating countries in the Military Assistance Program. It was also evaluated by the USAF in Vietnam.

7 August: The first Lockheed YF-12A (60-6934) made its maiden flight from Groom Lake. This version of the Lockheed A-12 met the SOR-220 requirement for an advanced interceptor, replacing the cancelled North American XF-108 Rapier, and three A-12s already on order were thus modified. $90 million funding was agreed by Congress for 93 production F-12Bs, but Defense Secretary McNamara refused to sanction production.

16 October: During Operation *Greased Lightning*, a B-58A Hustler (61-2059) of the 305th Bombardment Wing, Bunker Hill AFB, IL set a new world record time of 8hr 35min 20sec flying 8,028 miles non-stop from Tokyo to RAF Greenham Common, Berkshire.

22 October: The Cessna YAT-37D, an armed version of the USAF's basic T-37 trainer, made its first flight.

22 October-21 November: Operation *Big Lift* was held, in which the USAF and US Army airlifted 14,893 men of the 2nd Armoured Division from Bergstrom AFB, TX to airfields

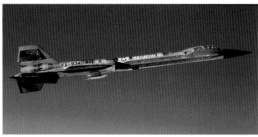

Lockheed YF-12A

in France and Germany, supported by fighter-bombers, reconnaissance aircraft and tankers.

November: The Tactical Air Warfare Center (TAWC, later AWC) was established at Eglin AFB, FL, to develop closer liaison between the test phase of weapons evaluation and their operational employment. THe 4485th Test Squadron was formed as the Center's flying unit in April 1971.

20 November: Service use of the F-4C Phantom began at MacDill AFB, FL, initially with the 4453rd CCTS for training and then with the 12th Tactical Fighter Wing. Three more wings in TAC received F-4Cs in the following years.

17 December: The Lockheed C-141A StarLifter was flown for the first time at Marietta, GA. It was the first pure-jet transport designed specifically for the strategic transport elements of the Air Force.

31 December: President Johnson approved the deployment of Lockheed U-2s to Vietnam, where the 4028th Strategic Reconnaissance Squadron began operating them out of Bien Hoa two weeks later.

31 December: At the end of the year (shortly before formal US involvement in the region), a total of 117 USAF aircraft had been deployed to Vietnam.

The 4400th Combat Crew Training Squadron flew many of the first USAF missions in Southeast Asia. The Douglas B-26 Invader shown in Ronald Wong's Jungle Jim Goes to War *is on a typical night operation against the Ho Chi Minh Trail in Southern Laos.*

Jungle Jim Goes to War by Ronald Wong BSc(Hons), GAvA, GMA, ASAA

The Viet Cong enjoyed a number of important military successes in the spring, capturing the town of Kien Long and sinking the USS *Card* in Saigon harbour, while the North Vietnamese Army mounted a successful invasion of 'neutral' Laos. This led to increased US air activity, with Air Force RF-101Cs carrying out reconnaissance missions, although North Vietnam was still 'off limits' to the Voodoos and US Navy aircraft with which they shared the task of photographing the Viet Cong infiltration routes from the North. The situation took a further turn for the worse in June, when a US Navy RF-8A and F-8D were shot down by anti-aircraft fire. US retaliation was inevitable, and the 511th TFS deployed to Da Nang with its F-100D Super Sabres, supported by four KC-135s. The F-100s mounted a series of strikes against AAA batteries in Laos, thus commencing hostilities which were officially declared (after the attacks on US Navy warships in the Gulf of Tonkin) by President Johnson on 7 August.

Until 1965, only US Navy units were 'officially' assigned to operational missions, USAF aircraft being used in support of the Army of the Republic of Vietnam (ARVN) and 'covertly' in Laos. Assets stationed in the theatre for these operations included two squadrons of B-57Bs at Bien Hoa, and nine ground-attack units flying F-100s and F-105 Thunderchiefs. The only USAF air defence fighters thus far deployed were still the F-102s of the 509th FIS

North American XB-70A Valkyrie

based at Da Nang – not a large interceptor capability, but one which was still far superior to that of the North Vietnamese. However, doubts were placed on this position of superiority, when it was reported that MiG-15s and MiG-17s were being supplied to the NVAF by China, along with aircrew instruction.

It was the B-57 force which suffered the USAF's first ground casualties of the war, five being destroyed by a Viet Cong mortar attack on their base at Bien Hoa. The Viet Cong was an increasingly well-equipped force, and in an attempt to stop supplies from being transported down the Ho Chi Minh trail, Operation *Barrel Roll* was launched in December. This involved armed reconnaissance flights over eastern Laos, which followed the successful operations by A-1 Skyraiders that had attacked Viet Cong positions in two provinces, inflicting over 400 casualties. The resilient Viet Cong forces remained on the offensive in spite of these continuing and heavy attacks.

An historic event for SAC occurred in April, when it was announced that the Command had for the first time as many ballistic missiles on ground alert as it had manned strategic bombers. This illustrated the growing importance of missiles as a deterrent over aircraft – a situation which

would become more noticeable as the years progressed.

The test programme using the cancelled B-70 Valkyrie (scrapped due to budget restrictions and an increasing reliance on missiles back in 1959) was further cut back. Now only two XB-70s were to be built for experimental high-speed research, and hopes that the USAF had for production of 60 RS-70 reconnaissance variants also fell by the wayside. The first of these two XB-70As flew in September. Three months later, the Lockheed SR-71A made its maiden flight from Palmdale, CA, in the hands of Robert Gilliland. This Mach 3+ strategic reconnaissance aircraft was the successor to the A-12 and incorporated numerous improvements over that type, including new sensor systems and increased fuel capacity. Service entry would follow two years later, after a successful flight test programme that had been greatly hastened by experience gained through development of the A-12 and YF-12.

The big Douglas C-133A Cargomaster, shown here in Robert T McCall's painting, played an important part in transporting heavy loads of military equipment during the Vietnam War. It was the first strategic transport able to carry Air Force IRBMs and ICBMs. This painting is from the Air Force Art Collection.

North American F-100D Super Sabre

The pages for 1964 generously supported by Jeppesen – A Times Mirror Company

C-133 Transport Mission by Robert T McCall ASAA

6 January: In a tactical training exercise, 18 Lockheed F-104 Starfighters deployed from George AFB, CA to Moron AB, Spain. The 6,150 mile flight took 10hr 20min and required air-to-air refuelling six times.

29 February: President Johnson officially revealed the existence of the Lockheed A-12 programme, but incorrectly referred to it as the A-11 and held up a picture of the YF-12A interceptor prototype, that was still secret.

5 March: The B-70 Valkyrie research programme was cut back, with only two XB-70 prototypes now to be completed for high-speed aerodynamic trials. An unsuccessful attempt was made to obtain funds for an operational fleet of RS-70 reconnaissance-strike versions.

1 April: The USAF Europe's (USAFE's) tactical airlift functions were re-assigned to the Military Air Transport Service (MATS).

21 April: ICBMs became equal in numbers to manned bombers on ground alert.

18 May: Maiden flight of the first production standard RF-4C Phantom (63-7740).

June: President Johnson announced the increase in numbers at the Air Force Academy from 2,500 to 4,417.

9 June: For the first time, SAC air-refuelling tankers were used to support combat operations in Southeast Asia. Four KC-135s from Clark AB, Philippines refuelled eight F-100 Super Sabre fighter-bombers en route to strike Pathet Lao gun emplacements on the Plain of Jars in northern Laos.

10 July: A six-month test of the effects of sonic booms ended

Piasecki SH-21B Workhorse

with mixed reactions from the inhabitants of Oklahoma City. Supersonic USAF aircraft had created a total of 1,253 booms to simulate the effect of supersonic airliners regularly crossing the US.

16 July: Ryan's Model 43 (XV-5A) experimental VTOL 'fan in wing' aircraft made its first vertical take-off and landing at Edwards AFB, having previously made a conventional flight on 25 May.

August: The Cessna T-41A Mescalero – a standard Cessna 172 acquired 'off-the-shelf' by the USAF, had its first flight. A total of 170 T-41As was ordered for use in primary flight screening of Air Force pilot candidates on 31 July 1964.

August: The first Northrop F-5 tactical strike fighters were delivered to the 4441st Combat Crew Training Squadron at Williams AFB, where they were used to train crews for the countries being supplied with F-5s under the Military Assistance Program (MAP).

5 August: A major build-up of USAF forces in Southeast Asia began with the arrival of 36 Martin B-57s, 12 F-102 Delta Daggers, eight F-100 Super Sabres, and six additional RF-101 Voodoos at bases in Vietnam. Ten F-100s and eight F-105 Thunderchiefs were also deployed to Thailand.

7 August: The US government put the country on a war footing after the so-called Gulf of Tonkin Resolution. The destroyers USS *Maddox* and *C Turner Joy* destroyers had been attacked by the Viet Cong on 2 August.

10 August: USAF officials reported that China had delivered MiG-15 and MiG-17 fighters to Hanoi, together with pilots to train North Vietnamese airmen.

21 September: The first of two prototype North American XB-70A supersonic research aircraft flew for the first time. Powered by six General Electric YJ93-GE-3 turbojets, it had a design speed of 1,980 mph at 80,000ft and an unrefuelled range of 7,500 miles.

29 September: First conventional take-off made by the LTV XC-142A VTOL transport aircraft, which could be used by the US armed forces. All three services were interested in the XC-142A, which bore 'Tri-Service' wording on its tail. The

four turboprops were mounted on a wing that could pivot upwards through 90°.

November: Major developments started at Grand Forks AFB, ND, to house the 321st Strategic Missile Wing and its ICBMs.

November: USAF C-130E Hercules flew to Ascension Island, where they embarked 543 Belgian para-commandos and airlifted them to the Congo.

1 November: The first USAF ground losses in South Vietnam occurred, when five Martin B-57s were destroyed and 15 more damaged, together with an H-43 helicopter, by a Viet Cong mortar attack on their base.

December: Two Martin RB-57Fs were used by the 7907th Combat Support Wing, from bases in Germany, for intelligence-gathering missions around and over Eastern bloc boundaries. The aircraft used passive sensors together with a high-altitude camera (HIAC) as well as electronic devices.

2 December: Four TAC F-4 Phantoms, refuelled several times by SAC KC-135 Stratotankers, completed an 18-hour flight of 10,000 miles, in an endurance test of long-range deployment capabilities.

9-10 December: USAF Douglas A-1H and A-1E Skyraiders inflicted more than 400 Viet Cong casualties during air strikes in Quang Tin and Binh Din provinces.

14 December: USAF tactical fighters launched Operation *Barrel Roll*, an attack on the vital Communist supply route in northern Laos known as the 'Ho Chi Minh Trail'.

21 December: First flight of the General Dynamics YF-111A was made at Fort Worth. Development of the variable-geometry type started in the late 1950s when TAC's need for a replacement for the Republic F-105 first began to be studied.

23 December: The first prototype Lockheed SR-71A Mach 3+ strategic reconnaissance aircraft (64-17950) was flown.

22 December: President Johnson approved the development of the Lockheed CX-HLS heavy logistic transport to supplement the C-141 StarLifter and to increase the MATS airlift capability. Following a design competition between Boeing, Douglas and Lockheed, the latter company was named winner in October 1965 with the Model 500 C-5 Galaxy.

The increasing intensity of Viet Cong mortar attacks on USAF and VNAF airfields, such as that on Pleiku on 2 February which destroyed seven fixed-wing aircraft and 18 helicopters, led to Operation *Flaming Dart* being launched. This saw USAF, US Navy and VNAF aircraft attacking the enemy barracks at Dong Hoi in the North. However, VC attacks continued, requiring a longer-term offensive campaign known as *Rolling Thunder*. It was given approval by President Johnson on 13 February after consultation with his Joint Chiefs of Staff, who had formulated a list of targets for attack. These were mainly important supply and storage facilities. The cities of Hanoi and Haiphong were not to be bombed, to avoid undue casualties amongst civilians, while any NVAF aircraft seen were not to be engaged unless they attacked first.

Over 100 aircraft began *Rolling Thunder* on 2 March, striking the Quang Khe naval base and an ammunition store at Xom Bang. Four of these aircraft were shot down by anti-aircraft fire. Unwelcome improvements to the North Vietnamese air defence system (including the formation of MiG squadrons) led to further losses – two F-105s attacking a road and rail bridge were 'downed'

Boeing B-52D Stratofortress

Douglas EB-66C Destroyer

before the escorting F-100s were able to engage the attacking MiG-17s.

The arrival of the 45th TFS, with the first F-4C Phantoms to be deployed to the theatre, provided better support to strike aircraft on *Rolling Thunder* missions. Indeed, two aircraft from the 45th scored the USAF's first air-to-air kills of the conflict in July, claiming a pair of NVAF MiG-17s with their AIM-9 Sidewinders.

In May there was the first of what were to become regular 'bombing halts', to demonstrate to Hanoi that the bombing need not be relentless. When Hanoi did not react to the break, *Rolling Thunder* moved on into its second phase. The intensity of the strikes was stepped-up, and November saw a re-organisation of missions. North Vietnam was divided into Route Packages which were split between the USAF and the Navy. Thereby, attacks on the areas around Hanoi and the borders of Laos were the Air Force's responsibility, the Navy dealing with the coastal regions near to Haiphong.

The North Vietnamese air defence network was constantly improving, with the growing numbers of AAA positions and SA-2 surface to air missile (SAM) sites presenting an increasing danger. In November, attempts to identify and 'knock out' SAM sites began with the first operational use of F-100Fs under the *Wild Weasel* programme. These Super Sabres, of the 388th TFW at Korat, were fitted with radar homing and warning devices,

McDonnell RF-101C Voodoo

and armed initially with rockets and a 20-mm cannon (the AGM-45 anti-radiation missile not yet being available for use). The unit claimed its first destruction of an SA-2 site in December. Meanwhile, the EB-66C Destroyer was the only type of aircraft suitable for Electronic Countermeasures (ECM) and Electronic Support Measures (ESM) and was brought in to jam AAA fire-control radars.

Alongside *Rolling Thunder*, the start of *Arc Light* missions in June brought B-52 Stratofortresses into the war for the first time. The units participating were rotated, the 7th BW being most heavily-involved in 1965 with a four-month tour of duty. Andersen AFB in Guam was the operating base for the initial attacks on Viet Cong bases, with U-Tapao in Thailand and Kadena in Japan later taking some of the burden. Early in the campaign, accuracy was lacking. The first raids had involved up to 30 aircraft each, but were actually of little real value. However, the efficiency of these operations had improved significantly by the end of the year, with B-52s flying close-support missions from November.

Experiments earlier in the year with single FC-47 gunships had been so successful, that a squadron was formed and moved to Tan Son Nhut in November. By the year's end they proved the gunship principle in both day and night operations. The aircraft were re-designated AC-47s to reflect their 'attack' rather than 'fighter' role.

The pages for 1965 generously supported by Arkells Brewery Limited

1965

January: The 4252nd Strategic Wing, SAC was activated at Kadena AB, Okinawa to provide KC-135 Stratotanker air refuelling for Pacific Air Force fighter-bombers engaged in air operations over Vietnam.

11 January: The first transition to horizontal flight was made by the LTV XC-142A research aircraft. As an operational transport it was the first US V/STOL aircraft to be designed for service use.

February: The Military Aircraft Storage and Disposal Center (MASDC) was established at Davis-Monthan AFB, AZ, to 'process' surplus aircraft, helicopters and missiles from all branches of the Department of Defense.

7 February: A Viet Cong mortar attack was made on Pleiku, in which five helicopters were damaged and nine personnel killed, resulted in Operation *Flaming Dart* in which retaliatory air strikes were made against North Vietnam.

13 February: The President authorised Operation *Rolling Thunder*, the sustained bombing of targets in North Vietnam associated with Viet Cong support of armed attacks on South Vietnam.

19 February: First use of Air Force jet aircraft was made in the offensive role in South Vietnam, when 24 Martin B-57s attacked the Viet Cong 9th Division's base camp near the Cambodian border.

2 March: The first *Rolling Thunder* attacks were made by 110 aircraft against Xom Bang ammunition base and the naval base at Quang Khe.

3 April: Operation *Steel Tiger* commenced. Two Martin B-57s, accompanied by a flare-dropping C-130 Hercules, carried out the first night jet interdiction mission against enemy forces moving down the Ho Chi Minh trail.

4 April: Two Republic F-105s were shot down by North Vietnamese aircraft whilst attacking the Ham Rung bridge at Thanh Hoa. F-4C Phantoms of the 45th Tactical Fighter Squadron were moved to Ubon to give fighter cover to F-105s.

1 May: A new world speed record of 2,070.102 mph was set by Colonel Robert L Stephens in a Lockheed YF-12A, two examples of which set a total of nine world records on this

day. A new height record, in level flight of 80,258ft (24,462-m) was also achieved.

12 May: The first RF-4C Phantoms arrived in England with the 10th Tactical Reconnaissance Wing at RAF Alconbury, Cambridgeshire.

22 May: F-105 Thunderchiefs attacked an NVA barracks in North Vietnam, the first attack above the 20th Parallel.

4 June: A US space endurance record of 97hr 30min was set by USAF Majors James A. McDivitt and Edward H White on the Gemini 4 mission. Major White became the first American to 'walk' in space.

18 June: Operation *Arc Light* commenced when the first Boeing B-52s attacked targets in North Vietnam; 27 B-52Fs of the 7th and 320th Bombardment Wings flying from Andersen AB in Guam to attack the Binh Duong area.

10 July: The first USAF air-to-air kills in Vietnam occured when two F-4C Phantoms of the 45th Tactical Fighter Squadron based at Ubon downed two MiG-17s of the North Vietnamese AF with AIM-9 Sidewinder missiles.

16 July: The North American YOV-10A prototype made its maiden flight. Designed for the US Marine Corps, the Bronco later saw USAF and Navy service.

17 July: First flight of the second, and last, North American XB-70A Valkyrie took place.

23 July: The first F-4C Phantom was brought down by a Soviet SA-2 Guideline missile south of Hanoi.

30 September: Authorisation was given by Defence Secretary McNamara for full development of the USAF's C-5 Galaxy, the production contract for which was awarded the following month to Lockheed.

4 October: The 81st Tactical Fighter Wing at RAF Bentwaters, Suffolk, England, received its first F-4C Phantoms.

6 October: TAC issued Qualitative Operational Requirement 65-14-F, which defined the need for an air superiority fighter to replace the F-4 Phantom. This eventually resulted in the F-15 Eagle.

23 October: The Northrop F-5A Freedom Fighter arrived in Vietnam with the 4503rd Tactical Fighter Squadron.

Douglas C-54D Skymaster

26 October: The first four F-100F Super Sabre *Wild Weasel* electronic countermeasures aircraft deployed to Vietnam commenced operations with the 388th TFW at Korat.

28 November: F-100Fs of the 388th TFW destroyed the first SA-2 battery.

December: The USAF began 'Big Belly' modifications to the Boeing B-52D, whereby it was adapted to the role of conventional iron-bomb carrier rather than as a strategic nuclear delivery bomber. This modification allowed the B-52Ds to carry 84 x 500lb bombs internally and up to 24 x 750lb bombs externally.

8 December: Plans were announced to phase out all Convair B-58A Hustlers and Boeing B-52C, D, E and F models by June 1971.

8 December: The USAF issued a request for proposals on the F-X tactical air superiority fighter to 13 manufacturers.

15 December: The first daylight USAF gunship missions took place over Vietnam by Douglas FC-47s (later AC-47s) of the 4th Special Operations Squadron at Bien Hoa. The gunships were fitted with three General Electric SUU-11A 7.62-mm Miniguns. These were followed by the first night sorties on 23 December.

Probably the smallest aircraft involved in the Vietnam War, the Cessna O-1 Bird Dog was the standard mount for Forward Air Controllers providing identification of enemy targets for attacking aircraft. This painting by Walter Richards is from the Air Force Collection.

Cessna O-1 Bird Dog by Walter D Richards

After a Christmas and New Year 'bombing halt' the third phase of *Rolling Thunder* commenced in January, although the list of targets was limited to the southern half of North Vietnam in order to try to encourage further peace negotiations. When these failed, Phase Four began in March with a much wider range of targets. During this period, the F-100 Super Sabres employed in the *Wild Weasel* role were replaced by F-105F Thunderchiefs, numbers of which rose as more SA-2 sites were discovered. Over 100 SAM sites were identified during 1966.

A re-deployment of USAF units in Southeast Asia led to two wings of F-4 Phantoms being stationed in South Vietnam, augmented by three equipped with F-100 Super Sabres and one each with F-105 Thunderchiefs and F-104 Starfighters. These units had as their primary mission attacks on targets in the 'southern route package' across North Vietnam. Meanwhile, the two wings of F-105s and one of F-4s stationed in Thailand executed strikes to the north and west of Hanoi. In a joint attack with Navy A-4 Skyhawks, F-105Ds from the 355th and 388th TFWs hit targets around Hanoi and Haiphong for the first time – previously, these areas had been 'off-limits'.

The expansion of the strike force with further F-100, F-105 and F-4 deployments was coupled with an increase in bombing accuracy. The use of so-called blind bombing techniques made attacks possible in bad weather and at night. However, missions were increasingly being hampered by the growing presence of North Vietnamese MiG-21 fighters. A September strike operation by F-4Cs was curtailed when they were 'bounced', requiring the Phantom crews to jettison their bomb loads in order to defend themselves in combat against the enemy fighters.

The *Arc Light* operations by B-52 Stratofortresses were, from April, undertaken by modified 'Big Belly' B-52Ds from the 28th and 454th Bomb Wings, which at this point were flying some 450 sorties each month. The conversions, begun the previous year, saw the 'BUFF' being adapted to carry conventional iron bombs as opposed to nuclear weapons – a maximum load of 60,000lb was possible, carried both internally and externally. An indication of the B-52s' increased utilisation and the larger bomb loads being carried was provided in October, with an estimate that 638,000 tons of bombs would have been dropped on Communist targets by the end of the year. This was more than the total achieved during the 1941-45 Pacific campaigns. The majority of this was down to the B-52 missions. Sorties by the re-designated Douglas AC-47D *Spooky* gunships were achieving their objectives, with the 4th Special Operations Squadron at Bien Hoa building up to a 16-strong squadron.

At Beale AFB, CA, the 4200th Strategic Reconnaissance Wing (later to be re-titled the 9th SRW) became the first unit to operate the Lockheed SR-71A. Without an official name allocated to it, the SR-71 was dubbed *Blackbird* due to its overall black finish. To support these reconnaissance operations, a special variant of the KC-135 Stratotanker, designated KC-135Q, was put into service in June. These aircraft were modified to carry the SR-71's special JP-7 fuel. While these 'new' types were introduced to service, SAC retired its last two B-47E Stratojets in the bomber role during February from the 100th Bomb Wing and the 9th Strategic Wing. After this, only the B-52 and the (soon to be retired) B-58 made up the Command's manned bomber force.

The troubled development of what was to have been the Stratofortress' replacement, the North American B-70, continued when the second XB-70A was destroyed after a collision with an F-104N Starfighter during a photographic sortie. The F-104 pilot and the XB-70's co-pilot both lost their lives in the resulting crash of the two aircraft.

Lockheed C-130E Hercules

The Douglas A-1 Skyraider was used in Vietnam for ground attack operations and as a support fighter for search and rescue helicopter missions. William Phillips' painting shows a single-seat A-1H returning from a rescue mission and is from the Air Force Art Collection.

The pages for 1966 generously supported by Airclaims Limited

Survivor on Board, Heading Home by William S Phillips ASAA

January: The first Minuteman II was placed on alert.

1 January: The USAF directed that the Military Air Transport Service (MATS) would become Military Airlift Command (MAC).

7 January: Delivery of the first Lockheed SR-71 was made to an operational unit, the 4200th Strategic Reconnaissance Wing at Beale AFB, CA.

17 January: A SAC B-52G Stratofortress from Seymour Johnson AFB, NC, returning from a ten-hour patrol of the Soviet border with four 1.5 megaton thermonuclear weapons on board, collided with a Boeing KC-135A from which it was refuelling. Both aircraft crashed near Palomares in Spain.

11 February: SAC retired its last two Boeing B-47E Stratojets, the final bomber variants of the type in service. Other B-47s continued after modification for specialist roles.

2 March: Authorisation was given to the USAF for the development of a rocket-powered research craft for evaluation of lifting-body designs to allow controlled re-entry from space missions.

7 March: French President, Charles de Gaulle, announced that he was taking his country out of NATO and requested the withdrawal from French soil of all non-national military forces. This affected a number of USAFE units based in France.

10 March: An A-1E Skyraider of the 1st Air Commando Squadron landed on the A Shau airstrip, to rescue a downed pilot colleague, after it had been overrun by North Vietnamese troops. The pilot of the A-1E, Major Bernard Fisher, was awarded the Medal of Honor in January 1967, for this action.

15 March: After a two-month search, a 1.5 megaton nuclear bomb that had fallen from the wreckage of the B-52 and KC-135 that had collided over Spain on 17 January was finally located in the sea. The other three had been found on land. The 5,000lb, ten foot-long bomb was retrieved from a depth of 2,500ft, five miles off the coast.

22 March: The 36th Tactical Fighter Wing at Bitburg AB, Germany, received its first F-4D Phantoms.

25 March: A General Dynamics F-111A flew from Edwards AFB, CA to Fort Worth, TX using a newly developed terrain-following radar that was designed to keep the aircraft at a constant height above undulating ground.

1 April: Modified 'Big Belly' B-52D Stratofortresses of the 28th and 454th Bombardment Wings were flown on subsequent *Arc Light* operations over Vietnam. Some 450 sorties per month were flown, reaching 600 per month by the end of the year.

25 April: The 447th Strategic Missile Squadron became fully operational. It was the first to be equipped with the LGM-30F Minuteman II.

3 May: The first air-snatch of a man off the ground by an aircraft in flight using the Fulton Recovery System was successfully completed by an HC-130H Hercules.

June: The 21st Composite Wing was formed at Elmendorf AFB, AK, operating the F-102A Delta Dagger and C-130D Hercules. The base's strategic position ensured that it provided facilities to aircraft deploying to and from Southeast Asia during the Vietnam War.

8 June: The second North American XB-70A was destroyed, along with a Lockheed F-104N, at the end of a photographic assignment, which also involved a Northrop F-5, a T-38 and an F-4B Phantom.

25 June: The 4200th Strategic Reconnaissance Wing at Beale AFB, CA was reorganised as the 9th Strategic Reconnaissance Wing. The 349th Air Rescue Squadron, 100th Strategic Wing, was formed from the 349th (Strategic Reconnaissance

Grumman HU-16B Albatross

Squadron) to operate the dedicated Boeing KC-135Q tanker fleet in support of the SR-71.

29 June: Strategic targets in Hanoi and Haiphong, North Vietnam were attacked by USAF aircraft for the first time, namely F-105 Thunderchiefs from the 355th and 388th Tactical Fighter Wings.

30 July: The plan for modified Lockheed A-12s (known as M-12s) to carry D-21 'mini-Blackbird' drones piggy-back ended in tragedy when the first live launch of the drone saw it collide with the mother ship on release.

September: Operation *Thayer* was held during which five battalions of the 101st Airborne Division were dropped by C-123 Providers in the Cay Giep mountains in Vietnam.

3 September: Substantial numbers of new MiG-21 fighters were encountered by US pilots over North Vietnam. Operating from five bases in the Hanoi area, which could not be attacked, the MiGs forced the F-4C Phantoms to divert from their primary strike mission in order to fly counter-air operations.

October: During a nine-day battle against regular NVA forces in the Suoi Da area, tactical aircraft flew 2,500 sorties including 487 immediate requests for close air support. In addition, 330 tactical airlift sorties delivered 8,900 tons of cargo and airlifted 11,400 men.

November: The *Muscle Shoals* (later *Igloo White*) program came to operational fruition in Vietnam, as Lockheed EC-121Rs of the 553rd Reconnaissance Wing operating from Nakhon Phanom began monitoring and relaying data on North Vietnamese movements along the Ho Chi Minh Trail, from sensors dropped initially by Navy OP-2Es and subsequently by Air Force F-4Ds.

14 November: The first landing of a jet aircraft in Antarctica was made by a C-141A StarLifter, at McMurdo Sound.

28 November: Development of a USAF combat rescue model of the Sikorsky H-53 helicopter began, when the first of two Marine Corps CH-53As was loaned to the Air Force.

29 December: The USAF ordered 145 Cessna 0-2As (military variants of the Cessna 337 Skymaster) to operate in the forward air controller role in Vietnam.

In Vietnam frustration had mounted during 1966 amongst USAF pilots at the lack of opportunities for air combat. North Vietnamese fighter bases were not on the list of approved *Rolling Thunder* campaign targets. In an attempt to draw NVAF fighters into combat and use the capabilities of US pilots and aircraft to inflict losses on the enemy, Operation *Bolo* was mounted on 2 January. The operation was devised by pilots of the 8th TFW at Ubon, with a major contribution from the unit's commander, Colonel Robin Olds. This was an elaborate plan, in which F-4Cs of the 8th and 366th TFWs simulated F-105s, which were normally laden with weapons and attractive targets for NVAF MiGs. The Phantoms were supported by F-105F *Wild Weasels*, EB-66 radar jammers and escorting F-104C Starfighters, making a total of 366 aircraft. With 'escape routes' to China and the enemy airfields at Gia Lam and Phuc Yen covered by F-4s, NVAF MiG-21s were successfully drawn into combat and seven were shot down – almost half the total North Vietnamese fleet strength of this type, with no USAF losses. A further two MiG-21s were destroyed during another ruse four days later, that saw F-4Cs simulating an unarmed RF-4C reconnaissance mission.

After this early bout of air combat, inclement weather halted further such operations for some time, though it was resumed in April. The authorisation of attacks on the NVAF airfields at Kep and Hoa Lac resulted in 26 enemy fighters being destroyed on the ground by the end of May. From the following month, there were no more North Vietnamese aerial operations until August.

The USAF introduced the F-4D Phantom to service in Southeast Asia from May onwards, operating with the 555th TFS, 8th TFW at Ubon. This was the first cannon-armed version of the F-4, having a 20-mm M-61 pod. There were initial successes, but new enemy tactics employed from August saw MiG-21s remaining at low level before executing climbing attacks. Several F-4Ds were lost due to this tactic while on an escort mission to

Yen Vien railyard. A further widening of the *Rolling Thunder* campaign allowed strikes to be carried out on Phuc Yen, an important NVAF fighter base and air defence control centre, with nine MiGs destroyed in an attack on 25 August. However, the danger posed by North Vietnamese SA-2 SAMs was ever-growing. Not only were more and more launchers appearing, but new tracking devices, that were not affected by the USAF's jamming operations, had been introduced. When coupled with the developments being made by the enemy in terms of air defence tactics, the situation remained dangerous.

The *Arc Light* B-52 missions met their original target of 800 sorties per month in February, while still operating from Andersen AFB, Guam. This led to overcrowding, and the U-Tapao naval base in Thailand became home to Stratofortresses from the following month. This was closer to North Vietnam, and thus eliminated the need for in-flight refuelling. The 10,000th *Arc Light* mission was reached in May, the sortie rate having virtually doubled in 1967. Since the campaign commenced in June 1965 almost 200,000 tons of bombs had been dropped.

In November, raising the monthly target to 1,200 missions led to more B-52D deployments by SAC which was forced to use a third base, this time Kadena AB,

Douglas AC-47D Magic Dragon

Boeing RB-47H Stratojet

Okinawa. B-52s were also involved in *Rolling Thunder*, Phase V of which saw continuous pounding of North Vietnamese targets except for a brief pause during peace negotiations in August. A combination of artillery, naval forces and air power also undertook a concentrated strike on Communist targets in North Vietnam and Viet Cong units deployed in the South as Operation *Neutralize*. This stopped enemy attacks on the US base at Con Thien, though there were reports of NVA forces building up near Khe Sanh – movements which would lead to a much more serious situation.

At Offutt AFB, NE, the end of an era arrived as SAC retired its last Boeing RB-47H from service with the 55th SRW – the final Stratojet of any type in service. It was flown to Davis-Monthan AFB, AZ, to join many of its previous counterparts in storage. The aircraft, in its many variants, holds the distinction of having been deployed in greater numbers than any other post-war US bomber. Meanwhile, the USAF welcomed an advanced new type to its operational inventory during October, the General Dynamics F-111A – first flown in December 1964. It was the responsibility of the 4480th TFW at Nellis AFB, NV, to introduce the variable-geometry tactical strike aircraft to service following a troubled early development. The first five F-111As were subjected to a very intensive trials programme before initial operational capability (IOC) was reached.

The pages for 1967 generously supported by Short Brothers plc

2 January: Implementation of Operation *Bolo* – a plan to draw North Vietnamese AF MiG fighters into combat.

February: A contract was placed by the Air Force with the Cavalier Aircraft Corporation for 15 rebuilt, two-seat F-51 Mustangs, which were supplied to Bolivia, Dominica and Guatemala under the US agreement to provide military aircraft for these countries.

February: *Arc Light* B-52 Stratofortress bombing missions finally reached the authorised level of 800 sorties per month.

22 February: Operation *Junction City Alternate*, one of the few parachute drops of the Vietnam War, involved 845 paratroopers of the 173rd Airborne Brigade who were dropped by 14 C-130 Hercules, to attack enemy bases north of Tay Ninh City.

6 March: The USAF issued a request for proposals to a total of 21 aircraft companies for design studies of a low-cost attack aircraft – designated A-X.

10 March: An F-105 attack bomber flown by Captain Max Brestel shot down two MiG-17 fighters on a single mission.

10-11 March: F-105 Thunderchiefs and F-4C Phantoms attacked the Thai Nguyen iron and steel works near Hanoi, disrupting production.

Sikorsky HH-3E

11 March: For the first time, USAF aircraft attacked the Canal des Rapides road and rail bridge, four miles north of Hanoi.

15 March: The Sikorsky HH-53B heavy-lift helicopter (66-14428) was flown for the first time. The 'Super Jolly', which was intended for use by the USAF's Aerospace Rescue and Recovery Service, became operational in June.

22 March: A B-52 Stratofortress base was set up at U-Tapao in Thailand to help relieve the congestion at Andersen AFB, Guam which had reached maximum operating capacity.

25 March: The 6th Strategic Wing was re-designated at Eielson AFB, AK, with the primary role of strategic reconnaissance. It employed a variety of Boeing RC-135 versions including the RC-135S *Cobra Ball* and RC-135X *Cobra Eye*.

10 April: B-52 Stratofortresses began operating from the Royal Thai Naval Base at U-Tapao, Thailand, thus eliminating the need for tanker support on combat sorties.

28 April: The McDonnell Aircraft Corporation and the Douglas Aircraft Company merged to form the McDonnell Douglas Corporation.

6 May: Since the *Arc Light* operation began on 18 June 1965, B-52s had flown 10,000 sorties over Southeast Asia.

1 June: The first non-stop helicopter flight across the North Atlantic was made, when two Sikorsky HH-53Es arrived at the Paris Air Show at Le Bourget. The helicopters traced the route taken by Charles Lindbergh in 1927 and en route were refuelled in the air nine times.

30 June: The first cannon equipped version of the Phantom, the F-4E (66-0284) had its maiden flight. This was to be the most numerous of the Air Force's F-4s.

30 July: First flight of the General Dynamics FB-111A for SAC was made at Fort Worth. It was converted from an F-111A.

15 August: The Air Force began trial operations with the Cessna A-37A Dragonfly close support aircraft. They replaced Douglas A-1 Skyraiders at Bien Hoa, Vietnam, operating with the 604th Air Commando.

21 August: US pilots attacking targets in North Vietnam counted 80 SA-2 surface-to-air missile launches, a record for a single day in the war. In all, 149 SAMs were counted by pilots

during August. Sixteen US aircraft were lost, ten to enemy fighters and AAA and six to SAMs.

28 August: The new Lockheed U-2R, for which Lockheed had received a production contract in 1966, was flown for the first time. It was designed in the light of operational experience to offer improved performance, better payload and somewhat less demanding flight characteristics. Twelve were built initially, with six going to the CIA and six to the Air Force.

September: The Sikorsky HH-53B entered service with the 34th Aerospace Rescue and Recovery Squadron at Udorn AB.

3 October: The rocket-powered North American X-15 research aircraft set the absolute world speed record for non-orbiting manned aircraft. Launched from a Boeing B-52 carrier aircraft, the X-15 reached a speed of Mach 6.7 (4,543 mph) and a height of 102,100ft.

16 October: The first operational General Dynamics F-111A variable-geometry tactical strike aircraft was delivered to the 474th TFW at Nellis AFB, NV.

23 October: The Fighter Weapon Center at Nellis AFB, NV received the first F-4E Phantoms to enter Air Force service.

15 November: The third North American X-15 crashed after a flight to Mach 5.2 (3,570 mph) and a height of 266,000ft.

29 December: Under Operation *Eagle Thrust*, the largest and longest airlift ever attempted into a combat zone was completed, when USAF transport aircraft deployed the 101st Airborne Division to Vietnam. The airlift required 413 missions by C-141 StarLifters and C-133 Cargomasters, transporting 10,355 troops and 5,118 tons of equipment including 37 helicopters, from 17 November.

29 December: The last Boeing RB-47H (53-4296) was withdrawn from service with the 55th Strategic Reconnaissance Wing, Offutt AFB, NE. This was the final operational flight made by a Stratojet.

Keith Woodcock's specially commissioned painting shows a Martin B-57B on an interdiction mission over Vietnam. This US adaptation of the British Canberra bomber saw service with the Air Force in Southeast Asia from 1957 to 1974.

Martin B-57B on Interdiction Mission, Vietnam by Keith Woodcock GAvA

Reports of enemy troop movements near the American base at Khe Sanh were confirmed, as it became encircled by NVA and Viet Cong units (totalling some 40,000) who were supported by a large number of anti-aircraft guns. This made an approach to the airfield extremely hazardous, and once on the ground aircraft remained exposed to mortar fire. USAF transport assets in the theatre comprised six squadrons of C-7A Caribous, four of C-123 Providers and three of C-130 Hercules on temporary duty (TDY) deployments. 7,000 US Marines and South Vietnamese army troops were based at Khe Sanh, and urgently required the delivery of supplies which could only be brought in by air.

Special operational tactics had to be employed, in order to keep aircraft on approach to Khe Sanh out of the range of the heavy enemy AAA fire for as long as possible before executing the final descent to land. Aircraft maintained height for as long as possible, before 'diving-down' to land on the runway. On days of heavy AAA activity, C-130s often made use of the Container Delivery System (CDS) – dropping loads by parachute at low level. These CDS cargoes totalled 14 to 16 one-ton pallets on every sortie. For larger loads, the Low-Altitude Parachute Extraction System (LAPES), with reinforced containers being pulled out by large parachutes at an altitude of only a few feet, was an initial solution. Unfortunately this damaged Khe Sanh's temporary runway, so the Ground Proximity Extraction

Lockheed C-130E Hercules and Fairchild C-123 Provider

System (GPES), using a hook and cable to offload the pallets, was developed and proved more successful.

Attacks on enemy forces around the base's perimeter continued throughout the airlift, with missions by B-52s and fighter-bombers delivering some 96,000 tons of bombs, the most concentrated period of attack so far in the Vietnam conflict. By the time the siege ended on 15 March, USAF transports had parachuted 8,120 tons of medical supplies into Khe Sanh, with 4,136 tons of additional equipment and 2,676 personnel also being flown in. Casualties were much lighter than had been anticipated – the Air Force lost only one C-123, though many aircraft were damaged by enemy fire. The C-130 operations were especially successful, delivering 92% of the total tonnage airlifted into the base. It was a most visible illustration of the Hercules' unique tactical capabilities.

The *Rolling Thunder* strikes entered their final stage in January, as the North Vietnamese launched the Tet Offensive in the South. This was an unsuccessful campaign which saw great losses inflicted on NVA and Viet Cong troops. At the forefront of operations against the enemy were the Douglas AC-47s, which provided defence for US bases. In an attempt to hasten peace negotiations with the North, bombing north of the 20th Parallel was halted on 31 March. The invitation to talks was taken up by the Hanoi government, and as a result the cessation of air strikes was extended to the 19th Parallel. At the end of October, it was announced that all bombing of targets in North Vietnam would end, and on 1 November an F-4D of the 8th TFW attacked a target near Dong Hoi – the last *Rolling Thunder* mission. This was the start of the process of 'Vietnamisation' in which President Johnson planned to gradually withdraw US military units and thereby allow South Vietnam to take over its own defence.

A number of new aircraft types commenced operations in Southeast Asia during 1968. The *Combat Lancer* mission was the first deployment of the General Dynamics F-111A, six aircraft of the 428th TFS being

Fairchild Hiller AC-119K

based at Takhli, Thailand for evaluation. Three of these were lost within a month, but there were no further casualties before the trials ended in October. The 9th SRW established a detachment at Kadena AB, Okinawa to operate the Lockheed SR-71A over Vietnam for photo-reconnaissance and ELINT work, initially supplementing a co-located CIA unit flying the earlier A-12. Another Lockheed aircraft to see its first operational service during the year was the AC-130A *Spectre* Hercules gunship variant, that was initially used by the 16th Special Operations Squadron. Equipped with low-light level TV equipment and armed with four GE SUU-11A/A 7.62-mm Miniguns and four 20-mm Vulcan cannon, the AC-130 (like the earlier AC-47, which from 1968 was replaced by the Fairchild AC-119G) proved successful from the outset. Unlike the AC-47 (mainly used for local defence, such as that around Khe Sanh), the AC-130 was used for longer-range search and destroy missions, especially along the Ho Chi Minh Trail.

The McDonnell Douglas F-4 Phantom was the Air Force's most significant fighter development during the conflict in Southeast Asia. Entering service in 1965, the RF-4C reconnaissance version replaced RF-101s and remained in front-line service for over two decades. RF-4C at Udorn, Thailand by George Akimoto is from the Air Force Art Collection.

The pages for 1968 generously supported by Colonel Mary M Tripp, United States Air Force

RF-4C at Udorn, Thailand by George Akimoto

1 January: Air Defense Command was re-designated Aerospace Defense Command (ADC).

22 January: A B-52G Stratofortress carrying four free-fall nuclear bombs crashed on sea ice at North Star Bay, whilst attempting an emergency landing at Thule AB, Greenland. It took months for the area to be cleared of all detectable radioactive debris.

14 January: Following a new all-out offensive by the North Vietnamese, an additional 26 B-52s were flown from the US to Kadena AB, Okinawa. They were to support the 1,200 sorties per month authorised by the Defense Secretary, under Operation *Niagara*, targeting Communist positions near to the demilitarised zone.

29 January: It was announced that the successful North American X-15 programme was to be terminated by the end of the year.

29-30 January: North Vietnam launched the Tet Offensive, a large-scale attack by Viet Cong and NVA units throughout South Vietnam.

27 February: Following successful trials over Laos, and the delta, the first operational use was made of the AC-130A Hercules gunship over the Ho Chi Minh Trail in Vietnam.

March: Air support kept almost 7,000 isolated US Marines and South Vietnamese army troops at Khe Sanh from being annihilated by an estimated force of 40,000 North Vietnamese and Viet Cong surrounding the plateau.

3 March: A patrol of Douglas AC-47s repelled a Viet Cong night attack. Since the Tet Offensive was launched on 31 January, these AC-47s, which were armed with three six-barrelled 7.6-mm SU-11A Miniguns, had been keeping a constant watch over US bases in Vietnam.

25 March: Operation *Combat Lancer* commenced when six F-111As of the 428th Tactical Fighter Squadron that had been deployed to Takhli, Thailand on 17 March, flew their first combat missions over Vietnam. Two were lost during the month and a third in April. Eventually 55 sorties were completed before the F-111s returned to the US.

31 March: Bombing north of the 20th Parallel in Vietnam was stopped.

6 April: Selected by the USAF in 1966 as an attack fighter adapted from the US Navy Corsair II, the first of two LTV YA-7D prototypes made its first flight.

10 April: The Kadena-based detachment of the 9th Strategic Reconnaissance Wing began operations over Vietnam with the SR-71A.

17 June: The first McDonnell Douglas C-9A aeromedical transport for the USAF, was rolled out at Long Beach, CA.

18 June: B-52 Stratofortresses completed three years of war operations. They had flown more than 25,000 sorties, dropping over 630,000 tons of conventional bombs.

30 June: The first of five development Lockheed C-5A Galaxy transports made its first flight. Eventually 81 were built for MAC.

13 July: The first production General Dynamics FB-111A strategic bomber had its maiden flight. It was intended as an interim replacement for the retired Convair B-58A and the cancelled North American B-70A.

July: The 340th Bombardment Group was formed at Carswell AFB, TX, to conduct crew training on the FB-111A.

8 August: Maiden flight of the USAF's first C-9A Nightingale.

11 September: The largest research balloon ever made, developed by the USAF's Cambridge Research Laboratories, was launched from California. It flew for 18 hours to a height of 158,000ft with instruments designed to measure the upper atmosphere and the interaction of the sun with the stratosphere.

26 September: The Air Force's first A-7D Corsair II (67-14584) made its maiden flight.

30 September: Bids were requested for the USAF's F-X single-seat air superiority fighter programme.

McDonnell Douglas F-4E Phantom II

Cessna O-2A

October: The third operational fixed-wing gunship entered operational service in Vietnam, when an AC-119, a Lockheed converted Fairchild C-119 transport, commenced operations. Adapted in the Project *Gunship III* programme, the AC-119s soon replaced Douglas AC-47s.

1 October: The completion of a four-month airlift, following an exercise on redeployment, from West Germany of the US 24th Infantry Division, the 3rd Armoured Cavalry Regiment and some USAF units. This was a record 33,000 military personnel, 3,700 tons of cargo and 15,000 dependants in one operation.

1 November: The last attack of *Rolling Thunder* was made against a target near Dong Hoi by an F-4D Phantom of the 8th Tactical Fighter Wing.

1 November: President Johnson called to a halt *Rolling Thunder* operations against North Vietnam, as part of a planned drawback of US military units to transfer the defence of South Vietnam to its own people. Attacks were to continue only in the demilitarised zone between North and South Vietnam.

30 December: F-4 Phantoms commenced operations as a night escort and flak suppression aircraft for the Lockheed AC-130 gunships, to deter attacks on them by North Vietnamese interceptors.

A further bombing halt had begun on 1 November of the previous year and the Vietnamisation process was now well under way. Both of these combined to reduce the number of operations in Southeast Asia. However, the failure of peace talks and the continuing aggression by the North Vietnamese Army and Viet Cong forced a resumption of bombing on 5 June. *Arc Light* raids by B-52 Stratofortresses recommenced, although the number of sorties was reduced from 1,800 per month to 1,400 by the end of the year, with further cutbacks following. Evidence of the gradual US withdrawal was to be seen in July, when C-141A StarLifters flew back to McChord AFB, WA, the first American combat unit to be pulled out of Southeast Asia.

During this latest 'bombing halt' the only US aircraft that flew north of the border were reconnaissance aircraft such as the RF-101C or the SR-71. However, in South Vietnam and in Laos, operations continued and B-52 *Arc Light* raids were much in evidence although not at previous years' totals. In particular the forces in the south concentrated on the Ho Chi Minh trail and attempted to prevent the North from using the halt to build up their forces and reserves of equipment.

The F-4 Phantom had become the major tactical fighter and began to replace the F-100 Super Sabres, while specially modified F-4Cs were taking over the *Wild Weasel* role from the F-105F Thunderstreak. 1969 also became known as the year of the O-1 Bird Dog and the O-2 Skymaster, operating at low-level and often below tree top height, in support of ground forces. Able to speak directly with the troops on the ground, the 'little guys' were able to call in their 'big brothers', the F-100s, F-4s or other offensive support. By the beginning of June the talks were stalled and the 'halt' was over, with limited strikes again permitted north of the border.

A veteran aircraft that was retired from service during the year was the A-26A Invader. Originally known as the B-26K, the Invader had been equipped with modern

Lockheed T-33As of the 317th FIS

avionics and served principally in the counter-insurgency role. Its tasks were taken over by Northrop F-5As of the 10th Fighter Commando Squadron and Cessna A-37s, both of which were subsequently transferred to the Vietnamese Air Force. The other piston-engined attack aircraft, the long-serving Douglas A-1 Skyraider, remained in service for close support duties, providing particular assistance for helicopter rescue missions.

Away from Vietnam, the 340th Bombardment Group at Carswell AFB, TX received its first General Dynamics FB-111As from October onwards. First flown in July 1968, the type was capable of employing the AGM-69 SRAM and other nuclear weapons, and had originally been intended as a stop-gap measure following retirement of the B-58A Hustler and cancellation of the B-70 Valkyrie. However, only 76 examples of SAC's first new bomber since the B-58 were delivered, also serving with the 380th Bomb Wing at Plattsburgh AFB, NY and the 509th BW at Pease AFB, NH.

The final chapter in the troubled history of the B-70 Valkyrie project was closed in February, with the retirement of the only remaining XB-70A. Its flight research programme ended in January, and the Valkyrie was flown from Edwards AFB to the US Air Force Museum at Wright-Patterson AFB, OH. An indication of SAC's manned bomber future was to follow in November, when the USAF put out a request for initial proposals for its Advanced Manned Strategic Aircraft (AMSA) programme. This eventually resulted in the Rockwell B-1.

Cessna A-37A

The pages for 1969 generously supported by Lockheed Martin Tactical Aircraft Systems

January: The USAF began experimenting with one-man helicopters for stranded pilots.

7 January: Almost ten years after the first flight of the type, Northrop delivered the 1,000th example of its T-38 Talon supersonic trainer for USAF service.

4 February: Its flight research programme having ended, the sole surviving XB-70 Valkyrie was flown from Edwards AFB, CA to Wright-Patterson AFB, OH to be preserved in the USAF Museum.

9 February: Tacsat, the largest tactical communications satellite then built, was launched into geostationary Earth orbit. It was designed to provide a large capacity communication system for the US armed forces.

20 February: SAC initiated a satellite-basing concept, in which small numbers of bombers and tankers were placed on ground alert at bases other than those routinely used for this purpose.

19 March: Despite opposition from the USAF, an order for 12 Hawker Siddeley Harrier V/STOL ground attack fighters, designated AV-8A, was announced for the US Marine Corps.

17 April: The Martin X-24A lifting-body research vehicle made its first unpowered flight from the underwing position of a B-52 Stratofortress. It had an 8,480lb thrust XLR11 rocket motor together with two 500lb thrust hydrogen peroxide engines for flare and landing control.

21 May: A C-5A Galaxy set a new world record by taking-off at a gross weight of 728,100lb.

Kaman HH-43B Huskie

Boeing KC-135A Stratotanker and Republic F-105D Thunderchiefs

5 June: USAF bombers renewed their attacks on North Vietnam, the first since the ceasefire had been announced by President Johnson the previous November.

10 June: The Manned Orbiting Laboratory programme (MOL) was cancelled. It would have placed a long-term 'workshop' in Earth orbit.

1 July: The USAF Air Rescue and Recovery Service completed its 2,500th rescue in Southeast Asia.

8 July: As part of the overall plan of 'Vietnamisation' – handing over to the South Vietnamese – coupled with the phased withdrawal of US forces from Vietnam, the first combat unit departed to the US in C-141A StarLifters from Tan San Nhut AB and returned to McChord AFB, WA.

8 October: The 340th Bombardment Group at Carswell AFB, TX received the first operational General Dynamics FB-111A (67-7193).

3 November: The USAF issued a call for proposals to meet the requirements of its advanced manned strategic aircraft (AMSA). The AF sought a high-subsonic, high-altitude stand-off bomber, to be designated B-1.

6 November: A 34 million cubic ft balloon, twice as tall as the Washington Monument, and the largest balloon ever launched, lifted a payload of 13,000lb over Holloman AFB, NM.

15 November: Due to escalating costs, the Department of Defense reduced the order for C-5A Galaxy transports from 155 to 81.

17 December: The USAF closed Project *Blue Book*, its 22-year investigation into unidentified flying objects (UFOs).

22 December: An F-111A crash at Nellis AFB, NV, resulted in all F/FB-111s being temporarily grounded.

23 December: The Defense Secretary announced McDonnell Douglas as the winner of the F-X air superiority fighter competition for a single-seat fighter, later named the F-15 Eagle.

Bob Cunningham not only captured the B-58 Hustler on canvas, but also designed the high visibility paint scheme for the initial batch of test aircraft for the manufacturer, Convair. In this painting, Firefly, he shows the SAC bomber in a characteristic setting, at high speed above the clouds. It is reproduced here by courtesy of Lockheed Martin Tactical Aircraft Systems.

Firefly by Robert E Cunningham ASAA

One of the first actions by Richard Nixon, following his inauguration as President, had been to permit attacks by B-52 Stratofortresses on targets in Cambodia. The actual locations of these targets were not revealed, as they were in a neutral country. These B-52 operations were stepped up in the early part of the year, after threatening North Vietnamese manoeuvres in February. The following month, American troops joined with the South Vietnamese to launch a series of incursions into Cambodia, in order to strike NVA forces there. During April and May, Stratofortresses flew 4,308 sorties and dropped 120,528 tons of bombs. From this point onwards, the US gave support to the Cambodian army in its war against Pol Pot's Khmer Rouge. B-52s carried out 763 missions in two months, mostly in support of ground operations. However, B-52 missions were banned by Congress later in the year following violent demonstrations against them across the USA. Strikes on targets in North Vietnam also continued following attempts by the enemy to shoot down USAF reconnaissance flights.

There had been a US assumption that they had an agreement whereby unarmed reconnaissance flights over the North would not be fired on. However, the North Vietnamese observed no such agreement and when reconnaissance flights began to be fired at, strikes in retaliation were permitted. Initially, these first missions were called 'protective reaction strikes', but this was later changed to 'reinforced protective strikes' to give more flexibility. Whatever the title, US Navy and Air Force aircraft completed some 500 sorties against anti-aircraft artillery (AAA) and SAM sites north of the demilitarised zone (DMZ) during the first four days of May.

One of the major operations mounted by the USAF in Southeast Asia during 1970 was the attempt, on 20-21 November, to rescue around 100 prisoners of war from the Son Tay camp near Hanoi. This night mission was to have involved the prisoners being airlifted out by Sikorsky CH-53E helicopters, with support provided by A-1

Lockheed HC-130P Hercules and Sikorsky HH-3E Jolly Green Giant

Skyraiders, F-105G *Wild Weasel* Thunderchiefs and F-4D Phantoms. Unfortunately the rescue had to be aborted as the prisoners had been moved away from that camp several months previously. The *Igloo White* programme, that monitored movements along the Ho Chi Minh Trail using aircraft-dropped sensor equipment, continued to be a success, but with some tactical alterations. The dropping of sensors was now being undertaken by F-4D Phantoms of the 8th TFW and the information relay element of the operation was handed over in December 1970 to the 554th Reconnaissance Squadron and its Beechcraft QU-22Bs. These aircraft, codenamed *Pave Eagle*, were modified versions of the civilian Beech Bonanza four-seat tourer. They were capable of being remotely-piloted and presented a smaller target than the Lockheed EC-121Rs previously used. Their operational life, however, was rather short – but much cheaper.

With the entry into service the previous year of the General Dynamics FB-111A swing-wing bomber, SAC now retired its final two B-58A Hustlers from service with the 305th Bomb Wing at Grissom AFB, IN. This last pair

joined 82 other Hustlers in the storage facility at Davis-Monthan AFB, AZ. Two, however, were preserved, one by the USAF Museum at Wright-Patterson AFB, OH and another at SAC's own Museum located at Offutt AFB, NE. The first General Dynamics F-111Es arrived at RAF Upper Heyford, UK in September, replacing F-100 Super Sabres with the 20th Tactical Fighter Wing. By now, many of the variable-geometry strike aircraft's initial technical problems had been ironed out. The F-111 immediately provided USAFE with major improvements in terms of weapons payloads, range and mission capability. Should the Cold War have developed into actual conflict, the Upper Heyford-based 'Aardvarks' would have spearheaded deep penetration missions into hostile airspace, in order to carry out either conventional or nuclear strikes.

The definitive service version of this long-range tactical fighter bomber, the Republic F-105D Thunderchief was operated effectively in Vietnam until November 1970, when it was replaced by the F-4 Phantom. This painting, The Song Begins *by William Phillips, comes from the Air Force Art Collection.*

The pages for 1970 generously supported by Colebrand Limited

The Song Begins by William S Phillips ASAA

January: The first *Crested Cap* exercise was held, in which F-4D Phantoms from US-based units deployed to Spangdahlem and Hahn ABs, West Germany, to take part in the inaugural *Reforger* manoeuvres that demonstrated the 'dual-basing' Wing concept.

16 January: The last two B-58A Hustlers, of the 305th Bombardment Wing, Grissom AFB, IN were withdrawn from SAC and flown to Davis-Monthan AFB, AZ.

17 February: B-52 Stratofortesses commenced the first bombing raids against North Vietnamese and Pathet Lao troops that were threatening the Plaine des Jarres in the north of the country.

18 March: In conjunction with a US/South Vietnamese thrust into Cambodia to engage North Vietnamese forces there, B-52s began a series of night sorties against Cambodian targets and in the following two months flew 4,308 sorties and dropped 120,528 tons of bombs.

19 March: The first powered flight of the Martin X-24A (SV-5P) lifting-body research vehicle. After release from its parent B-52, it made a rocket-boosted flight to Mach 0.865 (571mph) at a height of 44,384ft.

7 May: The USAF issued requests for proposals on the A-X attack aircraft and asked 12 companies to bid.

1 June: The C-5A Galaxy became operational with MAC at Scott AFB, VA and took its place alongside the C-141A

McDonnell Douglas F-4E Phantom

StarLifter on supply flights to Europe and Southeast Asia.

5 June: Following a request to bid on the USAF advanced manned strategic aircraft (AMSA) programme, North American Rockwell was awarded a contract to design and build the supersonic B-1A as SAC's B-52 replacement.

11 June: Weelus AB, near Tripoli, Libya, was closed after 26 years of operation, just as Colonel Gadaffi came to power. It had been the USAF's primary weapons training centre outside of Continental USA (CONUS).

15 June: The 354th Tactical Fighter Wing returned from deployment in South Korea to be re-equipped with the A-7D Corsair II at Myrtle Beach AFB, SC.

8 July: A contract was awarded to Boeing to develop and integrate an airborne warning and control system (AWACS) into the Boeing 707-320B airframe.

6 August: Spain and the US signed a renewal of their mutual defence agreement, allowing the US continued use of air bases in Spain. In return, Spain would receive considerable military equipment to modernise its armed forces.

19 August: The first LGM-30G Minuteman III ICBM was placed on alert at Minot AFB, ND. 550 of these missiles were eventually to be deployed at four bases.

20 August: Two Sikorsky HH-53Cs completed the first non-stop trans-Pacific crossing by helicopter, from Eglin AFB, FL to Da Nang, South Vietnam. They were refuelled en route by HC-130 Hercules tankers.

12 September: Two General Dynamics F-111Es, out of an eventual 72, arrived at RAF Upper Heyford. Forward-basing F-111s was viewed as vital to the success of any missions which may have involved penetrations of hostile European airspace.

2 October: The first of 141 Bell Model 212 twin-turbine helicopters, designated UH-1N was delivered to the Special Operations force.

14 October: First supersonic flight by the Martin X-24A.

28 September-31 October: USAFE airlifted two US military hospitals and medical personnel to Jordan to treat victims of the civil war under Operation *Fig Hill*.

4 November: The USAF contracted Bell to produce 30 HH-

Martin B-57B

1H helicopters for local base rescue purposes, as a replacement for the HH-43 Huskie. Deliveries began in October 1971 and were completed two years later.

6 November: The USAF launched Project 647, a military reconnaissance satellite that was to go into geostationary orbit above the Indian Ocean. It was reputed to have sensors able to detect infra-red emissions from rocket plumes. Unfortunately, there was an incomplete burn due to engine failure and it did not reach the planned orbit.

20-21 November: Under cover of heavy diversionary air attacks, US Special Forces flew Sikorsky HH-3 and HH-53 helicopters 400 miles (645km) from bases in Thailand to Son Tay prison camp, NW of Hanoi. A-1E Skyraiders provided escort for the helicopters in a mission to rescue American POWs believed to be imprisoned in a compound there. In the event, the prisoners had been moved and the mission was aborted.

December: The data relay element of the *Igloo White* project in Vietnam was taken over by Beechcraft QU-22Bs, variants of the civilian Bonanza, of the 554th Reconnaissance Squadron. However, the type was withdrawn in August 1971 and the dropping of sensors along the Ho Chi Minh Trail was then taken over by F-105 or F-4 aircraft.

18 December: Four prototypes of two competing designs (by Northrop and Fairchild Republic) were ordered by the USAF for its A-X ground attack aircraft programme.

A series of heavy and concentrated strikes on important military targets took place throughout the year, beginning with Operation *Slugger*, also known as Operation *Louisville Slugger*, in February, with the destruction of SAM sites, missile transporters and vehicles along the important Ban Karai pass, during the 67 sorties flown. Despite this, the North Vietnamese attempted to improve their communication and supply lines, constructing new routes through the de-militarised zone (DMZ) into the South. Gunship operations by the AC-130 Spectres, now including improved AC-130E versions, continued over the Ho Chi Minh Trail in an attempt to slow the stream of enemy movements between the North and South. However, the enemy air defence system now had much-improved radar control facilities, combined with an increasing number of MiG-21 fighters in service. Also the limitations placed on US air strikes, forbidding the bombing of many front-line NVAF air bases, placed the Americans' superiority in air combat under a serious threat. In an attempt to counter this, an improved airborne early warning service was brought in, using Lockheed EC-121D Constellations. Authorisation was finally provided in November for strikes against NVAF airfields.

These began on 7-8 November, when a force made up of F-4Ds and *Wild Weasel* F-105Gs effectively put the bases at Quan Lang, Dong Hoi and Vinh, out of action. With enemy operations thus severely restricted, targets south of the 20th Parallel that had previously been defended by NVAF aircraft from these airfields, could now be attacked to good effect. The intensity of operations mounted, with the last four days of 1971 seeing 1,025 missions being flown against objectives in this area, with the heaviest air strikes since the bombing halt in 1968. Despite this, North Vietnamese ground forces were apparently back on the offensive, with US reconnaissance reports indicating that NVA and Viet Cong troops were massing in enormous numbers just north of the DMZ.

McDonnell F-101B Voodoos

1971 saw the withdrawal from Southeast Asia of some of the USAF's longest serving aircraft and types that had borne the brunt of offensive work since the conflict started. In June, the last O-1 Bird Dog was handed over to the South Vietnamese Air Force and its 'big brother', the F-100 Super Sabre, finally left South Vietnam in July. But surprisingly unmarked and almost unknown, the *Patricia Lynn* RB-57E reconnaissance operation finally wound down. Never more than five aircraft, they had provided up to 94% of all battlefield intelligence and were widely viewed as the most effective reconnaissance system in the conflict.

The addition of the 475th Military Airlift Wing's C-5A Galaxy fleet to the 'air bridge' of supplies to the Vietnam theatre, was a major improvement to the assigned transport fleet, as the giant aircraft, that had first entered service in June 1970, started to play a significant role. Alongside them, C-130 Hercules, that were no longer employed on inter-theatre transport work, and C-141 StarLifters, had replaced the C-124s, C-133s and C-135s used earlier for the longer-range missions. The last defoliation missions by Fairchild UC-123B/Ks took place in early 1971 under the control of the 315th Tactical Airlift Wing. They had been in progress since the start of the *Ranch Hand* programme in 1962. During those nine years, some 6.2 million acres of forest had been sprayed using 100,000,000lb of herbicides, mainly Agent Orange. On their return to the US, these aircraft were almost immediately employed to deal with a different menace, a virus known as Venezuelan equine encephalomyelitis, which first spread through Texas and then other states causing several deaths. The ex-*Ranch Hand* UC-123Ks and additional Douglas C-47s used the same spraying techniques as had been employed over the jungles of Southeast Asia in order to help battle the illness.

The pages for 1971 generously supported by The Royal International Air Tattoo

28 January: The last *Ranch Hand* defoliation mission was carried out in Vietnam by Fairchild UC-123B sprayers of the 310th Tactical Airlift Squadron operating with US Special Air Services.

February: The USAF launched Operation *Louisville Slugger* in North Vietnam. In 67 sorties, strike aircraft destroyed five SAM sites, 15 SAM missile transporters and 15 vehicles in the Ban Karai pass area.

1 March: The 4950th Test Wing was activated at Wright-Patterson AFB, OH, as the flying unit of the test aircraft operated by the Aeronautical Systems Division.

12 April: The USAF announced the use of the so-called 'daisy cutter' bomb in Vietnam. This was a conventional high-explosive bomb designed to clear jungle areas.

26 April: A Lockheed SR-71A strategic reconnaissance aircraft of the 4,200th Strategic Reconnaissance Wing, Beale AFB, CA completed a record breaking flight. It was airborne for 10hr during which it covered 15,000 miles (24,140 km) which included two round trips across the north and central US and a circuit of central states. Most of the flight was above 80,000ft and Mach 3, except for the refuelling contacts with the KC-135Q tankers. The crew were awarded the USAF's McKay Trophy for 'the most meritorious flight of the year'.

May: It was reported that the 24 General Dynamics F-111Cs built for the Royal Australian Air Force, but not delivered, were possibly to be converted into electronic warfare EF-111s.

26 June: The 35th Tactical Fighter Wing started to leave Phan Rang AB, Vietnam, thus ending front-line operation of the F-100 Super Sabre.

July: Over a two-week period, six USAF Fairchild UC-123K spray aircraft battled a new and unusual foe – a virus called Venezuelan equine encephalomyelitis, which had killed more than 100 Texans since it was first detected at Brownsville early in the month.

1 July: The first General Dynamics FB-111A was placed on alert by the 509th Bomb Wing at Pease AFB, NH.

16 July: Brigadier General Jeanne M Holm was appointed as the first female General Officer in the Air Force.

26 July-7 August: The Apollo 15 mission to the moon had an all-Air Force crew (Scott, Worden and Irwin) and saw the first use of the Lunar Roving Vehicle.

Lockheed EC-121T Constellation

August: In an attempt to restrict enemy road construction across the Demilitarised Zone into South Vietnam, USAF aircraft flew 473 missions, seeding the road with munitions and sensors.

August: The last Martin RB-57Es, that had been operating the *Patricia Lynn* reconnaissance tasks, were withdrawn. They had been among the first USAF aircraft in the area and had provided front-line intelligence throughout all the halts and changes of policy.

21 September: 196 USAF tactical aircraft, flying in poor weather, hit three POL storage areas south of Dong Hoi and destroyed some 350,000gal of fuel. This was the first all-instrument air strike of the Vietnam War carried out using LORAN (Long range aid to navigation).

1 November: The 15th Air Base Wing was formed as the primary unit at Hickam AFB, HI.

7-8 November: USAF aircraft carried out very heavy air attacks to neutralise the North Vietnamese airfields at Dong Hoi, Vinh and Quan Lang.

26-30 December: US aircraft launched the heaviest air strikes in Vietnam since 1968, when 1,025 sorties were flown against targets south of the 20th Parallel.

When 82 Boeing KC-97s were passed to Air National Guard units, they were given the added boost of two underwing, podded GE J47 turbojets. In this specially commissioned painting by John Young, a KC-97L of the Ohio Air Guard is refuelling an F-84F Thunderstreak.

General Dynamics FB-111A

Top-up by John Young GAvA, VP ASAA

The initial signs of a major North Vietnamese build-up north of the demilitarised zone at the end of 1971 had not halted the continuing withdrawal of US forces from the area. However, as it became clear that a fresh enemy offensive was on the way, the USAF began several redeployments in order to prepare for further offensive missions. More B-52 Stratofortresses were flown to Anderson AFB, Guam, after an increase in sorties to 1,200 per month was authorised. The North Vietnamese attack commenced in the early hours of 30 March, with rockets, artillery and mortars being fired across the DMZ preceding an invasion by around 40,000 troops. Assisted by regular NVA units already stationed in the South, these forces crushed the less powerful South Vietnamese army, leaving USAF and VNAF aircraft to provide defence.

The Joint Chiefs of Staff again raised the authorised B-52 sortie rate to 1,800 per month. The Stratofortress force was now also starting to include B-52Gs with a smaller bomb load than the 'big belly' B-52Ds, but possessing a longer unrefuelled range. Other immediate deployments under the *Constant Guard* programme of reinforcements included nine squadrons of F-4 Phantoms, a further F-105G *Wild Weasel* unit and another deployment of

McDonnell Douglas F-4D/E Phantoms

F-111As. In support of these, two squadrons of C-130 Hercules were also moved to Southeast Asia, together with several more SAC KC-135 Stratotanker units, for rapidly expanding air-to-air refuelling operations.

As hostilities again escalated, the peace talks taking place in Paris came to an end on 4 May and by 10 May the start of Operation *Linebacker I* signalled resumed bombing in the North, while continuing strikes were made against supply routes. Attacks on the principal cities, Hanoi and Haiphong, made use of new tactics in order to avoid the unusually capable defences employed around these two important centres. A group of about 20 strike aircraft with electronic warfare aircraft and fighter escorts in support, was a common 'attack package'. Laser-guided and electro-optically-guided 'smart' weapons were used more against particularly important targets. The *Wild Weasel* technology had improved such that it was now equipping F-105Gs and F-4C Phantoms to work in conjunction with better jamming equipment used by RB-66 Destroyers and Boeing EC-135s. Illustrating the effectiveness of the new weaponry, the Paul Doumer Bridge over the Red River, west of Hanoi, was finally destroyed in May by an F-4 Phantom using a single M18 laser-guided bomb. A strike the previous day using smaller such weapons had been unsuccessful. The bridge had been a target since 1967 and had often been badly damaged, but never irreparably. Sorties by B-52s reached a new peak of 3,150 during June alone, with *Arc Light* missions from U-Tapao, Thailand and Andersen AB, Guam totalling almost 56,000 by the beginning of July since the Communist invasion had begun. At around the same time, the pressure of the ever-heavier air strikes was beginning to tell on the North Vietnamese, whose offensive came to a halt on the ground. Peace talks were resume in Paris, but bombing continued even after President Nixon had announced a halt to such operations, to start in October. This was the end of *Linebacker I*, and the resulting 'breathing space' gave time for the formulation of plans for

even heavier attacks, as ceasefire negotiations again failed.

Linebacker II commenced on 15 December, with the USAF providing several wings of F-4 Phantoms, F-111As, three newly-arrived squadrons of A-7D Corsair IIs and over 200 B-52s. All were used between 18-29 December, when extremely heavy bombing raids by B-52s were launched against storage and fuel depots, airfields, SAM sites, power stations and rail installations, as well as targets in Hanoi itself. In spite of losses, the Stratofortresses continued on operations after a brief Christmas break. A 220-aircraft raid, of which 120 were B-52s, on ten targets on 26 December being the most concentrated wartime bombing mission ever. Three days later, there appeared to be progress regarding peace talks, and *Linebacker II*, the heaviest air strikes of the war, ended. 729 sorties by B-52s had dropped over 15,000 tons of bombs, with 5,000 more tons being delivered by other aircraft.

The entry into service of the AGM-69A short-range attack missile (SRAM) with SAC's 42nd Bomb Wing at Loring AFB, ME, added still further to the Command's air-launched ordnance capabilities. It carried a 170 kiloton W-69 nuclear warhead, and had a range of up to 100 miles. A total of 281 B-52Gs and 'Hs were modified to carry 20 AGM-69As. Meanwhile, the Air Force ordered four prototypes each of the two contenders for its Lightweight Fighter (LWF) requirement, namely the General Dynamics YF-16 and the Northrop YF-17. The competitive fly-off between the two, to be held at Wright-Patterson AFB, OH, was the first such comparison to be undertaken in 20 years. The winner of TAC's earlier interceptor order, the McDonnell Douglas F-15A had its maiden flight in late July.

A total of 284 Lockheed C-141A StarLifters was built for the Air Force between 1963 and 1966 and were immediately pressed into service with MATS (later MAC). In this painting from the Air Force Art Collection, Charles Carroll shows an early C-141A Landing at Thule in Greenland.

The pages for 1972 generously supported by Lockheed Martin Aeronautical Systems

Landing at Thule by Charles J Carroll Jnr

1972

6 January: The USAF issued a request for proposals for a lightweight fighter (LWF). It was required to have a maximum speed of Mach 1.6, operational ceiling of up to 40,000ft and a take-off weight of under 20,000lb.

24 January: The USAF issued a request for proposals on an advanced medium STOL (AMST) transport, that could be developed eventually into a larger successor to the C-130 Hercules tactical airlifter.

26 January: The last Republic F-84 variant (an RF-84F Thunderflash) was withdrawn from USAF service, having served finally with an ANG unit.

8 February: The Joint Chiefs of Staff authorised a B-52 Stratofortress sortie level of 1,200 per month, following a suspected build-up of Communist forces in South Vietnam. A further 29 B-52s were deployed to Andersen AFB, Guam to meet this objective.

9 February: The first of two AWACS prototypes was flown. These Boeing EC-137Ds were converted B707-320B civil airliners and equipped with a Westinghouse AN/APY-1 radar system complete with a large external radome.

20 February: A new world record for unrefuelled flight by a turboprop aircraft was set by a USAF HC-130H Hercules, flying between Ching Chuan Kang AB, Taiwan and Scott AFB, IL.

1 March: NASA announced a joint co-operative programme between the USAF and the US aerospace industry to develop a quiet experimental STOL transport (QUESTOL) – and the advanced medium STOL transport (AMST).

30 March: B-52 Stratofortress bombing sorties were increased yet again – this time to 1,800 per month. A further 28 B-52Gs were deployed to Guam - this version could not carry the bombload of the modified B-52Ds, but were able to fly round-trip missions without refuelling.

13 April: The USAF ordered four prototypes of two contenders (the General Dynamics YF-16 and Northrop YF-17) for its LWF programme.

15 April: The first AGM-69A SRAM (short-range attack missile) was placed on alert.

27 April: Four USAF aircraft destroyed the Thanh Hoa bridge with Paveway laser-guided 'smart' bombs, after 872 earlier missions against the bridge using conventional bombs had all failed.

29 April: The prototype YRF-4C Phantom (62-12200), subsequently modified with some F-4E features, became the first aircraft to be flown in the US fitted with a fly-by-wire control system.

10 May: Operation *Linebacker I*, the intensified bombing of North Vietnam, commenced.

10 May: The Fairchild YA-10A prototype (71-1369) made its first flight. After competitive evaluation against the Northrop YA-9 during 1972, the YA-10 was adopted for production in January 1973. It was designed to carry large ordnance loads and be able to withstand extensive battle damage.

10 May: The key Paul Doumer bridge, west of Hanoi, was destroyed yet again by F-4E Phantoms. On an important supply route for the North Vietnamese, it had been a major target for several years.

30 May: The Northrop A-9A (71-1367), the second competitor in the AX close-support fighter aircraft competition, had its first flight.

2 June: A Sikorsky HH-53 helicopter flew deep into North Vietnam on a daring daylight rescue mission to rescue a downed F-4 Phantom pilot who had been evading North Vietnamese forces for 23 days.

27 July: The prototype McDonnell Douglas YF-15A Eagle (71-0280) air superiority fighter was flown for the first time. The type had been named as the winner of the Air Force design competition for a new advanced tactical fighter in December 1969.

4 August: The first operational AGM-69A SRAM (short-range nuclear-tipped attack missile) was delivered to the 42nd Bombardment Wing, Loring AFB, ME.

9 August: The USAF received a new Boeing VC-137C (72-7000), a more modern 707-353B conversion, which took over the 'Air Force One' duties.

11 August: First flight of the Northrop F-5E Tiger II was made.

Lockheed HC-130H Hercules

The 425th Tactical Fighter Training Squadron at Williams AFB first received F-5Es and Fs for the training role from early the following year.

28 August: Captain Richard S Ritchie downed his fifth MiG-21 and became the first USAF ace of the Vietnam war.

23 October: Operation *Linebacker I* was terminated. All tactical bombing north of the 20th Parallel was brought to a halt, as once again the North Vietnamese returned to the peace talks.

27 October: The first flight was made by the Beech C-12/U-21 Super King Air.

27 October: USAF Systems Command launched the world's largest balloon, with an internal volume of 47.8 million cu ft, from Chino, CA. It reached a new altitude record of 170,000ft carrying a 250lb load of scientific instruments.

7 December: The all-Air Force crew (Cernan, Evans and Schmitt) of Apollo 17 made a lunar landing. They made use of a Lunar Roving Vehicle and a 75-hour stay on the lunar surface was the longest of the Apollo missions.

18 December: Operation *Linebacker II* commenced, following the breakdown of peace talks in Paris, with 125 B-52 Stratofortresses resuming operations against the Hanoi area.

29 December: At midnight of day eleven of *Linebacker II*, all bombing operations against North Vietnam were brought to a halt. Over 1,800 sorties had been flown during this campaign.

The *Linebacker II* raids at the end of the previous year, often known as the 'Eleven-Day War', inflicted such a heavy blow on the North Vietnamese that they returned to the Paris peace talks. On 23 January, agreement was reached on the terms of a ceasefire, and four days later US military operations in Vietnam were officially concluded after eight years of war. However, the bombing of targets in Laos continued into April, and that of Cambodia until 15 August.

Since the declaration of hostilities in 1965, the Air Force had lost 2,257 aircraft on operations (out of a total of 5,511 aircraft lost by all US forces in Southeast Asia), while 2,118 Air Force personnel had been killed. No B-52 Stratofortresses were lost to North Vietnamese interceptors but two MiG-21s were claimed by B-52 tail gunners. A total of 17 B-52s were lost to SAMs, although at least six of these were only written off after reaching their bases where the damage was considered beyond repair. There were also eight B-52s destroyed in accidents, including mid-air collisions.

It was a very expensive and wholly unsatisfactory conflict from almost all points of view, not least the eventual outcome. On the whole, airpower was not used wisely or effectively, with the exception of helicopters and close air support – during the USAF's 12 years of heavy involvement in Vietnam. Very often, politics had a major influence on the selection of weapons and targets for US raids in North Vietnam. There were too many sanctuaries and rules of engagement, which proved costly in terms of aircraft and aircrew, and too many pauses in the bombing, which allowed the Communists to recover and convince themselves that the US was not fully committed to the war. Surgical strikes in a high-threat air defence environment without 'smart' weapons proved mostly ineffective. On 15 August, with the end of bombing missions against the Khmer Rouge in Cambodia, US involvement in Southeast Asia was finally concluded.

While one commitment had all but ended, another began. In October, MAC again demonstrated the enormous increase in its strategic airlift capabilities offered by the C-141A StarLifter and C-5A Galaxy. It began to transport what would eventually total over 22,000 tons of supplies to Israel, that had been attacked by Arab forces, at the start of what was known as the Yom Kippur War. Won by the Israelis, this victory would spark the 1973 oil crisis, when the defeated Arabs quadrupled prices in an attack on the West's support for Israel. With the C-5 and C-141, MAC could airlift a far greater range of cargoes over longer distances than ever before, and its response to directions for transport operations was all the more effective.

The year saw the maiden flight of the Boeing E-4A, the Air Force's new Advanced Airborne National Command Post (AABNCP) which replaced the smaller, less well-equipped EC-135s previously used. A converted Boeing 747-200B, this was the first of three to be built to E-4A standard. All three were converted several years later to become E-4Bs, a fourth being delivered in this configuration. At the time, the type was the heaviest, most powerful and costliest military aircraft ever produced.

Another Boeing product, the T-43A, entered service in July with the 323rd Flying Training Wing at Mather AFB, CA. This all-weather navigation trainer was developed from the successful Boeing 737-253 passenger airliner. The Vietnam conflict had shown the requirement for improved navigator instruction, which could not be met by the existing Convair T-29s. With stations for 12 basic student navigators, four advanced trainees and three instructors, the new type offered a larger capacity than its predecessor.

Sikorsky HH-53B 'Super Jolly'

The pages for 1973 generously supported by Lockheed Martin Tactical Aircraft Systems

18 January: Fairchild Republic was awarded a contract for ten pre-production A-10A close-support aircraft, the first aircraft of this type ordered by the Air Force.

13 March: The Headquarters of USAFE closed at Lindsey Air Station, Wiesbaden and re-opened on the following day at Ramstein AB, West Germany.

4 April: The first F-5E Tiger II for the USAF was delivered to the 425th TFTS at Williams AFB, AZ. The USAF adopted the F-5E as a specialised aircraft for dissimilar air combat training (DACT), in which it was flown in the aggressor role against other combat types in USAF service.

10 April: The Boeing T-43A navigation trainer (71-1403), developed from the Boeing 737 series 200 airliner, was flown for the first time. Nineteen were subsequently delivered to the 323rd Flying Training Wing at Mather AFB, CA, the type replacing the Convair T-29.

May: USAF aircraft, including B-52 Stratofortresses, General Dynamics F-111s, A-7 Corsair IIs and AC-130 Hercules, launched strikes against Khmer Rouge insurgents assaulting the Cambodian capital, Phnom Penh.

13 June: The maiden flight was made by the first of four Boeing E-4A advanced airborne national command posts (AABNCPs).

They were designed and equipped to provide a communications link at all times between the US National Command Authority and the front-line forces of all three services.

5 July: The last Grumman HU-16 Albatross on active duty (51-5282) was retired, having set an altitude record for twin-engined amphibians of 32,883ft on the previous day.

1 August: The NASA/USAF Martin Marietta X-24B (13551) lifting-body (rebuilt from the redundant X-24A) made its first unpowered glide flight from a Boeing NB-52 'mother-ship'.

15 August: The bombing of Cambodia by Air Force B-52 Stratofortresses ended after over eight years of almost constant operations in Southeast Asia, and nine years of air strikes by fighter bombers.

15 August: A-7 Corsair IIs were the last US aircraft to carry out the final air strike in Cambodia.

9 October: The USAF began airlifting supplies in C-5A Galaxies and C-141 StarLifters to Israel, as the Arab-Israeli (Yom Kippur) conflict was rapidly evolving into a war of attrition.

1 November: The first flight was made by NASA test pilot Einar Enevoldsen and USAF Major Stu Boyd, in a General Dynamics F-111A fitted with a supercritical wing, to evaluate the benefits of this concept for military aircraft design – known

Boeing NB-52A and Martin X-24B

Boeing T-43A

as TACT (transonic aircraft technology). The new wing generated twice the lift of a conventional F-111A wing at transonic speed.

15 November: The first powered flight of the Martin Marietta X-24B lifting-body was made. It achieved a maximum speed of Mach 0.917 (597 mph) and a height of 52,764ft.

13 December: Roll-out of the first General Dynamics YF-16 was made at the company's Fort Worth, TX, facility.

"A lightning-lit background and a glistening wet aircraft serve to advertise the F-111's low-level, terrain-following, night, all-weather capability" is how Bob Cunningham describes his painting of this 20th TFW General Dynamics F-111E. It is reproduced here by courtesy of Lockheed Martin Tactical Aircraft Systems.

Lockheed SR-71A Blackbird

Night All-Weather by Robert E Cunningham ASAA

The genuine first flight of the General Dynamics YF-16 prototype on 2 February, the new fighter having lifted-off during high-speed tests on the Fort Worth runway on 20 January, heralded the start of an intensive flight-test programme. The operational requirement to be met by the F-16 had originally been known as the Lightweight Fighter (LWF) programme. This title was altered to become the Air Combat Fighter (ACF) and its mission adaptability was brought to the forefront. With potentially very large orders from the NATO European air forces to replace their F-104 Starfighters, the rewards for whichever company (General Dynamics or Northrop with its YF-17) was successful, were very rich indeed. The YF-16's range was longer than that of its competitor, and indeed its overall performance, thanks in no small way to its Pratt & Whitney F100-PW-100 turbofan, was superior to that of the early YF-17s. The consideration that purchasing the single-engined YF-16 was less costly than the twin-engined YF-17 also entered the equation, resulting in the former's selection the following year.

The USAF's other new fighter, the McDonnell Douglas F-15, entered service in November, when President Ford accepted the first two-seat Eagle on behalf of the service. It was delivered to the 555th Tactical Fighter Training Squadron at Luke AFB, AZ, where conversion onto the type began. Instructors started the work-up process on the two-seaters, compiling the vital training documents for the training and conversion of pilots for Eagle operations. At the time, its abilities as an air superiority fighter were unequalled. The F-15A, with its Pratt & Whitney F100 engines, boasted a higher power-weight ratio than any other similar aircraft, as well as more defensive and offensive electronics than had been used before. Addition of the FAST (fuel and sensor tactical packs), first tested in 1974, gave the Eagle some 71% more range with any weapons load. To illustrate this an F-15 thus equipped flew across the Atlantic in late August to appear at the Farnborough Air Show. There, it joined another very

Rockwell B-1 – First flight 23 December 1974

impressive USAF aircraft – the Lockheed SR-71A of the 9th SRW at Beale AFB, also making its European public début. This came after a record non-stop New York-London flight that took 1hr 54min 56sec, giving an average speed of 1,806.96 mph. Returning to its US base, the 'Blackbird' broke the London-Los Angeles record time by reaching California in 3hr 47min 39sec, at an average speed of 1,435.59 mph.

The inaugural flight also took place in December of the Rockwell B-1, only two months after it had been rolled out. This, the Air Force's new Advanced Manned Strategic Aircraft, was intended to be the third main element in the US strategic defence system, alongside land-based and submarine-launched ballistic missiles. With a potential weapons load of some 80,000lb, including such weapons as the Boeing AGM-69A SRAM and air-launched cruise missiles, and with a maximum range of over 6,000 miles, it was the most flexible. However, like the B-70 before it, the B-1 soon ran into technical and political difficulties.

Although its ground forces had been withdrawn from South Vietnam, the US was still supporting the South against the North. Remnants of the major air force were still based in Thailand, including A-7s, F-4s, F-111As and B-52s, with their attendant KC-135 tankers. These were held in readiness, able to return to help the South if a dangerous situation developed. The South Vietnamese Air Force was suffering a financial crisis, rendering it ineffective. It had been given a large number of aircraft, but lacked the funds to buy fuel and spares to operate them. Many of the aircraft were put into storage, including A-1 Skyraiders, 0-1 Bird Dogs, C-47s and C-119s, while the C-130As transferred from the USAF were proving too much for the SVAF and few of the 32 airframes were in flyable condition.

The enormous bulk of the Lockheed C-5A Galaxy is no more evident than when it is seen on the ground, towering above men and machines. Dick Kramer's painting, from the Air Force Art Collection, shows one of MAC's fleet at Dover AFB, DE.

The pages for 1974 generously supported by Lockheed Martin Aeronautical Systems

C-5 Galaxy at Dover AFB by Richard Kramer

4 January: Teledyne Ryan rolled out two YQM-98A RPV long-endurance prototypes. They were built for the USAF's *Compass Cope* programme and were designed to take-off and land on normal runways.

20 January: The first 'flight' was made by the prototype General Dynamics YF-16 (72-01567). This was an inadvertent lift-off during high-speed taxi tests. The first 90-minute official flight followed on 2 February, when it reached 15,000ft and 300 knots.

20 March: Fairchild Republic, McDonnell Douglas and Rockwell were awarded contracts for definition studies of the first advanced fighter integration (AFT-1) demonstrator aircraft.

10 April: A Martin Marietta Titan III-D launched an additional (eighth) *Big Bird* reconnaissance satellite into Earth Orbit from Vandenberg AFB, CA.

April: Defense Secretary James Schlesinger, announced that the USAF's lightweight fighter requirement, met by the competing YF-16 and YF-17, had been modified to provide an air combat fighter which could provide specific mission flexibility in foreign service.

May: The Air Force Rescue Co-ordination Center became operational. It was a single federal agency responsible for co-ordinating all search and rescue efforts.

9 June: The Northrop YF-17 (72-01569), Northrop's entry

General Dynamics YF-16

North American Rockwell OV-10A Bronco

for the Lightweight Tactical Fighter (LTF)/Air Combat Fighter program, had its maiden flight. It became the first US aircraft to exceed Mach 1 in level flight without reheat.

21 June: USAFE received its first two OV-10A Broncos, which were delivered to the 601st Tactical Control Wing.

28 June: Allied Air Forces Central Europe (AAFCE), was formed with its headquarters at Ramstein AB, West Germany, to control all Central Region NATO aircraft.

27 July: An F-15 Eagle made its first flight with the new FAST (fuel and sensor tactical) pack. This was a conformal tank or container which is attached to the sides of the engine intake trunk, to allow the combat radius and ferry range to be substantially increased.

1 September: An SR-71A of the 9th Strategic Reconnaissance Wing, Beale AFB, CA made a record non-stop flight from New York to London (landing at the Farnborough Airshow) in 1hr 54min 56sec, at an average speed of 1,806.96 mph.

13 September: An SR-71A set a new world record from London (departing from RAF Mildenhall) to Los Angeles in 3hr 47min 39sec, at an average speed of 1,435.59 mph.

16 September: The 3rd Tactical Fighter Wing replaced the 405th TFW at Clark AB, Philippines.

14 November: Service use of the F-15 Eagle began with the delivery of a TF-15A to start the training process at the 555th Tactical Fighter Training Squadron, 58th TFW at Luke AFB, AZ. The first TF-15As gave instructors an opportunity to work up on the new aircraft and devise training procedures.

23 December: The first prototype variable-geometry Rockwell B-1A (74-0158) had its maiden flight. The B-1A was designed to meet the requirement for an Advanced Manned Strategic Aircraft (AMSA) and was the West's largest aircraft featuring a variable swept wing.

Direct US involvement in Vietnam finally ended during 1975. The North Vietnamese launched a large invasion of the South resulting in the fall of Saigon on 30 April. Military support was therefore required for an evacuation of US citizens and those granted asylum in America from South Vietnam. This was effected as Operation *Frequent Wind*, which was at first executed by sea from Saigon and Vung Tau. However, as the need to complete the evacuation more speedily became evident, the USAF committed C-130E Hercules, C-141A StarLifters and C-5A Galaxies to the operation. Military Airlift Command flew 201 missions during April, despite the C-5 fleet having been grounded early on after an accident near Ton Son Nhut, Saigon, in which 206 people (mainly Vietnamese orphans) lost their lives. On the 27th, C-141s stopped operations, leaving C-130s to take over by themselves until the 29th. By this date the Evacuation Control Centre located at Tan Son Nhut airbase was under heavy North Vietnamese artillery fire, but because

aircraft loads had been allowed to exceed the normal peacetime figures, there were only 7,014 people left at the Centre and the US Embassy awaiting evacuation. They were airlifted by helicopters, including USAF Sikorsky CH-53s and HH-53s, to waiting US Navy aircraft carriers. The operation had evacuated over 51,000 people in total, this having taken 19,000 sorties in four weeks.

Retirement of the last Lockheed F-104 Starfighter from USAF Air National Guard Squadron service on 31 July illustrated the service's changing requirements for its front-line fighters were concerned. The type was the perfect example of an interceptor design of the 1950s, when such aircraft were developed simply with their missile-firing capabilities in mind. The Vietnam conflict had re-affirmed the need for dogfighting ability, a primary design feature of the F-15 Eagle and the YF-16. Elsewhere the F-104 continued to serve with many air arms including NATO countries, until replaced by F-16s in particular.

The production A-10A Thunderbolt II was flown for

the first time on 10 October, with the initial 'working-up' period commencing with the 355th Tactical Training Wing at Myrtle Beach, SC, the following March. This Fairchild Republic design had won the Air Force's A-X ground attack aircraft production contract in January 1973, after the YA-10A prototype had been involved in a comparative evaluation against the unsuccessful Northrop YA-9A. Experience gained during the Vietnam War, in which close support missions were undertaken by A-1 Skyraiders, Cessna T-37s and Martin B-57s amongst others, had shown the need for a dedicated aircraft for this task. It had to be highly-survivable, operationally flexible and effective in combat, qualities that were met by the A-10. It had the big GAU-8 Avenger rotating-barrel gun and provision for external stores, excellent agility and high levels of protection for the airframe, engines and pilot.

An electronic countermeasures (ECM) version of the General Dynamics F-111 was first proposed in 1970, to replace the veteran Douglas EB-66. At one stage consideration was given to converting the 24 F-111Cs that had been built for the Royal Australian Air Force, but not delivered. In January 1975, Grumman was appointed as prime contractor to convert two F-111As (66-0049 and 66-0041) as prototypes of the specialised electronic warfare EF-111A. This new version was to be capable of undertaking stand-off and penetration escort missions. Grumman was selected as it already had considerable expertise in the EW field, having produced the EA-6B Prowler for the Navy and Marine Corps.

The EF-111A was to have a 16ft long canoe-shaped radome to house the Raytheon AN/ALQ-99E tactical radar jamming system and a fin-top pod to accommodate the ECM receivers. It also embodied a greater degree of automation, so as to be effectively managed by just one electronics warfare officer (EWO). One set of wing pylons were to be retained to allow the EF-111 to carry AIM-9 Sidewinder missiles for self-defence. An aerodynamic prototype was flown for the first time on 15 December.

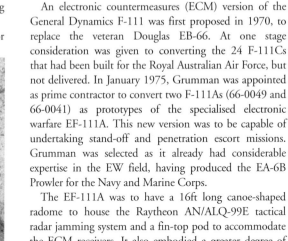

Northrop F-5E Tiger II – 57th FWW

The pages for 1975 generously supported by AIR & SPACE/Smithsonian Magazine

January: The first operationally-configured F-15A Eagle was delivered to the 57th Tactical Fighter Training Wing at Nellis AFB, NV.

1 January: Headquarters of the 8th Air Force was relocated to Barksdale AFB, LA from Andersen AFB, Guam.

13 January: The General Dynamics F-16 was chosen as the USAF's first air combat fighter. The Northrop F-17 was rejected following a competitive fly-off.

16 January-1 February: Operation *Streak Eagle* when an F-15A Eagle (72-119) operating from Grand Forks AFB, ND captured all eight world time-to-height records.

30 January: A contract was placed with Grumman Aerospace for the conversion of two F-111As as prototype electronic warfare (EW) aircraft.

4 April: A C-5A Galaxy (68-0218) crashed near Ton Son Nhut airfield in Saigon, with the loss of 206 lives (mainly Vietnamese orphans) on their way to Clark AB in the Philippines during Operation *Baby Lift*.

10 April: The first air-to-air refuelling of a Rockwell B-1A by a KC-135 Stratotanker was successfully tested.

30 April: Operation *Frequent Wind* ended in desperate efforts to evacuate US government personnel and South Vietnamese

granted asylum in the United States. A total of 7,014 US and South Vietnamese military, diplomatic and government officials were taken out in the final days before the North Vietnamese captured the city.

12 May: The SS *Mayaguez* was boarded and taken by Cambodians, sparking a raid by US forces that resulted in the rescue of civilian hostages. This was at the cost of two USAF crew members and 16 Marines killed, and three Air Force Sikorsky CH-53s destroyed.

20 June: Aircraft of the 601st Tactical Control Wing from Sembach AB, Germany, together with the Air Rescue and Recovery Service, evacuated US citizens from strife-torn Beirut.

30 June: The 1st Tactical Fighter Wing moved to Langley AFB, VA, from McDill AFB, FL, when the 56th TFW returned to the USA from Nakhon Phanom RTAFB, Thailand.

31 July: Retirement of the USAF's last Lockheed F-104 Starfighter from Air National Guard units after nearly 18 years of service.

August: The EC-130E Hercules of the 7th Airborne Command & Control Squadron were reassigned from Southeast Asia to Keesler AFB, MS.

28 August: First flight of the prototype four-turbofan

McDonnell Douglas YC-15 (72-1875), contender for the USAF advanced medium STOL transport programme (AMST). Boeing's YC-14 was the other AMST competitor in the search for a C-130 Hercules replacement, but neither it nor the YC-15 entered production.

September: The USAF's first Beech C-12A (73-1205) was delivered. Initially 30 were ordered to replace C-117Ds and C-131s providing support to US embassies around the world.

19 September: A USAF pilot flew the Rockwell B-1 bomber for the first time.

7 October: President Ford signed legislation allowing women to enter America's military academies. The first female cadets started training with the Air Force Academy the following June.

10 October: The first production Fairchild Republic A-10A Thunderbolt II (75-0258) was flown.

31 October: Maiden flight of the first definitive Boeing AWACS, the E-3A Sentry (73-1675).

November: The USAF and US Defense Advanced Research Projects Agency revealed a programme that had been running for some time that was aimed at the study in depth, and investigating the possibility of building, an aircraft with a very low radar-cross-section (RCS). This, it was hoped, would make them almost impossible to detect by radar and introduced 'stealth' technology through the *Have Blue* program.

29 November: The first *Red Flag* exercise was held at Nellis AFB, NV.

6 December: The F-4G *Wild Weasel* Phantom II (69-7254) was flown for the first time. Subsequently 116 were converted from F-4Es for the SEAD and SAM suppression roles.

23 December: Lockheed was given a contract for the strengthening of the C-5A Galaxy's wing-box assemblies.

McDonnell Douglas YC-15

The two-seat Convair F-106B, painted here by Andrew Whyte, is shown in the colours of the New Jersey Air National Guard, the last unit to fly the Delta Dart. The F-106 supersonic interceptor served with Air Defense Command from July 1959 until the last examples were withdrawn from the ANG in 1988. This painting is from the Air Force Art Collection.

F-106 New Jersey Air National Guard by Andrew C Whyte ASAA

On 9 August, the Boeing YC-14, second contender for the Air Force's advanced medium STOL transport (AMST) requirement, made its initial flight. Its competitor, the McDonnell Douglas YC-15, had got airborne for the first time in August 1975. The original request was for designs that could be developed into a C-130 Hercules replacement, making use of improvements in aerodynamics and powerplants. It had to be able to transport 27,000lb of cargo over 450 miles, from a take-off run of 2,000ft or less, and 38,000lb of cargo over 3,000 miles with unrestricted runway length. Both the YC-14 and YC-15 were extremely manoeuvrable, demonstrating this alongside each other at numerous international airshows. However, in spite of their use of the latest aerodynamic technology, particularly with

advanced wing, engine and flap configurations that delivered good short take-off and landing (STOL) performance, neither aircraft provided advances that were significant enough over the C-130's capabilities to merit the expenditure on progressing with the production of an entirely new type.

Development of the General Dynamics F-16 continued apace, with the first full-scale development (FSD) aircraft flying in December. Many changes and improvements had been made since the YF-16 first took to the air. The aircraft was now able to carry 11,000lb of weapon stores with a standard fuel load, compared to the 8,000lb originally intended when the aircraft was still seen as a lightweight fighter rather than the current multi-role air combat fighter. The first CCV (control-configured

vehicle) test aircraft commenced trials in March, using canards on the forward fuselage in conjunction with a computerised fly-by-wire system. This considerably increased the combat agility of the F-16, which would be the key to its future success.

On 20 April, RAF Mildenhall, Suffolk welcomed a second visit by a Lockheed SR-71A of the 9th SRW, Beale AFB, but for a rather longer period than the first. The 'Blackbird' stayed for ten days, being based alongside the same unit's co-located U-2R detachment. During its deployment, only two flights were made, but further SR-71s visited throughout the rest of the 1970s. A purpose-built hangar was constructed at the base in 1980, allowing longer periods of temporary duty (TDY). From Mildenhall, missions could be mounted along the borders of Eastern Europe, monitoring Warsaw Pact military movements. As the Cold War dragged on, the SR-71 was a valuable asset to NATO. Detachment 4 of the 9th SRW was enlarged to two SR-71s in 1982, and from then until 1990 was kept continually active. The type was in the news during 1976 for other reasons as well, when on 28 July, three aircraft broke the absolute world speed record, the 1,000km closed-circuit speed record and the sustained altitude record in level flight. None of them have been broken by any other 'conventional' air-breathing aircraft, as none has yet matched the SR-71's unique capabilities.

The first launch of the Boeing AGM-86A air-launched cruise missile (ALCM), from a B-52 Stratofortress, was also significant – this stand-off weapon, with a range of up to 750 miles, was intended to be procured for B-52s and the new Rockwell B-1A, for which funding was cut back by the Senate in August, deferring production.

Lockheed U-2R

There has always been something 'magical' about the Lockheed SR-71. The first Mach 3 aircraft to enter service with the Air Force, in 1966, its strategic reconnaissance value has been sought again some 30 years later. This painting of a Blackbird flown by the 9th SRW is reproduced here by kind permission of the artist, Wilf Hardy.

The pages for 1976 generously supported by Lockheed Martin Skunk Works

Black Magic by Wilfred Hardy GAvA

9 January: The F-15 Eagle entered service with the 1st Tactical Fighter Wing at Langley AFB, VA, with delivery of its first F-15A (74-0083). For more than a year, the TF-15 had been operated by the 555th Tactical Fighter Training Squadron at Luke AFB, AZ. Production was nine aircraft per month and the 1st TFW received its full complement by the end of the year.

1 March: The 4440th Tactical Fighter Training Group was assigned to Nellis AFB, NV, to co-ordinate *Red Flag* exercises.

5 March: The Boeing AGM-86A air-launched cruise missile (ALCM) made its first powered flight after being dropped from a B-52 Stratofortress carrier aircraft, at a height of 35,000ft over the White Sands Missile Range, NM.

16 March: First flight made by the General Dynamics YF-16 prototype (72-01567) that was re-engineered as a control-configured vehicle (CCV) testbed aircraft for fully-computerised fly-by-wire tests.

1 April: The 527th Tactical Fighter Training Aggressor Squadron was formed at RAF Alconbury, Huntingdon, operating the F-5E Tiger II.

20 April: The first period of temporary duty (TDY) at RAF Mildenhall was made by a Lockheed SR-71A of the 9th SRW. It heralded the start of 'Blackbird' operations from the base.

25 May: The first flight of a Boeing AWACS or E-3A Sentry

Cessna T-37A

North American T-39A Sabreliner

as the production versions were designated, with full mission avionics, was made at Seattle.

28 July: A Lockheed SR-71A, crewed by Major Adolphus Bledsoe Jr and Major John Fuller set a 1,000km closed-circuit speed record of 3,367.221km/h (2,092.29mph). Another SR-71A, flown by Captain Eldon Joersz and Major George Morgan Jr achieved 3,529.56km/h (2,193.17mph) – a new absolute world speed record – and a third, piloted by Captain Robert Helt and Major Larry Elliott achieved a sustained altitude record in level flight of 85,069ft (25,929.03m).

9 August: First flight of the twin-turbofan Boeing YC-14

(72-1873) contender for the AMST programme, was made. The YC-14's engines were positioned so as to blow their efflux over the inboard portion of the wing and trailing edge flaps in an upper surface blowing (USB) concept.

10 August: The US Senate voted a FY 1977 Defense Appropriations Bill which restricted expenditure on the Rockwell B-1 bomber until the following February – thus effectively deferring a full production decision until after the next US president would have assumed office.

9 September: The first flight of a fully guided air-launched Boeing AGM-86A ALCM took place over White Sands Missile Range, NM when the missile demonstrated guidance capabilities based on preset co-ordinates.

1 October: The 14th Air Force was deactivated at Colorado Springs.

November: The last General Dynamics F-111 (74-00188, an F-111F) was completed.

8 December: The inaugural flight of the first full-scale development (FSD) General Dynamics F-16 was made at Fort Worth. This version incorporated numerous changes and modifications to the original YF-16.

December: C-141 StarLifters of MAC delivered relief supplies (mainly tents and heaters) to Incirlik AB after more than 3,600 people died in an earthquake, on 24 November, in eastern Turkey. From Incirlik, MAC C-130 Hercules flew 40 missions to move supplies to Van Airport, often in difficult conditions.

Boeing YC-14

Echoes of the B-70 Valkyrie Bomber programme were perhaps to be heard during the year, when President Jimmy Carter cancelled the Rockwell B-1A programme. Instead of pursuing the advanced manned penetrating bomber route, the new President had decided to keep the B-52 Stratofortress fleet and their stand-off missiles, and to expand development of cruise missiles. The three B-1 prototypes already flying were to continue their research and development programme and completion of a fourth was to go ahead. This aircraft, which flew on 14 February 1979, was the first B-1 to be equipped with a complete suite of offensive and defensive avionics and weapons systems. Continuing the research programme was intended to provide an alternative to cruise missiles, should problems with their development have occurred, and to test new systems for possible use on a future B-52 upgrade programme which was being mooted. However, time would prove that the decision to cancel the B-1A was somewhat premature and ill-advised.

The Air Force gained an advanced airborne early warning capability in March, when the first Boeing E-3A Sentry was delivered to the 552nd Airborne Warning and Control Wing (AW & CW) at Tinker AFB, OK. Boeing's design submission had been selected as the USAF's Airborne Warning and Control System (AWACS) platform on 9 July 1970, and the company had converted a pair of 707-320B airliners to EC-137B standard in order to conduct comparative trials of Hughes and Westinghouse radar systems. The latter's AN/APY-1 installation was selected, mounted in a rotodome of some 30ft diameter on top of the fuselage. The first of the batch of 22 aircraft was delivered to the 552nd AW&CW, which assumed a role of continental US air defence two years later when personnel attached to NORAD, North American Air Defence started to join Tactical Air Command (TAC) crews on Sentry missions. The E-3's first 'operational' use, Exercise *Team Spirit* in Korea in 1979, illustrated the ability of the AWACS to monitor hostile aircraft, in this

Boeing E-3A Sentry AWACS

case those of North Korea. Through future deployments, the USAF's E-3 Sentries quickly proved to be a valuable tactical asset.

In Europe, the arrival of USAFE's first F-15A Eagles that equipped the 36th Tactical Fighter Wing at Bitburg AB, Germany in April was a very significant event. The type's impressive performance as an air superiority fighter made it the most potent NATO combat aircraft asset in Europe at the time, and the only aircraft with a greater capability than the Soviet MiG-25 *Foxbat*, which was then in service in large numbers in the Warsaw Pact states. Soon, the Bitburg-based wing comprised three squadrons of F-15s and became fully operational by the end of the year. This was the start of many years of Eagle operations in Europe, that were to provide USAFE and NATO with a formidable air combat capability.

A ceremony held at Myrtle Beach AFB, SC on 10 June marked the entry into USAF frontline service of the Fairchild A-10, the Air Force's first purpose-built close-support aircraft. Started originally as a counter-insurgency aircraft it was quickly developed into a 'tank-buster'. The

first operational wing was to be the 354th at Myrtle with the 355th at Davis-Monthan AFB already operating the A-10 in the training role. By far the most important deployment would be those to Europe where it would become the primary close support aircraft and available to blunt the Eastern Bloc tanks on any advance they would attempt across the plains of Europe.

Formation of F-5E, F-104G, F-4G and F-15A

The pages for 1977 generously supported by Paul Bowen and Tim Prince

1 January: The 479th Tactical Training Wing was formed at Holloman AFB, NM with three additional squadrons of T-38 Talons. These were fitted with gunsights and practice bomb dispensers, and were known as AT-38Bs.

11 February: President Jimmy Carter made his only flight in a Boeing E-4A NEACP aircraft, when he flew from Andrews AFB, MD to Robins AFB, GA. This was the first occasion on which a US president had flown in an aircraft of this type.

19 February: President Carter announced that development work would cease on an advanced tanker aircraft (ATCA), that SAC had been developing as a conceptual deployment-support aircraft.

March: Initial deliveries began of the A-10A Thunderbolt II to the 354th Tactical Fighter Squadron at Myrtle Beach AFB, SC. The A-10A was noted for its devastating firepower, which comprised the hardest-hitting aircraft gun in history and up to ten anti-armour missiles. It was also designed to withstand hostile gunfire.

10 March: First flight of the EF-111A Raven, after full modification as an electronic warfare aircraft. The conversions introduced a large fin-tip fairing to house the receiver and antennas of the AN/ALQ-99E tactical jamming system, the transmitters for which were installed in a long canoe-shaped radome under the fuselage.

24 March: The first E-3A Sentry was delivered to the 552nd Airborne Warning and Control Wing (later Division) at Tinker AFB, OK. The 552nd was to be the sole user of the Sentry, including the 963rd and 964th AWACS Squadrons at Tinker and the 960th and 961st AWACS Support Squadrons based respectively at NAS Keflavik, Iceland and Kadena AB, Okinawa, Japan.

24 March: In 1975, the USAF contracted with Lockheed to modify one C-141A StarLifter to have a 23ft 4in lengthening of the fuselage, air-to-air refuelling capability and a new wing root fairing. This aircraft (66-0186) flew as the YC-141B on this date

and, after successful testing, the USAF decided to modify the entire StarLifter force of 270 aircraft to this standard.

14 April: US defensive radar chiefs were embarrassed by a Soviet Tupolev Tu-95 *Bear* which appeared south of Charleston, SC, then dived beneath the radar and turned up again 60 miles from Jacksonville, FL.

27 April: The first deployment of the F-15A Eagle to Europe, at Bitburg AB, Germany. By the end of 1977, the 36th Tactical Fighter Wing was fully operational on the air superiority fighter at the base.

May: The de Havilland Canada DHC-6 Twin Otter was selected by the USAF Academy for cadet parachute training. Two aircraft were acquired 'off-the-shelf', being designated as UV-18Bs and stationed at Peterson AFB, CO – a few miles from the Academy.

30 June: President Carter cancelled the Rockwell B-1A bomber programme in favour of cruise missiles for strategic attack. The research and development on the three flying prototypes was authorised to continue, plus completion of a fourth prototype.

10 July: The phased array radar to monitor Soviet space activities known as *Cobra Dane*, became operational.

2 September: The first ten female Air Force pilots were awarded their 'wings'.

10 October: Two Soviet Tupolev Tu-95 *Bears* dropped metal foil over the destroyer USS *Spruance* in the Western Atlantic in an attempt to confuse US radar.

20 November: The USAF authorised McDonnell Douglas to commence production of the KC-10A Extender, a military tanker/transport developed from the company's DC-10 wide-body airliner. Twenty aircraft were ordered on 19 December after the Air Force had successfully obtained a reversal of President Carter's earlier decision on the advanced tanker/cargo aircraft (ATCA) and ordered 20 McDonnell Douglas KC-10As.

Over 1,000 examples of the Northrop T-38A Talon, the USAF's first supersonic trainer, have been flown by Air Force pilot training schools since the first aircraft was delivered to Randolph AFB in March 1961. Harold McCormick's painting, from the Air Force Art Collection, shows a Talon on a training sortie.

Beech C-12A Huron

Talon by Harold McCormick

When the new Carter administration put forward its first Defense Department budget in January it contained another significant programme cancellation, despite being the highest defence spending round yet presented to Congress. Funding was provided for the Air Force's new Lockheed TR-1 battlefield reconnaissance aircraft and the big McDonnell Douglas KC-10A tanker. However, the Advanced Medium STOL Transport (AMST) Program was scrapped, leaving the Boeing YC-14 and McDonnell Douglas YC-15 prototypes 'out in the cold'. This confirmed many more years of production for the C-130 Hercules as the Air Force's primary tactical and special mission airlifter. The withdrawal of government funding resulted in the YC-14 and YC-15 prototypes, after successful flight test trials, being returned to their respective manufacturers and subsequently placed in storage at Davis-Monthan AFB, AZ.

There were signs of a possible 'resurrection' for the AMSTs in June, when the Air Force issued requests for proposals for a wide-bodied cruise missile carrier (CMC), projected as being capable of operating as a stand-off launch platform for cruise missiles. This was intended to augment the B-52 Stratofortress penetrating bomber force, and among the designs put forward were YC-14 and YC-15 conversions, but the CMC was eventually deemed unnecessary. McDonnell Douglas had hoped to sell a variant of the YC-15 to civilian customers, who, it was felt, would be interested in its short take-off and landing capabilities. Nothing came of this, but the company used some of the expertise obtained through the YC-15 programme in developing its C-17 Globemaster III – an aircraft that bears more than a passing resemblance to its 1970s AMST predecessor.

While MAC had now lost its future advanced STOL tactical transport, its existing strategic transport equipment again proved its capabilities during two airlift operations in 1978. The first of these was in May, when Zaire was invaded from Angola by rebel troops. A call for assistance

Boeing B-52G Stratofortress and Convair F-106A Delta Darts

from President Mobutu was met by attacks on enemy positions by the Zairean Air Force, and the French and Belgians each supplied paratroops. These contingents were supported by the USAF, with 18 C-141A StarLifters (from the 437th and 438th MAWs) and C-5A Galaxies (of the 436th MAW) transporting French and Belgian equipment to the theatre and moving fuel and supplies from the capital Kinshasa to the south of the country. After the rebels had been defeated, MAC's C-141A fleet was again utilised, flying in 5,000 troops from African nations to support the Congolese Army in maintaining peace in Zaire, after the French had departed. In December, the collapse of the Shah's government in Iran and the subsequent revolution saw C-5As and C-141As in action again, evacuating 900 American military dependants from Teheran.

By the latter half of the year USAF plans for the Lockheed TR-1A, became clearer. Initial funding provided for the production line to be re-opened to produce 25

TR1s, a new and updated version of the U-2R, which itself was an enlarged U-2. Included in the build were two, twin-seat dual control trainers. The TR-1As were powered by J57-P-13 engines removed from scrapped Republic F-105s and that had their after-burners deleted during refurbishment. The mission equipment included a Hughes Advanced Synthetic Aperture radar incorporating a sideways looking facility. This allowed an aircraft flying over NATO territory to 'look' 35 to 40 miles into Eastern Europe. The new equipment was installed in a lengthened nose bay and into flush fitting wing pods. The original jigs were removed from store and the first aircraft was planned for entry into service by 1982.

The C-9A Nightingale is used for aeromedical evacuation duties. Ronald Wong's painting illustrates a C-9A of the 375th Aeromedical Airlift Wing on a mission over the United States. It is reproduced by kind permission of the artist.

The pages for 1978 generously supported by Royal Air Force News

Aeromedic Airlift by Ronald Wong BSc(Hons), GAvA, GMA, ASAA

1978

23 January: Following the announcement that funding was being withdrawn from the Advanced Medium STOL Transport Program, trials and development flying with the Boeing YC-14 and McDonnell Douglas YC-15 were stopped. However, provision for an improved Lockheed U-2R (designated TR-1A) and the McDonnell Douglas KC-10A was approved in the Defense Department budget.

February: Approval was granted for production of the *Pave Tack* airborne weapons system.

22 February: The prototype of the NAVSTAR Ground Positioning System (GPS) was placed in orbit.

March: Lockheed was granted a $24m programme to produce two new wing sets for the USAF C-5A Galaxy. One was for fatigue testing and the other for flight testing in 1980. The re-wing programme, if successful, would give a 30,000hr extension to the service life of the C-5As.

March: The USAF launched a test programme to select six enlisted women as KC-135 Stratotanker refuelling boom operators and ten others as C-141 StarLifter flight engineers. Another 40 USAF women officers and enlisted women began training as members of crews operating Titan II ICBMs.

1 March: The 6510th Test Wing was formed at Edwards AFB, CA as the flying component of the Air Force Flight Test Centre (AFFTC).

23 March: Captain Sandra M Scott became the first woman pilot to perform alert duty in SAC, whilst assigned to the 904th Air Refueling Squadron, Mather AFB, CA.

19-27 May: The Air Force airlifted French, Belgian and West African troops into the Shaba province of Zaire in response to an invasion from Angola, and supported the evacuation of Americans and Europeans from the country. During the operation, over 200 missions were flown by C-130 Hercules, C-141 StarLifters and C-5 Galaxies.

20 May: McDonnell Douglas delivered its 5,000th F-4 Phantom (an F-4E for the Turkish Air Force), 20 years after the first flight of the prototype.

Vought A-7D Corsairs

June: The USAF issued requests for proposals on a wide-body, cruise-missile carrier (CMC) which could be used as a stand-off launch platform for large numbers of pilotless cruise missiles. These were intended to supplement the B-52 Stratofortress manned penetrating bomber force, as funding had been added for Tomahawk and air-launched cruise missile developments.

1 July: The 7th Air Division was activated in Germany to provide command and control of SAC forces operating in Europe.

27 July: First overseas deployment of the A-10A Thunderbolt II was made when the first three aircraft for the 81st Tactical Fighter Wing arrived at the 'twin bases' of RAF Woodbridge and RAF Bentwaters.

September: For the first time, B-52 Stratofortresses began to practise conventional weapons delivery missions (as distinct from nuclear weapons) in support of NATO, during Exercise *Cold Fire 78*.

October: The 37th Tactical Fighter Wing reached initial operational capability with the F-4G Phantom at George AFB, CA. It subsequently entered service at Spangdahlem AB, Germany and Clark AB, Philippines.

9 December: Some 900 Americans were evacuated from Teheran by C-5 Galaxies and C-141 StarLifters after the collapse of the Shah's government.

Lockheed C-5A Galaxy

Strategic Air Command undertook its largest-ever exercise during the year. *Global Shield 79* tested the Command's Single Integrated Operational Plan (SIOP) to the maximum without actually launching missiles or dropping nuclear weapons. The exercise illustrated the equipment and operational changes that had taken place within SAC over the years. The 343 B-52 Stratofortresses and 65 General Dynamics FB-111As that made up its inventory looked set to remain in service for several years to come following cancellation of the B-1. While its ICBM strength outnumbered the manned bomber force with 1,228 Atlas and Minuteman missiles deployed, for the exercise its B-52s and FB-111s, supported by KC-135 Stratotankers, were dispersed away from their home bases and placed on full alert status. From these designated forward operating locations, the aircraft executed practice 'strikes' on radar bomb-scoring targets at various locations across the USA. This successful exercise was the first to

test SAC's 'battle plan' to its limits, and as such proved a valuable operation. The following few years would see further, expanded exercises along these lines taking place. There would also be several significant changes within SAC's assets to further heighten its capabilities.

Military Airlift Command (MAC) received the first of 270 'stretched' C-141B StarLifters later in the year, the prototype having flown in March 1977. In order to utilise the original C-141A's full potential, Lockheed added fuselage 'plugs' 23ft 4in long, fore and aft of the wing, giving a total aircraft length of 168ft 4in and a 35% increase in load-carrying capacity. The addition of an air-to-air refuelling receptacle above the cockpit was to further enhance the StarLifter's strategic capability. In effect, the 'stretch' programme provided MAC with the equivalent of some 90 additional aircraft, and for a much cheaper outlay. All but four test aircraft (known as NC-141As, and based with the 4950th Test Wing at Wright-Patterson

AFB) were converted to C-141B standard by June 1982.

The first production General Dynamics F-16A was delivered to an operational Air Force unit, the 388th TFW's 16th Tactical Fighter Training Squadron at Hill AFB, UT. This marked a significant milestone as the advances provided by the F-16 when compared with its predecessor, the F-4 Phantom, were considerable, given that the new aircraft was far lighter and cheaper to operate. The new type's abilities as an air-combat fighter were unrivalled thanks to its advanced fly-by-wire control system and radar. The expanded range of stores that production examples could carry combined with its 'dogfighting' capabilities made it an immediate favourite with pilots, in spite of some initial teething troubles including problems with the then-new F100-PW-100 powerplant. A second unit, the 56th TFW (the initial Replacement Training Unit for the F-16, based at MacDill AFB, FL) was formed in October.

In March Grumman was awarded a contract to produce the EF-111A, or as it was to become known, the *Spark Vark*. Two prototypes had been converted from standard F-111As in 1977 – the first was initially an aerodynamic test aircraft while the second was more representative of the production aircraft. At the heart of the EF-111A was its ALQ-99E, a tactical jamming system. This was a complex electronic system able to deal with more threats than any other system then current. Hostile radars were detected by receivers located in the new fin fairing and countered by jamming signals from up to ten transmitters located in a canoe shape ventral fairing. With extensive use of computerisation it was possible to programme the system to deal with expected threats, leaving the operator free to deal with the unexpected. The EF-111A could be operated as a 'stand-off' jammer, enabling it to remain over friendly territory clear of SAM threats and saturate the enemy's electronic capabilities. The performance of the aircraft also allowed it to accompany strike packages deep into enemy territory.

Fairchild A-10A Thunderbolt II

The pages for 1979 generously supported by Chevron Aerospace Limited

1979

1 January: E-3A Sentries assumed an air defence role, after NORAD personnel began augmenting TAC crews on missions flown from Tinker AFB, OK.

6 January: The first production General Dynamics F-16A to enter service with the USAF was allocated to the 16th Tactical Training Squadron, 388th Tactical Fighter Wing at Hill AFB, UT.

29 January: The Northrop RF-5A 'Tigereye' reconnaissance aircraft prototype made its initial flight.

27 February: The first flight of the improved F-15C Eagle took place at St Louis, MO. Entering full-scale production in June, the F-15C supplanted the F-15A from the mid-1980s, with the two-seat F-15D replacing the F-15B at the same time.

10 March: Two Boeing E-3A Sentry AWACS aircraft were deployed to Riyadh, Saudi Arabia to monitor hostilities between North and South Yemen.

May: The first Forward Operating Base (FOB) at Sembach, Germany was activated for the A-10 Fairchild Thunderbolt II close support aircraft from the 81st TFW, based at RAF Bentwaters, UK.

8-16 July: Operation *Global Shield 79*, the first complete exercise of Single Integrated Operational Plan (SIOP). This was one of the most comprehensive SAC exercises, involving hundreds of bombers, tankers and missiles generated to alert. The aircraft were dispersed to pre-selected bases, from which they flew sorties over radar bomb-scoring sites.

Boeing KC-135 Stratotanker

Lockheed C-140B JetStar

17 July: Start of a fly-off between the General Dynamics AGM-109 Tomahawk cruise missile and the Boeing AGM-86B air-launched cruise missile for SAC.

24 July: A Boeing KC-135A Stratotanker made its first flight with winglets installed at the wingtips. Developed as a joint USAF/NASA project it was intended to evaluate the potential fuel savings of drag-reducing winglets.

27 July: The first air-dropped free flight of the Rockwell Highly manoeuvrable aircraft technology (HiMAT) unmanned research aircraft was made from a B-52 carrier aircraft at 45,000ft over the Edwards AFB, CA test range.

July: The huge *Pave Paws* Phase Arrayed Radar System, able to detect surface-launched ballistic missiles, became operational at Beale AFB, CA.

1 October: Start of the de-activation of Air Defense Command, its responsibilities being transferred to SAC and TAC, with NORAD retaining operational control of its resources.

5 November: First flight of a 'production' C-141B StarLifter was made at Marietta, GA.

November: The Lockheed U-2R production line was re-opened to produce 37 new TR-1A tactical reconnaissance aircraft.

4 December: Military Airlift Command accepted its first C-141B StarLifter. Service use continued with the 14 squadrons in six wings originally equipped with C-141As.

12 December: NATO agreed to the deployment of cruise and Pershing II missiles to Europe.

In describing this action scene, Michael Turner says he has "tried to capture the transition between the enormous power of the F-15 and its seemingly effortless movement through the sky. A pair of high-flying Eagles, on an air exercise, spot their unsuspecting 'prey', their pilots punching in reheat for maximum power as they wing-over to dive down for the kill far below". Eagles Prey is reproduced by kind permission of the artist.

Eagles Prey by Michael Turner PGAvA

In April a mission was attempted to rescue the occupants of the US Embassy in Teheran who had been taken hostage in November 1979 by a group of militant Islamic students. This terrorist action was in retaliation to the US giving tacit support to the former Iranian regime, by allowing exile for the Shah. Of the 66 taken hostage, 13 were released later in November and they were able to provide good intelligence information which was to prove vital in planning a rescue attempt. Planning for such a mission began to take shape after 11 April when it was decided that negotiation would get nowhere. From this planning came Operation *Eagle Claw* and was to involve aircraft and helicopters of the USAF, Navy and Marine Corps.

An elite US Army unit, the 20th Delta Force, was assigned to undertake the recovery mission and was transported from Pope AFB to Frankfurt on 20 April, and then on to the Middle East. On the day of the operation, MC-130E Hercules of the 8th Special Operation Squadron airlifted these troops to the Desert One airstrip south-east of Teheran, from where they were to have been flown to Teheran by Sikorsky RH-53Ds of the US Navy. A flight of eight helicopters was allocated to take the rescuers into the Iranian capital and then return the hostages to the Desert Two airstrip closer to the city.

The eight RH-53Ds left the carrier USS *Nimitz* for the mission but one quickly became unserviceable and returned to the ship, whilst the remaining seven reached Desert One airstrip. On arrival, one was unfit to fly any further, leaving the declared absolute minimum of six for the mission to go ahead and when another RH-53D was found to be unserviceable the operation had to be called off completely. At this point the situation deteriorated rapidly as an RH-53D that was moving position to refuel, collided with a USAF EC-130H of the 7th Airborne Command and Control Squadron. The refuelling was being done from fuel bladders/blisters carried by the EC-130Hs. The collision and subsequent fire set off

Lockheed C-141B Starlifter

ammunition aboard the RH-53 resulting in eight deaths and damage to all of the helicopters. All seven RH-53Ds were abandoned and the surviving crews were evacuated by the remaining C-130s. The wounded were later flown to Germany for medical treatment using a C-9A Nightingale that had been allocated to the operation to evacuate the hostages.

Also assigned to Operation *Eagle Claw* were AC-130E Hercules gunships of the 1st Special Operations Squadron (SOS), to provide patrols around the US Embassy and Mehrabad air base, the home of the Iranian Air Force's F-4Es. These Hercules gunships were also tasked to deal with any ground fire and then destroy the embassy building. With the loss of eight lives, seven helicopters and one Hercules the operation was a costly failure.

The advent of new technology again played a major part in the USAF's year. The service completed its competitive evaluation of the General Dynamics

AGM-109 Tomahawk and the Boeing AGM-86B ALCMs in February, albeit two months behind schedule and following numerous failures by both missiles. Getting the ALCM into service (to equip the B-52 Stratofortress fleet) was a major priority after President Carter's cancellation of the Rockwell B-1A in favour of improved ALCM technology. In the end, in spite of two failures to achieve the required test objectives in its initial two flights, Boeing's AGM-86B contender was selected. Procuring the ALCM would cost $4 billion, the AGM-86B being seen as possessing better guidance and terrain-following capabilities, and the most cost-effective solution.

Entering service in December 1956, the Lockheed C-130 Hercules quickly became the universal workhorse for the Air Force. The C-130E version shown in Andrew Whyte's painting, making a low-altitude precision extraction of heavy cargo, was ordered and first flown in 1961. The painting is from the Air Force Art Collection.

The pages for 1980 generously supported by the Marshall Group of Companies

On-Spot Delivery by Andrew Whyte ASAA

McDonnell Douglas C-9A Nightingale

15 February: The USAF issued a draft request for proposals on a cargo aircraft requirement – known as CX – which called for a new military transport, with extreme STOL capability aircraft capable of lifting large and oversize loads.

14 March: Two B-52H Stratofortresses of the 410th Bombardment Wing completed the third non-stop global flight conducted by SAC (previous flights were in 1949 and 1957). The 22,256 mile trip was accomplished in 42hr 30min and involved five air-to-air refuellings.

25 March: The Boeing AGM-86B ALCM was selected to equip SAC's B-52 Stratofortresses in a stand-off role. This was to provide greater penetration capabilities in an operational role and extend the mission life of the aircraft by removing it from the worst air defence threats.

March: A top-secret group of Northrop engineers completed design work on the configuration of an Advanced Technology Bomber. With data obtained by the USAF *Have Blue* stealth programme, the design chosen was a flying-wing shape that was eventually built as the B-2A.

March: The Rapid Deployment Joint Task Force (RDJTF) was created to respond worldwide with conventional forces in crisis situations.

24-25 April: Operation *Eagle Claw* – the abortive attempt to rescue 66 American hostages held in Teheran, Iran since 4 November 1979, resulted in the loss of an EC-130H in a collision with a US Navy RH-53D. The subsequent explosion and fire claimed eight lives and a total of seven RH-53D helicopters.

28 May: The first women graduated from the USAF Academy.

29 June: Completion of *Global Shield 80*, an exercise by SAC that had first been held in the previous year. The operation had involved 437 aircraft from 44 bases, flying 1,035 sorties for a total of 5,506 flying hours. The exercise was sprung without prior warning to test reaction time to an emergency alert.

5 July: The USAF carried out an airlift to support Thailand with arms and ammunition, after Vietnam invaded on 24 June.

8 July: McDonnell Douglas first flew a modified FSD F-15B (71-291) to demonstrate the ground attack capabilities of the Eagle. This dual role 'Strike Eagle' had a re-designed front cockpit and the rear cockpit equipped for use by a Weapons Systems Officer.

12 July: The McDonnell Douglas KC-10A Extender cargo/tanker aircraft (79-0433) was flown for the first time. Procurement of the big tankers began in FY1978 with an order for two. Subsequent contracts brought the total purchased to 60.

21 July: In a special ceremony at Hill AFB, UT, the USAF formally assigned the name 'Fighting Falcon' to the General Dynamics F-16 fighter aircraft.

22 August: The US stealth fighter and bomber projects being worked on by Lockheed (F-117) and Northrop (B2) were made public.

24 August: The prototype F-15B Strike Eagle made the first unrefuelled trans-Atlantic flight by a jet fighter, landing at RAF Mildenhall, Suffolk. It later appeared at the Farnborough International Airshow.

16 September: A USAF Boeing RC-135 electronic surveillance aircraft from Hellenikon airbase, near Athens, was forced to take evasive action to avoid an attack by Libyan MiG-23 fighters during an electronic intelligence (ELINT) flight along the Libyan coast.

22-25 September: Exercise *Busy Prairie* was held to test the ability of the Strategic Projection Force to penetrate 'enemy' air defences. During the exercise 14 B-52H Stratofortresses of the 5th Bombardment Wing deployed from Grand Forks AFB, ND to Whiteman AFB, MO to conduct operations over the *Red Flag* training area in central Nevada.

29 October: Maiden flight made by the first two-seat A-7K Corsair II (73-1008), of which 31 were converted from standard single-seat A-7Ds.

McDonnell Douglas F-4G 'Wild Weasel' Phantom

In 1981 the latest version of the long-running U-2 family, the Lockheed TR-1A, took to the air for the first time and entered service with the USAF. It had come as a major surprise in early 1978, when the Defense Department's budget for Fiscal Year 1979 included funding for the 'new' aircraft. It was clear that production of the manned TR-1A would mark the end of development of Boeing's *Compass Cope* remotely-piloted vehicle (RPV) for battlefield reconnaissance, that the company was hoping to sell to the USAF.

The Lockheed production line had been re-opened in 1979 to produce the improved aircraft, which included many advances over its immediate predecessor, the U-2R. Among these were the 'superpods', modular sensor-carrying containers up to 24ft in length, mounted under each wing to house different forms of antennae for many tasks, alongside the photo-recce and signals intelligence (SIGINT) equipment that could still be carried in the TR-1A's Q-bay, behind the cockpit. Its extended nose-cone carried the ASARS-2 sideways-looking surveillance radar, used to provide information on the disposition of forces and combined with the aircraft's SIGINT fitment made up the Tactical Reconnaissance System package. TR-1As also introduced the Precision Location and Strike System (PLSS), enabling the exact location of enemy radars to be detected. The 9th Strategic Reconnaissance Wing at Beale AFB, CA, was the first unit to receive the TR-1A in September, followed by USAFE's 95th RS at RAF Alconbury, which was formed on 1 October and received its first aircraft in February 1983. A pair of two-seat TR-1B variants for conversion training purposes would also enter service in 1983, these being the fourth and fifth production TR-1s.

Another design from the same company, and one which would perhaps become almost as famous as the U-2/TR-1 family, made its initial flight in 1981 as well – the first Lockheed F-117 'stealth fighter' as it was popularly called. The Defense Advanced Research Projects Agency (DARPA)

McDonnell Douglas F-15C Eagle

had been studying 'stealth' technology since the 1970s, leading to the *Have Blue* programme that developed a flying prototype to test the low-observables technology. Two such proof-of-concept aircraft were produced by Lockheed Advanced Development Projects' famous 'Skunk Works' at Burbank, CA. Responsibility for the project had been passed to the Air Force in 1977, who took the decision the following year to commence full-scale development of the initial F-117 prototypes, using components from existing aircraft types to save on costs and ensure fewer teething problems during development. It incorporated F-16 flight control computers, for example.

The F-117 only took 31 months after the 1978 development decision for the first prototype to make its first flight, from which point until the type's official unveiling almost eight years later, virtually all sorties were conducted at night, initially from the top-secret test airfield at Groom Lake, NV, and when in service at the

equally remote Tonopah Test Range Airfield, NV.

There was the promise of new equipment for SAC as well, as President Ronald Reagan announced the resumption of development of the Rockwell B-1, as an interim measure, prior to Northrop's B-2 being fully developed. It was envisaged that 100 B-1Bs would be produced, with the first units reaching initial operating capability by 1987. The aircraft would have a wider range of roles in service than had originally been planned for the B-1A. The new bomber's nuclear role would be augmented by conventional and secondary maritime attack capabilities.

MAC was also to receive new equipment in the years to come, as McDonnell Douglas and its C-17 design was named as the winner of the USAF's C-X contract, to build a transport aircraft that combined the outsize airlifting capabilities of the C-5 Galaxy with the tactical qualities of the C-130 Hercules.

The pages for 1981 generously supported by the McDonnell Douglas Corporation

11 January: Delivery of the first two Boeing AGM-86B ALCMs made to the 416th Bombardment Wing, Griffiss AFB, NY.

26 January-16 February: Exercise *Global Shield 81*, the third annual SAC Emergency War Order practice. More than 120 SAC bombers were dispersed (some to overseas bases) in rehearsal for an emergency alert that involved 30 tankers. Some 100,000 SAC personnel were involved.

17 March: Delivery of the first operational KC-10A Extender (79-0434) to Barksdale AFB, LA. The first six were assigned to the 32nd Air Refueling Squadron, 2nd Bomb Wing, in November.

19 March: The first of 18 Boeing E-3A Sentry AWACS aircraft for NATO duty was delivered to the Dornier factory at Oberpfaffenhofen in Germany for mission avionics to be installed.

30 April: Research and development flights by the four Rockwell B-1A prototypes were terminated. The four aircraft had flown a total of 1,895 hours since the first B-1 made its initial flight on 23 December 1974.

18 June: First flight made by the multi-faceted Lockheed F-117 from a special facility in the Nevada desert. Originally developed under the code name *Have Blue*, Lockheed was given the contract for the production of a derivative aircraft described as CSIRS (covert, survivable, in-weather reconnaissance/strike), subsequently identified as the F-117A.

1 August: The first flight of the Lockheed TR-1A, the derivative of the U-2R, that had been designed to carry the Precision Location Strike System (PLSS) – an advanced sensing system to locate and identify hostile radar sites and to direct strike aircraft, or ground-based missiles, against them.

15 August: The first B-52G Stratofortress configured for air-launched cruise missiles, was delivered to SAC's 416th Bombardment Wing at Griffiss AFB, NY.

29 August: It was announced that the USAF had selected McDonnell Douglas as prime contractor to develop the C-17 long-range cargo aircraft as the winner of its C-X competition.

15 September: The first flight test was made by a B-52G Stratofortress carrying 12 AGM-86B ALCMs on underwing

Northrop T-38A Talons – Euro-NATO Jet Pilot Training

pylons. The entire SAC force of 172 B-52G aircraft was progressively modified to carry the weapon – each aircraft carrying six missiles under each wing on jettisonable pylons and eight on a rotary launcher in the bomb bay.

15 September: The 494th Tactical Fighter Squadron, equipped with the F-111F at RAF Lakenheath, became the first USAF squadron to be operational with the *Pave Tack* weapons delivery system (comprising a pod housing a laser transmitter/receiver and a precision optical sight).

15 September: The first Lockheed TR-1A (80-1066) was delivered to the 9th Strategic Reconnaissance Wing at Beale AFB, CA.

1 October: The 95th Reconnaissance Squadron of the 17th Reconnaissance Wing was activated at RAF Alconbury to operate Lockheed TR-1As that would be deployed to England in 1983.

1 October: The Euro-NATO Joint Jet Pilot Training Program (ENJEPT) was inaugurated at Sheppard AFB, TX.

2 October: President Reagan announced the resumption of

the Rockwell B-1 programme, as an interim strategic bomber pending development of the B-2 'stealth' bomber.

November: With the popular name of Raven, General Dynamics EF-111As began to enter service and were issued to the 388th Electronic Combat Squadron (becoming the 390th ECS on 1 April 1984) at Mountain Home AFB, ID.

23 November: Under Exercise *Bright Star*, eight B-52Hs of the 319th Bombardment Wing from Grand Forks AFB, ND and from the 5th Bomb Wing, Minot AFB, ND, flew the longest non-stop simulated bombing mission in the history of SAC. A 15,000-mile sortie, to carry out a simulated strike on a runway in Egypt, was accomplished in 31 hours, and involved three in-flight refuelling operations.

The last version of the Phantom to enter Air Force service, the F-4G was a modified F-4E airframe equipped with the AN/APR-38 radar and missile detection and launch homing system for Wild Weasel anti-radar tasks. Mark Waki's painting from the Air Force Art Collection shows a 37th TFW F-4G on a training exercise.

McDonnell Douglas F-4G *Wild Weasel* Phantom by Mark Waki

One of the USAF's longest serving workhorses, the KC-135 Stratotanker, started a new lease of life during 1982 when the programme for the conversion of many of the active-duty fleet to KC-135R standard started. The programme, that had been announced in 1980, involved replacing the original J-57 turbojets by four CFM International CFM-56 (military designated F108-CF-100) turbofans, each delivering some 22,000lb of thrust. They offered major advantages over the KC-135A's Pratt & Whitney J57s, being far quieter, cleaner and much more fuel-efficient, as well as allowing a much shorter take-off run. The new KC-125R models would have a bigger fuel capacity than their predecessors, at a total of 203,289lb, and have a greater range. The re-engined aircraft were scheduled to enter service with the 384th Air Refueling Wing at McConnell AFB, KS in July 1984.

SAC conducted its *Global Shield 82* exercise over eight days in July. This was another in its series of practice operations designed to bring about increases in the Command's already impressive operational capabilities. The exercise was expanded this time, involving aircraft of the Canadian Armed Forces Tactical Air Group which were set against SAC's bombers and tankers. This particular operation's enlarged scope saw a furthering of defensive tactics, which would allow any potential hostile attacks to be repulsed more effectively. Another important event for SAC during 1982 was its first mission flown by an all-female crew. They came from the 924th ARS at Castle AFB, CA operating the KC-135. This five-hour training mission was commanded by Captain Kelly Hamilton who was the Air Force's only female aircraft commander at the time. The co-pilot for the flight was First Lieutenant Linda Martin. It had been made possible by a ruling allowing women to enter the USAF Academy, the first officers having graduated in May 1980.

There was something of a setback for MAC's new jet transport programme in January, when the Defense Department cancelled the McDonnell Douglas C-17, that

Boeing KC-135R Stratotanker

had been ordered the previous year, in favour of the purchase of 50 new Lockheed C-5N Galaxy variants. However, a great deal of lobbying by the Air Force, that was in favour of continuing development of the C-17, was successful, as in July a $31.6 million contract was placed with McDonnell Douglas by the USAF for the type. Another new aircraft ordered during 1982 was the Fairchild T-46A. This two-seat primary jet trainer was selected as a Cessna T-37 replacement, with the procurement of 650 being envisaged, for planned service entry date in 1986.

The General Dynamics F-16XL, an advanced version of the Fighting Falcon featuring a 'cranked arrow' composite delta wing configuration, flew for the first time, in single-seat form, during July. A two-seat version followed on 29 October. The F-16XL was designed to increase the weapons-carrying capability offered by the basic aircraft,

and later competed for the multi-role strike/fighter contract, that was eventually won by the F-15E Strike Eagle. If the aircraft had been ordered by the USAF, single-seat versions would have been known as F-16Es and two-seaters as F-16Fs. However, in spite of the failure of the programme to win any military orders, the F-16XL prototypes both entered service with NASA and have since been used for tests of laminar-flow wing components.

The most enduring of Lockheed's Shooting Star variants was the T-33 trainer conversion, which first flew in 1948. Well over 5,000 were built and most US-based interceptor squadrons operated 'T-Birds' in a variety of training roles, including simulated enemy intrusion, until the late 1980s. In his painting Friendly Flight *Ronald Wong shows a grey camouflaged T-33A of 5021 TOS engaging a 43 TFS F-15 Eagle over the bleak, glacial landscape of Alaska. It appears here by courtesy of the artist.*

The pages for 1982 generously supported by Inflite Engineering Services Limited

Friendly Flight by Ronald Wong BSc(Hons), GAvA, GMA, ASAA

1982

Northrop Tacit Blue *stealth technology demonstrator*

26 January: A total of 480 F-16 Fighting Falcons was ordered for delivery between 1982 and 1985 – the largest multi-year procurement contract by the USAF to date.

26 January: Plans to procure the McDonnell Douglas C-17 were cancelled and 50 Lockheed C-5Ns ordered instead. The Air Force lobbied extensively for work on the C-17 to be continued.

5 February: The Northrop *Tacit Blue* stealth technology demonstrator aircraft was flown for the first time. It went on to make a further 135 test flights.

1 March: The first two of 27 F-15 Eagles were delivered to Elmendorf AFB, to replace the 21st Tactical Fighter Wing's F-4E Phantoms in Alaskan Air Command.

10 June: The first all-female SAC crew, from the 924th Air Refueling Squadron at Castle AFB, CA, completed a KC-135 Stratotanker mission.

29 June: The last of the stretched and up-dated C-141B StarLifter conversions was completed.

July: Exercise *Global Shield 82*, an eight-day intensive rehearsal for offensive and defensive operations, was held by SAC.

1 July: The 501st Tactical Missile Wing (TMW) was established at RAF Greenham Common, to operate Gryphon ground-launched cruise missiles.

2 July: It was announced that the Fairchild T-46A two-seat primary jet trainer had been selected to replace the Cessna T-37, with the first delivery planned for 1986.

3 July: The single-seat General Dynamics F-16XL was flown for the first time. It featured a 'cranked arrow' composite wing and a lengthened fuselage, together with a greater weapon-carrying capability.

26 July: A $31.6 million contract was received by McDonnell Douglas, following extensive lobbying, to allow continuation of the C-17 programme.

4 August: The first re-engined Boeing KC-135 Stratotanker, had its maiden flight. It was fitted with CFM-56 turbofan engines in place of turbojets giving significant performance improvements. This was the start of a major retrofit programme.

30 August: The first of three Northrop F-20 Tigersharks was flown. It was developed from the F-5 and at first designated F-5G, but no production ensued.

September: Seven KC-10A Extenders dispensed 65,000lb of fuel to each of 20 MAC C-141B StarLifters near Goose Bay, Labrador. The transports then flew non-stop to West Germany, where they air-dropped paratroopers, before returning to the US where another fuel transfer was made off the East Coast some 14 hours after the first refuelling.

1 September: The 602nd Tactical Air Control Wing for training forward air controllers was formed at Davis-Monthan AFB, AZ.

1 September: Air Force Space Command was activated.

21 September: Trials were completed of the US Navy's Harpoon anti-shipping missile by the 320th Bomb Wing's B-52 Stratofortresses.

16 December: The AGM-86B air-launched cruise missile (ALCM) reached Initial Operational Capability (IOC) at Griffiss AFB, NY. Sixteen B-52G Stratofortresses of the 558th Bomb Squadron, 416th BW were modified to carry 12 ALCMs on wing pylons.

During October, trouble flared up on the island of Grenada when its premier, Maurice Bishop, was first placed under house arrest and later killed along with some of his supporters in a coup that was viewed as having been inspired by Cuba. Coupled with this Communist threat was the potential problem posed by Grenada's location, north of the coast of Venezuela, which made it an ideal 'staging post' for Soviet aircraft flying to Latin America and as a base for international terrorists. It was decided to mount an operation to invade the island and evacuate US citizens. Operation *Urgent Fury* commenced on 24 October. MC-130E Hercules of the 8th Special Operations Squadron (SOS) were used to drop parachute troops from the US Navy's SEAL units and the Army's elite Delta Force to carry out reconnaissance of possible landing sites for the invasion. This was launched on the 25th, with the first landing by Marines.

MC-130s dropped paratroops from two Army Ranger battalions, with cover provided by AC-130H *Spectre* gunships of the 16th SOS. A relative lack of opposition allowed C-130E Hercules and C-141B StarLifters to fly in rather than drop the 82nd Airborne Division and support equipment. US Navy aircraft from the USS *Independence*

Lockheed F-117A 'Night Hawk'

Piper PA-48 Enforcer

executed a number of strikes on the enemy's defences, again aided by AC-130s, who also carried out sorties around the battle area, as the ground forces ran into some problems. These missions proved successful enough for further American landings to go ahead. The *Spectres* were in action again to rescue American students trapped on their university campus on the island. More attacks on enemy barracks and defensive positions followed, and the operation was eventually successful with all US citizens on Grenada being evacuated, and the possibility of terrorist attacks on the US being launched from the island was removed.

Development of SAC's new Rockwell B-1B began in earnest following the return of the second B-1A prototype to flight status in March. A number of modifications had been undertaken during the interim, in order to test systems which would be incorporated in production aircraft. SAC undertook its largest ever sea mining exercise in March. *Team Spirit 83* involved B-52D and B-52G Stratofortresses from the 43rd Strategic Wing and the 2nd and 19th Bomb Wings simulating laying mines along the South Korean coast. The exercise involved units from the Air Force, Army, Navy and Marines and the forces of South Korea, in a rehearsal of Joint Military Operations. This was the last major SAC exercise involving B-52Ds, with the last aircraft finally being retired from service with the 7th Bomb Wing in early October.

The pages for 1983 generously supported by Lucas Aerospace

1983

3 January: Northrop opened its Project CJ facility, where the development of the Advanced Technology stealth bomber was to be based.

February: The *Thunderbirds* resumed its traditional role of demonstrating the Air Force's front-line fighter capabilities, when it took delivery of F-16A Fighting Falcons to replace its T-38 Talons.

9 February: First flight of the C-5A Galaxy transport fitted with newly-designed wings in order to overcome fatigue problems which had been encountered with the existing model.

12 February: First overseas deployment of the Lockheed TR-1A, to RAF Alconbury where the 17th Reconnaissance Wing's 95th RS had been formed in 1981 to operate the type.

17 February: Bell Helicopter and Boeing Vertol presented their design proposal for a tilt-rotor, multi-purpose aircraft to fill the Joint Services Advanced Vertical Lift Aircraft (JVX) USAF/USN programme. The design was selected in the April. The V-22 Osprey was based on the successful testing of two Bell XV-15 prototypes. The Army dropped out of the programme in 1988.

23 February: The first flight of the two-seat Lockheed TR-1B was made.

7 March: Exercise *Team Spirit 1983*, the biggest peacetime sea mining exercise ever held, involved ten SAC B-52Ds and B-52Gs from the 43rd Strategic Wing and the 2nd and 19th Bombardment Wings, simulating laying mines off the coast of South Korea.

23 March: The second (modified) prototype Rockwell B-1A was returned to flight testing.

6 April: The report of the Scowcroft Commission recommended an ICBM modernisation programme.

9 April: First flight of the Piper PA-48 Enforcer, a modified F-51 Mustang which was evaluated by the USAF at Eglin AFB and Edwards AFB but was not proceeded with.

18 April: The US Embassy in Beirut was bombed by terrorists.

30 April: The USAF completed extensive studies of advanced capabilities for the F-15 Eagle. Four differently-configured aircraft were used to evaluate and demonstrate varying

F-16A Fighting Falcons – the Thunderbirds

combinations of mission and load-carrying.

18 June: First launch of the LGM-118 'MX' Peacemaker ICBM from Vandenberg AFB, CA. A total of 50 were subsequently deployed.

July: The first F-16A Fighting Falcon was delivered to the Air National Guard. The 169th Tactical Fighter Group of the South Carolina ANG formally accepted the aircraft at McEntire ANGB, SC.

8 July: The 1,000th General Dynamics F-16 was rolled out by General Dynamics at Fort Worth. The total included export aircraft built in Europe for Belgium, Denmark and the Netherlands. The USAF planned to procure 2,165 examples.

15 July: The first Boeing E-4B (E-4A up-grade) was delivered to the Electronic Systems Division. One operational E-4B was airborne at all times with a crew of up to 94, together with a senior officer on board capable of assuming command of US forces in extreme emergency. With an unrefuelled endurance of more than 12 hours the E-4Bs were cleared and crewed to fly missions lasting up to 72 hours.

September: Systems Command awarded concept definition study contracts for an advanced tactical fighter (ATF) to replace the F-15 Eagle at the turn of the century.

16 September: The first of three C-20A Gulfstream IIIs (83-0500) was delivered to the 89th Military Airlift Wing at Andrews AFB, MD for VIP transport duties. Initially operated under a lease/purchase agreement, the Gulfstream IIIs replaced the thirstier C-140B Jetstars.

25 September: Operation *Rubber Wall*, the re-supply of friendly forces in Lebanon, was concluded. Some 4,000 tons of supplies, mostly ammunition, was airlifted by C-130 Hercules, C-141 StarLifters and C-5 Galaxies in 113 sorties.

1 October: The last B-52D Stratofortress was retired from SAC's 7th Bombardment Wing and flown to the storage facility at Davis-Monthan AFB, AZ. Other B-52Ds had earlier been retired to 24 locations for preservation at museums and Air Force bases.

23 October: A US Marine barracks was bombed in Beirut, with 241 killed and 78 injured in the terrorist attack. Eight C-141B StarLifters and twelve C-9A Nightingales were involved in a major medical evacuation.

24 October-4 November: Operation *Urgent Fury* enabled the evacuation of US civilians from Grenada. Offensive air support was provided by AC-130 *Spectre* Hercules gunships, while troops of the 82nd Airborne Division were flown in by C-141B StarLifters of the 437th Military Airlift Wing.

26 October: The Lockheed F-117A attained Initial Operational Capability with the 4450th Tactical Group at Tonopah Test Range Airfield, NV. The unit operated five F-117As and 18 A-7D Corsairs at this time, the latter being flown for crew proficiency and 'security' cover. All F-117 flights were made at night until November 1988.

The North American OV-10As shown in George Guzzi's painting belonged to the 549th Tactical Air Support Group based at Patrick AFB, FL. First flown in 1966, the Bronco was used effectively in Vietnam and subsequently as a forward air control aircraft. The painting is reproduced by kind permission of the artist.

OV-10A Broncos at Patrick AFB by George Guzzi ASAA

In February the F-15E Strike Eagle was selected for the Air Force's dual-role fighter requirement, rather than the competing General Dynamics F-16XL. The service's order for 392 of the aircraft was an investment for future operational flexibility since the Strike Eagle would provide the F-15C's air-to-air combat capabilities alongside the ability to deliver a wide range of ordnance in all weathers. The F-15E was planned to carry 23,500lb of stores. The second two-seat F-15B built had been reconfigured as a Strike Eagle development prototype for a 'private venture' project by McDonnell Douglas. The first production aircraft was scheduled for delivery in 1988.

The latest version of the Fighting Falcon, the F-16C made its maiden flight in June, and soon began to enter service, replacing the earlier F-16As. The two-seat F-16D followed shortly afterwards, superseding the F-16B. The initial 'Block 25' examples of the F-16C were powered by the improved Pratt & Whitney F100-PW-200 engine, and equipped with the Hughes APG-68 multi-mode radar, offering increased range and clarity. They were also the first F-16s to have the provision to carry the AGM-65D Maverick missile, and included various improvements to the avionics system.

In October, the first Rockwell B-1B was airborne on its maiden flight from Palmdale, CA, and immediately entered an intensive test and trials programme. This particular aircraft was permanently assigned to test duties. The B-1B's gross weight had increased to some 477,000lb, while the configuration of the bomber's weapons bay, that was capable of carrying 67,000lb of ordnance, and its avionics system, had been substantially modified. The power of its four General Electric F101-GE-102 turbofans with afterburner, providing 30,780lb maximum thrust, gave the aircraft a maximum speed at altitude of 825mph (Mach 1.25), and a low-level penetration speed at 200ft of over 600mph.

During September, SAC's existing equipment was heavily utilised for the *Gallant Eagle 84* exercise, the

Boeing B-52G Stratofortress with ALCMs

largest such operation in the US for 24 years. It tested conventional forces only and was controlled by US Central Command. A total of 44 B-52 Stratofortresses participated, flying 182 sorties with 309 more missions being flown by KC-135 Stratotankers and KC-10A Extenders providing air-to-air refuelling support. Alongside SAC, both TAC and MAC were also heavily involved, with aircraft operating out of many bases across the USA.

The first British-designed aircraft type to be ordered by the Air Force since the English Electric Canberra was built as the Martin B-57 in the 1950s, the Shorts C-23A Sherpa, flew for the first time in August 1984. A $115 million contract was placed with the Belfast-based company in March by the Air Force, for 18 military variants of the Shorts 330 light utility transport. The first

C-23 entered service in November, being used to meet the European Distribution System Aircraft (EDSA) requirement. This task involved ferrying high-priority cargoes such as urgently-needed front-line aircraft spares between USAFE air bases. The 10th MAS at Zweibrucken AB, Germany, operated the C-23As on a network of regular routes around Europe.

Painted in 1984, the year after the USAF's aerial demonstration team the Thunderbirds *re-equipped with the General Dynamics F-16A, the late Bob Cunningham depicts the two solo performers completing the dramatic* Crossover Break. *This painting was donated by the artist to the* Thunderbirds *museum at Nellis AFB, the team's home base. It is reproduced here by courtesy of Lockheed Martin Tactical Aircraft Systems.*

The pages for 1984 generously supported by Lockheed Martin Tactical Aircraft Systems

The Crossover Break by Robert E Cunningham ASAA

January: The *Seek Igloo* programme was completed. It formed a chain of radar stations from Cape Lisburne AFS in the north down to Cold Bay AFS in the south. The 13 radar sites fed information into both the Regional Operations Center and NORAD Headquarters in Cheyenne Mountain.

January: The 419th Tactical Fighter Wing at Hill AFB, Utah became the first USAF Reserve Unit to fly the F-16A Fighting Falcon when they were delivered to the 466th Tactical Fighter Squadron to replace the last F-105 Thunderchiefs in service.

3 February: The 42nd ECS received its first EF-111A Raven at RAF Upper Heyford, Oxfordshire.

4 February: The first Sikorsky HH-60A Night Hawk was flown. It was a combat-rescue version of the military H-60 Black Hawk series for the Air Force, capable of performing unescorted missions day or night at treetop height. Production funding was not obtained and the project was subsequently abandoned.

24 February: The F-15E Strike Eagle was selected as the two-seat, dual-role fighter rather than the General Dynamics F-16XL. The Air Force's stated requirement was for a total of 392 aircraft.

2 March: The USAF announced that it had selected the Shorts 330-200 Sherpa to fulfill its requirement for an European Distribution Systems Aircraft, designated as C-23A.

Shorts C-23A Sherpa

13 March: Roll-out of the first Gates Learjet 35A configured for the USAF's Operational Support Aircraft (OSA) requirement. It was designated C-21A in service.

20 March: The last of 713 A-10A Thunderbolt IIs was delivered to the USAF.

6 April: The first three C-21A Learjet 35As were delivered to the 375th Aeromedical Airlift Wing at Scott AFB, IL.

June: The first Schweizer TG-7A motorglider was delivered to the 94th Air Training Squadron, part of the USAF Academy at Colorado Springs. The TG-7As were for use as powered gliding trainers for cadets.

16 June: The improved General Dynamics F-16C was first flown at Fort Worth. It featured a GEC wide-angle HUD and Hughes APG-68 multi-mode radar.

20 June: The first re-engined KC-135R Stratotanker (61-0293) was delivered back to an operational unit, the 384th Air Refueling Wing at McConnell AFB, KS. This followed two years of extensive test and evaluation trials.

21 June: A KC-10A Extender of the 22nd Air Refueling Wing, operating from Christchurch International Airport, New Zealand, carried out three in-flight refuelling operations on a MAC C-141B StarLifter making air-drop deliveries to Antarctic bases at McMurdo Sound and at the South Pole. A further flight was conducted two days later.

July: The 432nd Tactical Fighter Wing was re-activated at Misawa AB, Japan, to operate the F-16A Fighting Falcon for air defence of the area to the north of the country.

18 July: The 552nd Airborne Warning and Control Wing received its first improved E-3B Sentry. This development had improved advanced computers, secure communications, a limited maritime capability and five more crew work stations.

19 July: The first General Dynamics F-16C Fighting Falcon was delivered to the Air Force.

6 August: The Shorts C-23A Sherpa, a development of the Shorts 330 utility transport and short-haul airliner, made its first flight from Belfast. It was accepted into the Air Force inventory on 1 November.

29 August: The second Rockwell B-1A was lost in an accident

Grumman X-29A

on its 127th flight, killing one crew member and seriously injuring the other two.

4-12 September: Exercise *Gallant Eagle 84* – the biggest military exercise in the US for 24 years, involved 44 SAC bombers. It incorporated aviation elements from Strategic Air Command, Tactical Air Command and Military Airlift Command.

18 October: The first Rockwell B-1B (82-0001 *Leader of the Fleet* and carrying the name *Star of Abilene*) was flown at Palmdale, CA.

December: As part of the relief efforts in Ethiopia, two C-141B StarLifters carried supplies to Sudan, where famine victims had taken refuge.

14 December: The unusual Grumman X-29A (82-0003), a forward-swept wing research aircraft for the DARPA programme, was flown for the first time. Two X-29As were built, the second being 82-0049.

17 December: A C-5A Galaxy set a national record for taking off at the highest all-up weight, becoming airborne with a total weight of 920,836lb (418,562kg).

The first flight of the latest C-5B Galaxy in September signalled the start of a big increase in Military Airlift Command's total airlift capability – a shortfall had previously been envisaged, with the number of long term and emergency operations in which the Command had been so heavily involved. Fifty new production aircraft were ordered from Lockheed, to augment the 76 C-5As remaining in service. Changes compared to the earlier aircraft included a better, automated flight control system and a modified undercarriage, which replaced the 'A' model's crosswind landing gear. With the benefit of these improvements, the new aircraft were cleared to operate at weights up to 837,000lb, whereby the transport's already impressive maximum payload of 291,000lb could now be carried for a distance in excess of 3,400 miles. Production of the C-5Bs followed the programme to re-wing the C-5A models with strengthened units.

In October, the new Fairchild T-46A jet trainer, that was intended to replace the long serving Cessna T-37B, flew for the first time. This launched the Air Force into

Boeing E-4B Advanced Airborne Command Post

Fairchild T-46A

what turned out to be a very long-running procurement programme. A total of 650 examples of the aircraft, which had won the contract resulting from the Next-Generation Trainer (NGT) requirement, were to have been procured. In addition, an armed AT-46 variant had also been mooted for sales to potential export markets. The distinctive twin-finned T-46 was powered by two Garrett F109-GA-100 turbofans, a specially-designed powerplant which was intended to give a quiet, fuel-efficient performance. Indeed, the new trainer performed well during its flight testing schedule. However, the whole order for the T-46A was eventually cancelled. The NGT requirement was dropped largely as a result of poor programme management.

One important aircraft that did enter service in 1985 was the Rockwell B-1B, although delivery of the first

aircraft was not without its own problems. The USAF's first example was flown to Offutt AFB, NE, the SAC Headquarters location, on 27 June, and was to have been delivered on to the 96th Bomb Wing at Dyess AFB, TX two days later. It was scheduled to have been handed over to the unit on the 30th anniversary of the initial acceptance of the B-52 Stratofortress into service, but unfortunately the B-1B was grounded due to foreign object damage and remained at Offutt. The Commander-in-Chief of SAC, General Bennie L Davis, flew to Edwards AFB to collect the only other airworthy B-1B, the fleet prototype (82-0001) and delivered it to Dyess on 7 July for its formal acceptance by the 96th BW. The Wing subsequently received the first 29 examples of the swing-wing supersonic bomber and proved its operational capabilities.

The pages for 1985 generously supported by the B-52 Stratofortress Association

27 February: The first of four Boeing EC-18Bs modified as Advanced Range Instrumentation Aircraft (ARIAs) had its maiden flight. Eight ex-American Airlines Boeing 707-323s had been acquired in 1981 for conversion to C-18 standard. These aircraft were operated by the 4950th Test Wing at Wright Patterson AFB, OH.

4 March: An F-16 Fighting Falcon began flight tests with a TERPROM (terrain profile-matching) navigation system, developed jointly by General Dynamics and British Aerospace.

12 April: The slogan 'Peace is our Profession', that had stood outside SAC Headquarters at Offutt AFB, NE for 27 years, was removed and replaced by standard USAF plaques.

May: The first successful guided test launch of the AIM-120A AMRAAM (Advanced Medium-Range Air-To-Air Missile) was accomplished from an F-16 Fighting Falcon.

June: The 384th Air Refueling Wing at McConnell AFB, KS became the first SAC unit to fully re-equip with the updated KC-135R Stratotanker.

29 June: The first F-15 Eagle was delivered to an Air National Guard unit, the 159th Tactical Fighter Group at NAS New Orleans.

4 July: The 13th TFS was the first squadron of the newly formed 432ndTFW to take delivery of F-16 Fighting Falcons at Misawa AB. It was the first USAF combat squadron to be based in Japan for 14 years.

7 July: The first Rockwell B-1B (82-0001) was delivered to the 96th Bombardment Wing at Dyess AFB, TX. The aircraft was flown in by General Bennie L Davis, C-in-C of SAC.

6 August: The Precision Location/Strike System (PLSS) had its first full operational test flight on a Lockheed TR-1A reconnaissance aircraft.

September: The first of four Boeing C-22Bs was delivered to Detachment 1, District of Columbia ANG at Andrews AFB, MD. These were former National Airlines and Pan American Airways Boeing 727-035s, that were modified for Air Force use for various transport duties. Two more C-22s were later purchased, one from the FAA (designated C-22A, for use by the C-in-C, US Southern Command) and the other from

Gates C-21A Learjet

Singapore Airlines (a stretched C-22C, used by HQ, US Central Command)

10 September: The first of 50 Lockheed C-5B Galaxies had its maiden flight. The new aircraft were cleared to operate at weights up to 837,000lb.

13 September: An F-15 Eagle launched an ASAT (anti-satellite) missile and destroyed a target in space for the first time. The ASAT hit and destroyed the Defense Department P78-1, that had been launched into orbit in 1971 and was travelling at 17,500mph at an altitude of 290 miles.

17 September: Initial test flight was made by a B-52 Stratofortress fitted with a common strategic rotary launcher (CSRL) weapon carrier.

15 October: The first flight of the prototype Fairchild T-46A trainer took place at Edwards AFB. The 72-minute flight was uneventful. The future of the programme was already in doubt as the USAF had grave concerns about what it described as 'management deficiencies'.

18 October: The first flight was made by the AFTI General Dynamics F-111A (63-9778) fitted with the mission adaptive wing (MAW).

22 October: The last of 80 C-21A Learjets was delivered to the Air Force (four more were later acquired for the Air National Guard). The C-21As were distributed between 16 USAF locations, the last aircraft going to the 1400th MAS at Kirtland AFB, New Mexico.

6 December: The USAF accepted the 18th and last C-23A Sherpa from the manufacturer, Shorts at Belfast, Northern Ireland. The aircraft was delivered to the 10th MAS of MAC at Zweibrucken AB, West Germany.

31 December: Reversing the Pentagon decision of January 1982, McDonnell Douglas was awarded a contract to design and develop the C-17A long-range, heavy-lift cargo transport. The aircraft was required to be able to lift C-5A Galaxy-size payloads into rough-field areas, normally accessible only to the C-130 Hercules.

First operational with SAC in 1955, the B-52 Stratofortress was destined to continue in active service for five decades. Shown here in Ronald Wong's painting is a B-52G of the 379th BW carrying ALCMs on an exercise flight. Soldiering On is reproduced by kind permission of the artist.

Soldiering On by Ronald Wong BSc(Hons), GAvA, GMA, ASAA

Mid-April saw the biggest air strikes undertaken by the USAF for some years, with the attacks on Libya. For the previous five years, terrorism on the part of the Palestine Liberation Organisation (PLO) and direct Libyan aggression against the West, had gradually been escalating, encouraged by the country's leader, Colonel Gadhafi (who was being supplied with arms by the Soviet Union). In March, US Navy aircraft operating off the Mediterranean coast were fired on by a Libyan SAM site, and then on 5 April a discothèque in Berlin attended by American servicemen was blown up by a terrorist bomb, killing one serviceman. The evidence pointed to Libyan involvement, and it was decided by the US government to retaliate by carrying out air strikes under the name Operation *El Dorado Canyon*.

Reconnaissance of possible military and terrorist targets in Libya was carried out by SR-71As of the RAF Mildenhall-based Det 4, 9th SRW, as well as U-2Rs and TR-1As from Det 3, 9th SRS at RAF Akrotiri, Cyprus, along with a number of 55th SRW RC-135s also operating from RAF Mildenhall. Tanker units from the continental USA began the deployment of KC-10A Extenders and KC-135 Stratotankers to the UK, where they were based at RAF Mildenhall and RAF Fairford. These additional aircraft augmented those already on temporary duty (TDY) detachments at the two stations. The USAF section of the strike force comprised 24 General Dynamics F-111Fs from the 48th TFW at RAF Lakenheath, the other attacking elements assigned being aircraft from the US Navy carriers *Saratoga*, *Coral Sea* and *America*. Alongside the tankers, other mission support was provided by 42nd ECS EF-111As from RAF Upper Heyford (radar jamming), 960th AW&CS E-3A Sentries (airborne early warning) and a 7th ACCS EC-135E (tactical command and control).

Having taken off from RAF Lakenheath at 1836hr BST, the F-111Fs started a 5,500 mile in-direct flight to their targets, as France and Spain had both denied

General Dynamics F-111F – 48th TFW

overflying rights. They crossed the Libyan coast (protected by the EF-111s), where the force split into two sections – one attacked Colonel Gadhafi's headquarters at Al Aziziyah barracks and a training camp at Sidi Bilal, whilst the other bombed the military side of Tripoli Airport. The AN/AVQ-26 *Pave Tack* target designation system was

The pages for 1986 generously supported by Hughes

being used operationally for the first time during *El Dorado Canyon*, the F-111s being equipped with 2,000lb GBU-10 Paveway II laser-guided bombs. These reached their prime objectives successfully, although there was more collateral damage around the main target in Tripoli, Gadhafi's HQ, than had been expected. Only one of the USAF strike force was lost, this being due to an apparent technical problem over the sea north of Tripoli. The US Navy attacks on another military barracks, an enemy airfield and air defence radars also caused much damage, which was illustrated by the post-strike recce missions completed by an SR-71A that was already airborne before the first aircraft had recovered to their operating bases.

Aircraft from Mildenhall were committed to another important operation later in April, but of a very different kind. The explosion at the nuclear power station at Chernobyl in the Ukraine occurred on the 26th of the month, first being detected by Sweden, whose Air Force carried out the initial monitoring flights to check on amounts and type of radioactive fallout, along with an RC-135U of the 55th SRW. Two days later, an EC-135H from the 10th ACCS at RAF Mildenhall confirmed that the explosion had occurred by 'listening-in' to Soviet communications. This was followed by the start of flights by a WC-135B of the 55th Weather Reconnaissance Squadron – this specialist aircraft flew through the easterly airstream, collecting air samples. Had this 'independent' evidence not been gathered, the Soviets might well have covered-up the facts about this major nuclear accident, which posed a great threat to many Western countries.

EF-111A Ravens of the 42nd ECS from RAF Upper Heyford, Oxfordshire, accompanied the El Dorado Canyon strike force to Libya in 1986. Here in this painting by Ronald Wong, one of the 'Spark Varks' flies a stand-off jamming pattern near the Libyan coast, providing electronic countermeasure support for the F-111Fs from RAF Lakenheath as they carried out their attacks over Tripoli. The painting is reproduced here by kind permission of the artist.

First Blood for the 'Spark Vark' by Ronald Wong BSc(Hons), GAvA, GMA, ASAA

January: Eight C-20B Gulfstream IVs were ordered. This version incorporated advanced mission communications equipment and a revised interior.

8 January: The first C-5B Galaxy was delivered to the 56th Squadron of the 443rd Military Airlift Wing at Altus AFB, OK. This followed an extensive flight test programme. The rest of the 50 aircraft were delivered over the next three years.

17 January: The Air Force began operational test and evaluation of the first Martin Aerospace LANTIRN (low altitude navigation and targeting infra-red system for night) targeting system at McChord AFB, WA.

24 March: The USAF issued a request for proposals on a new air defence fighter to replace F-4 Phantoms in eleven Air National Guard squadrons. The USAF planned to buy 60 aircraft each year in 1988, 1989, 1990 and 1991 to a total of 300 aircraft.

14-15 April: The USAF was involved in co-ordinated air strikes on targets in Libya, mounted from air bases in England under Operation *El Dorado Canyon*. Eighteen General Dynamics F-111Fs from the 48th TFW at RAF Lakenheath and five EF-111As from the 42nd Electronic Combat Squadron at RAF Upper Heyford made the 5,500-mile round-trip flight. They were refuelled by 28 KC-10As and KC-135s. One F-111F was lost in unexplained circumstances.

15 April: Terrorists fired five rocket bombs at Yokota AB in Japan.

McDonnell Douglas F-15E Strike Eagle

Cessna OA-37B

26 April: A major accident occurred at the nuclear power station at Chernobyl in the Ukraine. Boeing EC-135Hs, RC-135Us and WC-135Bs operating out of RAF Mildenhall were involved in gathering details of the explosion and collecting air samples.

10 May: A B-52H Stratofortress carried a full complement of 20 Boeing AGM-86B ALCMs for the first time.

June: Frances E. Warren AFB, WY (the oldest continually used base in the USAF) became the only facility to deploy the LGM-118A Peacemaker missile with 50 silos in place. The missile was cold launched from existing Minuteman III silos of which 200 were spread over 5,866 acres in Wyoming.

5 June: The Boeing 747 was selected as the next Presidential aircraft 'Air Force One', to replace the long serving Boeing VC-137s with the 89th Airlift Wing at Andrews AFB, MD.

17 June: The last Fairchild UC-123K Provider, used by the 907th Tactical Airlift Group for spraying operations, was retired from service.

12 July: The Air National Guard received its first C-141B StarLifter. It was assigned to the 183rd Military Airlift Squadron, of the 172nd Military Airlift Group at Allen C Thompson Field, Jackson, MS.

13 July: The Air Force Reserve took delivery of its first C-141B StarLifter. It went to the 756th Military Airlift Squadron of the 459th MAW, at Andrews AFB, MD.

1 October: The 96th Bombardment Wing at Dyess AFB, TX reached initial operating capability (IOC) with its new Rockwell B-1Bs.

1 October: The 43rd Electronic Countermeasures Squadron was activated at Sembach AB, West Germany, to operate EC-130H Hercules from May 1987.

7 October: The 1,715th, and last, Boeing AGM-86B ALCM was delivered to the 2nd Bombardment Wing at Barksdale AFB, LA. The ALCM was to be carried by the Rockwell B-1B as well as the B-52 Stratofortress.

31 October: The USAF announced that it had selected the Northrop/McDonnell Douglas and Lockheed/General Dynamics/Boeing consortia to build prototypes for the Advanced Tactical Fighter fly-off.

11 December: Initial flight made by the first 'production' McDonnell Douglas F-15E Strike Eagle (86-0183), a two-seat ground attack and air superiority fighter version of the basic Eagle. The aircraft was capable of operating on long-range deep interdiction missions in bad weather, day or night.

One of the year's major concerns were the alleged operational shortcomings of the new Rockwell B-1B. It was reported that the initial aircraft delivered to SAC's 96th Bomb Wing at Dyess AFB, TX did not meet the service's requirements in various important areas. Mainly its defensive avionics were seen as being inferior to what was required, particularly in the light of Soviet developments in this field. Also there was a considerable increase in the B-1B's gross weight when compared to the development B-1As, resulting in a significant loss of performance and particularly a shortfall in range. These reports were denied by the Air Force, who talked up the enhancements to the aircraft's terrain-following and flight control systems then about to come 'on stream'. It was admitted, however, that improvements would have to be made to the B-1B's ECM fitment.

A report by the House Armed Services Committee blamed the apparent problems on poor programme management by the USAF, who, it was felt, had not properly sought to report the B-1's shortcomings to higher authority. This led to fears of similar problems with the forthcoming Northrop B-2, and a 'bomber gap' between East and West should the B-1 prove to be unable to carry out its full mission. There were further difficulties later in the year, after the crash of a SAC B-1B following a birdstrike while on a low-level training flight. A total ban was placed on low-level operations by the bomber that lasted until early November.

The F-15E Strike Eagle's flight test and development programme continued well, with the start of night-flying trials at Edwards AFB, CA. These evaluated the dual-role fighter's cockpit displays in night-time conditions, for their brightness and clarity. McDonnell Douglas fitted prototype Martin Marietta LANTIRN (Low Altitude Navigation and Targeting Infra-red for Night) pods to the first F-15E during February, which gave the aircraft a long-range interdiction capability at night or in poor weather. Strike Eagle testing entered a new phase later in

the year, with intensive trials of its Hughes APG-70 radar and the navigation and terrain-following functions of the LANTIRN pods. It was also announced that the USAF was studying a *Wild Weasel* version of the F-15 as one of two F-4G Phantom II replacements, along with the F-16 Fighting Falcon.

The formation on 1 June of Air Force Special Operations Command (AFSOC) coincided with developments on two new aircraft that it would operate. Rockwell was awarded the contract in July to convert new-build C-130Hs to AC-130U Hercules gunship configuration, with 12 such aircraft scheduled for delivery to the 16th Special Operations Squadron at Hurlburt Field, FL. The new aircraft was to utilise a single 25-mm GAU-12 cannon with 3,000 rounds, as opposed to the 20-mm weapon of the AC-130H, whilst retaining the 40-mm L-60 cannon and 105-mm M102 howitzer. For the combat rescue role, the new Sikorsky MH-53J *Pave Low III* was first delivered to AFSOC on 17 July, with full service entry following at Hurlburt Field in 1988. With more powerful T64

turboshaft engines, as well as better AN/APQ-158 terrain-following radar and more advanced avionics equipment than earlier H-53 derivatives used for these operations, the new helicopter would soon become a very important Special Operations tool.

There were changes within USAFE during the year, following Spain's refusal to renew its Mutual Defense Assistance Agreement with the US, which dated back to 1953 and was scheduled to last until 1988. There had been on-going disagreements in Spain regarding its membership of NATO, continuation of which was approved by a small majority in a 1986 referendum. However, there were conditions attached to its membership, namely that Spain would not be a part of the alliance's military command structure and the basing or storage of nuclear weapons on Spanish soil was forbidden. A third demand was that the US military presence, at Torrejon, Moron and Zaragoza ABs, was to be cut back. Following negotiations, it was decided that the US would relinquish its operations at Torrejon in 1991.

Lockheed EC-130H Hercules

The pages for 1987 generously supported by Normalair Garrett Limited

January: It was reported that Whiteman AFB, MO, was undergoing $90 million worth of improvements in order for it to be the USAF's first operational B-2 'stealth' bomber base.

February: It was reported that a major issue in the forthcoming session of Congress would be President Reagan's Strategic Defense Initiative (SDI), concentrating primarily on the development of space-based weapons systems capable of 'downing' Soviet ICBMs.

February: The USAF Aeronautical Systems Division awarded General Dynamics a $33,225,649 contract to equip FB-111As and EF-111As with digital flight control systems.

3 February: Sikorsky Aircraft delivered the first UH-60A modified to *Credible Hawk* standard, which included extra fuel tankage, a fuel management system and an air-to-air refuelling probe. The UH-60As were allocated to the 55th Aerospace Rescue and Recovery Squadron at Eglin AFB, FL, where they were eventually fitted with *Pave Low III* forward looking infra-red systems to help with their intended role of long-range search and rescue missions.

13 March: The USAF contract for the T-46A trainer with Fairchild Industries was terminated following the previous year's decision to end the programme. Only two prototypes and the first production aircraft had flown and they were relegated to research and trials work.

14 April: A Rockwell B-1B made its longest flight to date. Departing from Dyess AFB, TX it flew 9,410 miles in 21hr 40min and involved five air-to-air refuelling sessions with KC-135 Stratotankers.

4 May: The 43rd Electronic Countermeasures Squadron at Sembach AB, West Germany received its first EC-130H Hercules.

5 May: The last LAM-25C Titan II ICBM was taken off alert at Little Rock AFB, AK.

8 May: The fourth and final *Pave Paws* phased-array radar was activated at Eldorado AFS, TX. The system was established to detect submarine-launched ballistic missiles and collect satellite data.

June: Trials were successfully completed under the *Apache Thunder* programme involving USAF A-10A Thunderbolt IIs and US Army AH-64A Apaches. It confirmed that the close-

Gulfstream C-20B

support aircraft was most effective when working in conjunction with the helicopter's laser ranging and tracking system.

1 June: Special Operations Command was established.

10 June: The first deployment of a Rockwell B-1B to Europe, when an example from the 96th Bomb Wing at Dyess AFB, TX arrived at Le Bourget for a static appearance at the Paris Air Show.

2 July: Rockwell International was awarded the USAF's $155.2 million contract to convert new-build C-130H Hercules into AC-130U *Spectre* gunships.

17 July: The first Sikorsky MH-53J *Pave Low III* was delivered, entering service at Hurlburt Field, FL the following year.

28 July: General Dynamics presented its F-16 'Agile Falcon' proposal to the Air Force. This programme, giving the Fighting Falcon 25% more wing area, was aimed at returning the heavily laden F-16C to the air combat performance of the F-16A.

31 July: Development of the E-8A J-STARS system began when the first Boeing 707-320 to be converted (86-0416) was delivered to the Grumman facility at Melbourne, FL.

August: The 150th Tactical Fighter Group, New Mexico ANG received the first A-7D Corsair II to be equipped with the Low-Altitude Night Attack (LANA) pod, allowing better target acquisition at night or in bad weather.

2 August: C-5 Galaxies airlifted US Navy RH-53D minesweeper

helicopters to Diego Garcia, in preparation for their possible involvement in the Persian Gulf.

17 September: The 70th production Rockwell B-1B broke nine records and set nine new ones during a five hour flight. It carried a load of 66,140lb over a distance of 3,107 miles (5,000km) at an average speed of 655mph.

28 September: A Rockwell B-1B was destroyed when it was damaged during a high-speed low-altitude training flight, following a bird strike (possibly a large pelican). It was the first of the type to crash.

19 November: An US Department of Defense contract worth $2 billion was awarded to Northrop for production of the B-2 'stealth' bomber.

November: Spain stated that it would renounce its 1950 Mutual Defense Assistance Agreement with the USA, unless its total of 10,000 personnel stationed at US air bases on Spanish soil was cut back.

Having reached IOC in September 1986 after a troubled and prolonged development, the swing-wing Rockwell B-1B went on to become an effective weapon system. Lou Drendel captures a Lancer at high-speed on a simulated low-level bombing run. The painting is reproduced by kind permission of the artist.

Low Level Bomb Run by Lou Drendel

The roll-out in November of the first prototype Northrop B-2A marked the culmination of several years of development of the USAF's Advanced Technology Bomber (ATB). It had started life as a 'black' programme (Project *Senior CJ*), known to only a very few key personnel. Those with access to the project, knew that procurement of 132 B-2s was intended. Funding for six prototypes was provided in 1982, three more being added soon after.

Originally, the B-2 was intended for a high-level penetration role, but when the ATB design was frozen in 1983 this had changed to a primary low-level mission. The type employed the latest 'low-observable' technology, having a flying wing design with no tail surfaces, and using composite materials to provide a radar-absorbent structure. To further assist this, the B-2's four General Electric F118-GE-110 turbofans were set back from and above the wing trailing edges in order to reduce its radar

signature. Similarly the aircraft's unique planform, with a saw-tooth trailing edge to its wing, combined with the pronounced sweepback of the leading edge, helped to 'trap' radar energy.

The B-2 could be equipped with 16 conventional or free-fall nuclear bombs for standard missions, though for stand-off strategic operations either AGM-69 SRAM II or AGM-192A cruise missiles could be carried. Further weapon options became available, notably the ability to carry B61 nuclear weapons. The bomber has an APQ-181 radar, which would only be used on operational sorties just before the B-2 reaches its target. An electronic warfare capability is provided by an APR-50 Radar Warning Receiver (RWR) and the ZSR-62 defensive aids system.

Following the initial procurement of nine aircraft while the B-2 remained a 'black' programme, three more were ordered in 1989, and then two each in both 1990 and 1991. The initial total of 132 aircraft that were to be

ordered had by then been reduced to 76, but then in 1991 procurement was halted at just 16 B-2s, all but one for active USAF service. Following Air Force demands that a minimum of 20 aircraft was required for operational effectiveness, five more were subsequently added at a higher 'fly-away' unit cost of $2,220 million each.

During December another aircraft with significant technological and electronic advances made its maiden flight. This was the first E-8A J-STARS airframe to be converted by Grumman. Providing the airborne element in the Air Force and Army's J-STARS (Joint Surveillance Target Attack Radar System) programme, the E-8 was developed to allow significant advances in reconnaissance and surveillance of the battlefield area, and facilitate better command and control, communications and intelligence gathering. It had a Westinghouse Norden multi-mode side-looking radar with up to 100 miles imaging range, which, through the Surveillance and Control Data Link is able to relay information to truck-mounted Ground Station Modules. These are similar to the operators' consoles in the J-STARS itself, of which the two E-8As have ten. The two E-8As carried a large amount of test equipment, but production E-8Cs would have additional operators' consoles and a higher-resolution radar. A pair of late-model, ex-airline Boeing 707-320s were purchased for initial modification as E-8As. The first airframe, after major overhaul, was delivered to Grumman in August 1987, the second being delivered to Grumman in December of the following year.

Boeing/Grumman E-8A J-Stars

Not officially revealed until November 1988, the secret F-117 'stealth' fighter was developed and built at the Lockheed Skunk Works. The first F-117 was flown on 18 June 1981 from Groom Lake, NV. Nearby Tonopah Test Range Airfield housed the 4450th Tactical Group that was declared operational with the F-117 in October 1983. Craig Kodera's painting shows two of these 'black' fighters after they had emerged from exclusive night operations. It is reproduced here by courtesy of the artist.

The pages for 1988 generously supported by Lockheed Martin Skunk Works

Darkness Visible by Craig F Kodera ASAA

January: Agreement was reached between the Spanish government and the US Department of Defense, over a reduction in US forces stationed in Spain. It was agreed that the F-16 Fighting Falcons of the 401st Tactical Fighter Wing would vacate Torrejon AB and re-locate to Italy.

January: At Spangdahlem, the resident 52nd Tactical Fighter Wing began partially re-equipping with F-16C/D Fighting Falcons to replace its F-4 Phantoms.

January: The 405th Tactical Training Wing at Luke AFB, AZ became the USAF's Replacement Training Unit (RTU), providing instruction on the new F-15E Strike Eagle. It was shortly followed by the 4th Tactical Fighter Wing as the first operational unit, based at Seymour Johnson AFB, NC, where the F-15E replaced the F-4E Phantom.

March: The 21st Special Operations Squadron with six Sikorsky MH-53Js moved to RAF Woodbridge, Suffolk.

March: The Air Force ordered six Fairchild Swearingen C-26A Metros (later increased to 13) to meet the ANGOSTA (Air National Guard Operational Support Transport Aircraft) requirement.

30 April: The 100th and last production Rockwell B-1B was handed over to the 384th Bombardment Wing at McConnell AFB, KS. There were still some unresolved concerns about the B-1's defensive and offensive capabilities.

23 May: The first of six prototype Bell/Boeing V-22A Osprey tilt-rotor transport aircraft was rolled out at Arlington, TX. It

Northrop B-2A

McDonnell Douglas KC-10A Extender

had been designed for use by all four US armed services.

27 May: The Alconbury, Cambridgeshire-based 527th Aggressor Squadron flew its last F-5E Tiger II mission, prior to moving to Bentwaters in July.

4 June: Italy approved a NATO request to permit re-location of the 401st TFW to Aviano.

7 July: The last F-106 Delta Dart was taken off air defence alert with the 177th Fighter Interceptor Group, New Jersey Air National Guard at Atlantic City, NJ. The type had served in this role since 1959. A number of the surviving aircraft were subsequently converted as drones.

7 September: First flight made by the McDonnell Douglas F-15 (71290) STOL and manoeuvre technology demonstrator (S/MTD) Agile Eagle, fitted with provision for two-dimensional thrust vectoring and thrust-reverser nozzles. The objective was to develop a F-15 that could safely operate from a 1,500ft runway at night or in bad weather.

8 September: Implementation of the terms of the Intermediate Nuclear Forces Treaty began when the first two of 18 BGM-109G Ground Launched Cruise Missiles were flown out of Alconbury, Cambridgeshire on board a MAC C-5B Galaxy, for scrapping in the US.

10 November: The shadowy form that appeared in photographs taken from the perimeter of Nellis AFB and published in aviation magazines, was finally revealed to be the Lockheed F-117A 'stealth' aircraft. The Air Force had worked

Northrop F-5E Tiger II

very hard to keep the F-117 hidden from view by flying it only at night from the Tonopah Test Range Airfield in a remote part of Nevada. It had flown for the first time in 1981 and became operational in 1983.

22 November: The first prototype Northrop B-2A (82-1066) was rolled out at Palmdale, CA.

29 November: The 60th and last KC-10A Extender was delivered to the Air Force. It was also the first to be equipped with wing mounted refuelling pods in addition to the centreline boom.

December: Improved 'Block 40/42' F-16C/D Fighting Falcons began to roll off General Dynamics' Fort Worth production line. These aircraft were fitted with two LANTIRN pods, APG-68(C) radar, a global positioning navigation system, an enhanced gunsight together with a strengthened airframe. They were known as Night Falcons.

9 December: The Air Defense Weapons Center at Tyndall AFB, FL received the first of two E-9A airborne telemetry relay aircraft, that had been developed from the de Havilland Canada DHC-8 Dash 8.

22 December: The second E-8A J-STARS airframe (86-0417) was delivered to Grumman, and the first (86-0416) made its maiden flight during the month.

29 December: The first F-15E Strike Eagle interdictor was delivered to the 405th TTW (which had replaced the 58th TFTW at Luke AFB) for training purposes.

The Panamanian dictator General Manuel Noriega had, for several years, been causing concern to the US government through his involvement in drug trafficking, for which he was indicted by a Federal court. This escalated into the mistreatment and murder of American servicemen in Panama, and by mid-December he had 'declared war' on the US government. Numbers of US troops in the Central American country were almost immediately doubled, with MAC C-141B StarLifters, C-130 Hercules and C-5 Galaxies, supported by KC-135 Stratotankers and KC-10A Extenders of SAC, carrying out more than 150 missions in Operation *Nimrod Dancer*. This included the transport of the Fort Bragg-based 82nd Airborne Division from Pope AFB, NC in C-141Bs. Aircraft from regular MAC units were augmented by those of the Air National Guard and Air Force Reserve.

Returning transport flights to the US evacuated many thousands of 'non-essential' military personnel from Panama as the situation worsened. Operation *Just Cause* commenced on 20 December, with initial strikes around the capital, Panama City, including attacks by AC-130H Hercules of the 16th SOS on PDF (Panamanian Defense Force) targets. These continued throughout the brief conflict, supported by AC-130As of the 711th SOS, AFRes and a number of other Special Operations assets,

Sikorsky MH-53J Pave Low III

Lockheed AC-130H 'Spectre' Hercules

including the MH-53J *Pave Low III* and HC-130 tankers.

There were relatively few USAF combat aircraft involved in *Just Cause*. A deployment of six A-7D Corsair IIs from the 112th TFS, Ohio ANG, already stationed at Howard AFB on a regular Guard detachment, carried out a number of close-support strikes for Army forces before being replaced by aircraft of the 175th TFS, South Dakota ANG. More significantly, at least in the eyes of the media, was the inaugural combat use of the Lockheed F-117A, with aircraft of the 37th TFW reportedly flying non-stop from their home base at Tonopah Test Range, supported by tankers, to execute strike missions against a PDF barracks next to Rio Hato airfield, west of Panama City. These missions were targeted on an anti-aircraft battery next to the airfield and 'frightening' enemy troops.

The only other USAF aircraft engaged in 'operational' missions during the conflict were Cessna OA-37Bs of the 24th Tactical Air Support Squadron, which flew forward air control and patrol sorties. Additionally, 388th TFW F-16As were initially resident at Howard AFB to perform anti-drug smuggling missions, but returned to the USA in December. During the last days of 1989, General Noriega took refuge in the Vatican embassy, but gave himself up on 3 January 1990 and was flown to Florida under arrest in an MC-130E Hercules of the 8th SOS. After this, PDF forces soon collapsed.

The pages for 1989 generously supported by the McDonnell Douglas Corporation

9 January: Budget cuts were announced by the outgoing Reagan administration. These involved the cancellation of the Bell/Boeing V-22 Osprey.

10 January: First launch was made of *Tacit Rainbow* from a B-52 Stratofortress.

18 January: A team of Soviet observers flew to the UK to conduct a 'close-out inspection' of facilities at RAF Molesworth following the removal of the last Gryphon Ground-Launched Cruise Missile (GLCM).

28 February: The 485th Tactical Missile Wing was deactivated at Florennes in Belgium following the ALCM phase-out in Europe.

30 March: The first General Dynamics F-111E to be subjected to the Avionics Modernisation Program (AMP) arrived at McClellan AFB, CA.

17 April: After more than eight years, the Riyadh, Saudi Arabia-based *Elf One* Boeing E-3 Sentry detachment formally terminated with the return of the final aircraft to Tinker AFB, OK.

17 April: The 50th and last C-5B Galaxy was delivered to MAC's 436th Military Airlift Wing at Dover AFB, DE.

May: President Bush announced proposals for significant cuts in the overall strength of conventional forces in Europe.

10 May: The McDonnell Douglas F-15 'Agile Eagle', modified with thrust-vectoring nozzles and fitted with a flying foreplane, made its first flight.

11-18 May: US forces in Panama were reinforced in Operation *Nimrod Dancer*, when 85 missions airlifted 2,679 soldiers and Marines, together with 2,950 tons of equipment.

16 May-29 June: Almost 6,000 non-essential US personnel were evacuated from Panama in Operation *Blade Jewel*.

June: The USAF selected the F-106A Delta Dart as its future target drone, to replace the PQM-102A Delta Dagger and eventually the QF-100D/F Super Sabre.

10 June: Captain Jacqueline S Parker became the first woman graduate of the Air Force Test Pilot School.

17 July: The prototype Northrop B-2A made its first flight from Palmdale to Edwards AFB, CA.

August: C-5B Galaxies and C-141B StarLifters of MAC started to fly into RAF Greenham Common to airlift the based cruise missiles back to the US.

29 August: A request was issued for proposals on the USAF's tanker and transport training system (TTTS) programme – a design to be based on an existing executive or business jet.

September: After hosting standard 'stove-pipe' engined KC-135A Stratotankers for several years, RAF Fairford's 11th Strategic Group received the re-engined KC-135R derivative for the first time when aircraft from the 19th Air Refueling Wing began temporary duty.

September: The 425th Tactical Fighter Training Squadron was de-activated at Williams AFB, AZ.

September: The 316th Tactical Airlift Group, formed at Clark AB, Philippines in November 1973 as MAC's primary asset in the Far East, was inactivated when its parent unit, the 374th Tactical Airlift Wing, moved to Yokota AB in Japan.

14 September: The prototype Bell/Boeing V-22 Osprey performed its first full transition from helicopter to wing-borne flight. It made a conventional run-on landing without attempting a second transition to vertical flight.

October: Having been active since February 1963, the 320th Bombardment Wing was inactivated at Mather AFB, CA.

3 October: Last of the new production Lockheed U-2Rs (9), TR-1As (26) and TR-1Bs (2), was delivered to the USAF.

Lockheed C-5B Galaxy

Boeing C-22B

4 October: The first C-5B Galaxy to land in Antarctica delivered 168,000lb of cargo and 72 passengers on a re-supply mission.

November: Not having achieved its original planned complement of 18 aircraft, the 527th Aggressor Squadron at RAF Bentwaters began disposing of the F-16C Fighting Falcon prior to de-activation.

22 November: It was announced that the Lockheed SR-71A was to be grounded after all funds for continuing operations were deleted from the FY 1990 US Defense Department budget.

1-9 December: The Joint Task Force Philippines, including aircraft of the 3rd Tactical Fighter Wing, supported government forces after the attempted coup against President Aquino.

20 December-4 January: Operation *Just Cause* commenced in Panama, which was a US invasion to rescue American citizens. Lockheed F-117As of the 37th Tactical Fighter Wing carried out their first operational mission – an attack on a military barracks in Panama with 2,000lb laser-guided bombs.

With the last of 60 KC-10 Extenders delivered to the USAF in 1988, and the F-15E Strike Eagle entering service in the same year, the McDonnell Douglas combination is an appropriate subject for Mike Machat. The painting, from the Air Force Art Collection, is reproduced by kind permission of the artist.

McDonnell Douglas KC-10 and F-15E by Mike Machat ASAA

In the early hours of 2 August, troops of Iraq's Republican Guard crossed the border into Kuwait, making rapid gains to take control of the entire country. Four days later King Fahd of Saudi Arabia made a request for foreign assistance to strengthen the defence of his country against a likely attack by Iraq. This was met by President George Bush, with the launch of Operation *Desert Shield*, in what became the largest ever military airlift, starting with the deployment of the 82nd Airborne Division to Saudi Arabia. By the end of the operation's third week, the C-5 Galaxy fleet alone had transported a greater tonnage than that achieved during the entire Berlin Airlift. They were supported in the strategic transport role by the whole C-141B StarLifter inventory and the mobilised Civil Reserve Air Fleet (CRAF). Air National Guard and Air Force Reserve C-141 and C-5 units were officially called up for active duty on 23 August, the first ANG or AFRes elements to be deployed.

McDonnell Douglas F-15E Strike Eagle

By the end of October, over 220,000 troops and their equipment had arrived in the region.

The initial deployment of USAF combat aircraft to the Persian Gulf came on 8 August, when 48 F-15C Eagles of the 1st Tactical Fighter Wing flew non-stop from Langley AFB, VA to Dhahran in Saudi Arabia, making the longest ever Air Force operational fighter deployment. They were supported by KC-135 Stratotankers en route. This heralded the start of a build-up of aircraft from many front-line combat aircraft units, including the 4th TFW and its new F-15E Strike Eagles. On 20 August, the first Lockheed F-117As from the 37th TFW arrived at Khamis Mushait AB, Saudi Arabia. Like the Strike Eagle, this was the first operational deployment of the 'stealth' fighter. Joining the F-15Cs of the 1st TFW in the air defence role, more Eagles were sent from the 33rd TFW at Eglin AFB and the Bitburg-based 36th TFW. Fighter-bomber assets alongside the F-15Es were F-16 Fighting Falcons of the 50th, 52nd, 363rd, 388th, 347th and 401st TFWs, and the 138th TFS New York ANG and 157th TFS South Carolina ANG.

Both the UK-based F-111 units, the 20th TFW (F-111Es) and the 48th TFW (F-111Fs) despatched aircraft to Incirlik, Turkey and Taif, Saudi Arabia respectively, while the 366th TFW from Mountain Home AFB sent some of its EF-111As to Taif. More Ravens from the Upper Heyford-based 42nd ECS went to Incirlik AB, Turkey where the majority of USAFE's assets 'on call' for Gulf operations were based under the 7440th Composite Wing. Aircraft from three A-10A Thunderbolt II units were relocated, namely the 354th, 23rd and 10th TFWs, and the 926th TFG of AFRes, as well as OA-10A forward air control platforms of the 602nd Tactical Air Control Wing. The 35th and 52nd TFWs sent F-4G *Wild Weasel* Phantoms to Bahrain, joining the RF-4Cs of the 106th Tactical Reconnaissance Squadron, Alabama ANG, with more based at Incirlik alongside USAFE's 26th TRW. SAC, meanwhile, sent a number of B-52G Stratofortresses to Diego Garcia in the Indian Ocean to make up the

4300th Bomb Wing (Provisional). E-3 Sentries flying from Riyadh and Incirlik mounted 24-hour standing patrols. These, together with RC-135s of the 55th Reconnaissance Wing monitored the Iraqi air defence system and gathered ELINT information.

During *Desert Shield*, Lockheed U-2Rs and TR-1As were used for stand-off reconnaissance missions, providing extensive intelligence from far into Iraq. Meanwhile RF-4C Phantoms from the 106th TRS, Alabama ANG equipped with a LOROP (Long-Range Oblique Photography) capability flew cross-border reconnaissance operations. Such flights enabled the Coalition commanders, under the C-in-C Central Command, General Norman Schwarzkopf, to establish the direction which any conflict between the Allied nations and Iraq would take from its outset. On 29 November the UN Security Council passed Resolution 678 which set a deadline of 15 January 1991 for Saddam Hussein to withdraw his forces from Kuwait, after which member countries were authorised to use 'all necessary means' to remove the occupying Iraqi forces.

One significant Air Force type that did not see action in the Gulf was the Lockheed SR-71A, that was officially retired in January. 'Blackbird' operations by the 9th SRW had ceased in November 1989, but the Wing's two detachments at Kadena and Mildenhall did not return their aircraft until January. The last example to depart Mildenhall (64-17967) left for California on 19 January and the Air Force bade farewell to the SR-71 six days later at Beale AFB, CA. Three aircraft were transferred to NASA at Edwards AFB for use on high-speed research programmes.

Specially painted for 'Sabre to Stealth' by Ronald Wong, the first Northrop B-2 is momentarily caught by the light of the disappearing sun as it flies over the Mojave Desert on a test flight. Its all-important stealth features are achieved through smooth blending, instead of the multi-facetted approach of the Lockheed F-117, its flying wing design harking back to Northrop's early experiments in that field.

The pages for 1990 generously supported by Northrop Grumman

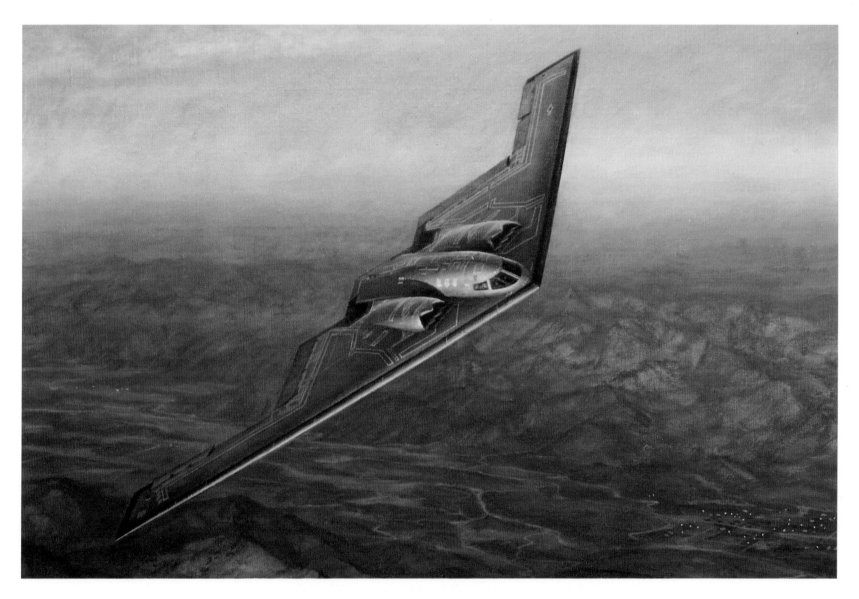

All quiet over the Mojave by Ronald Wong BSc(Hons), GAvA, GMA, ASAA

25 January: After more than 20 years service in the strategic reconnaissance role, the Lockheed SR-71A 'Blackbird' was retired from operational flying at a farewell ceremony at Beale AFB, CA. The 'official' retirement date was 26 February.

26 January: The Boeing VC-25A, a specially modified Boeing 747-200, for use by the President and VVIPs, had its first flight.

21 February: It was announced that the Beechcraft Model 400T Beechjet had been selected as the new multi-engine trainer to replace the T-38 for transport aircrew training. It was given the Air Force designation T-1A and named Jayhawk.

6 March: A Lockheed SR-71A (64-17972) established four speed records on its final flight. It set a new trans-continental coast-to-coast record of 1hr 8min 7sec across a distance of 2,404 miles, at an average speed of 2,112 mph.

24 April: Delivery of the first of six British Aerospace C-29As (BAe 125-800) was made to the 1467th Facilities Checking Squadron of the Air Force Communications Service at Scott AFB, IL. The arrival of the C-29A allowing AFCS to retire four long-serving C-140A Jetstars and two T-39A Sabreliners.

22 May: Air Force Special Operations Command with headquarters at Hurlburt Field, FL, was activated as part of the unified US Special Operations Command.

1 June: Withdrawn from strategic bombing duties with SAC, the 59 General Dynamics FB-111As were re-assigned to Tactical Air Command. The first were handed over to TAC at

Boeing VC-25A – 'Air Force One'

Cannon AFB, NM and redesignated as F-111Gs.

15 June: 'Global Reach – Global Power' – the White Paper outlining the US administration's post-Cold War strategy was issued.

12 July: The last of 59 Lockheed F-117As was delivered to the 37th Tactical Fighter Wing.

24 July: The final *Looking Glass* continuous airborne alert was made by SAC's airborne command post after 29 years and five months operational service.

July: The last operational sortie was flown from RAF Fairford, Gloucestershire by a KC-135 Stratotanker from the 11th Strategic Group, as part of the European Tanker Task Force.

August: The USAF selected the Alenia (Aeritalia) G222 as its Rapid Response inter-theater airlifter (RRITA). The aircraft was subsequently designated C-27A Spartan. The raw airframe was to be modified by Chrysler to USAF specification with the first aircraft available in 1991.

8 August: Start of Operation *Desert Shield*. The first US combat aircraft to arrive in the Persian Gulf were F-15C Eagles of the 1st TFW, that deployed to Saudi Arabia.

9 August: Alaskan Air Command was deactivated and became the 11th Air Force under the Pacific Air Force (PACAF).

17 August: The US Civil Reserve Air Fleet (CRAF) Stage One was activated for the first time in support of the military build-up in the Gulf. Thirty-nine aircraft, comprising 18 passenger and 21 cargo airliners plus crews were placed under the authority of MAC.

19-20 August: The first Lockheed F-117As were deployed from their home base via Langley AFB, VA to Saudi Arabia.

23 August: The first Boeing VC-25A (82-8000), for use by President Bush under call sign 'Air Force One', was delivered to the 89th Military Airlift Wing at Andrews AFB, MD. It completed its first overseas task on 7 December, flying President Bush to Helsinki, Finland. The second example (82-9000) was delivered on 30 December.

27 August: The Northrop/McDonnell Douglas YF-23A had its maiden flight. It was the first of the two Advanced Tactical Fighter contenders to fly.

Lockheed/General Dynamics/Boeing YF-22A

Northrop/McDonnell Douglas YF-23A

September: General Curtis E LeMay, SAC's Commander-in-Chief during the crucial 1950s, died. He had retired from military service in 1960.

September: The Air Force's 'Aggressor' training units were axed, with four squadrons (Bentwaters, Kadena, Nellis and Tyndall) being disestablished as part of a budget-trimming exercise.

29 September: The first flight was made by the prototype Lockheed/General Dynamics/Boeing YF-22A, the second of the ATF contenders.

14 November: The last C-23A Sherpa departed the European theatre after the type was withdrawn from USAFE service with the 10th Military Airlift Squadron at Zweibrucken AB, Germany.

By mid-January, after five months of building up forces in the Persian Gulf, the US and its Coalition partners were ready for direct confrontation with Iraq. On Thursday 17 January, with the deadline for Saddam Hussein to withdraw his forces from Kuwait having passed two days earlier, Operation *Desert Storm* commenced at 0300hr local time. The first wave of Air Force attacks was made by ten Lockheed F-117As of the 37th TFW, their targets being elements of the enemy air defence system. They were quickly followed up by a further 14 F-117As. A number of important Iraqi command and communications centres, including several in Baghdad itself, were destroyed by precision bombing. Further strike packages, including 4th Wing F-15E Strike Eagles, employing the new LANTIRN pods, and 53 *Pave Tack*-equipped 48th TFW F-111Fs, supported by KC-135 and KC-10 tankers, executed strikes on Iraqi Scud missile launch sites, Iraqi airfields and missile storage facilities. Supporting the waves of attacking aircraft, F-4G *Wild Weasel* Phantoms carrying AGM-88 HARM missiles, were launched to provide a defence suppression capability. Air defence assets, particularly Air Force F-15C Eagles, were kept busy. An F-15C, piloted by Captain Jon 'JB' Kelk of the 33rd TFW, scored the first Coalition 'kill' of the Allied campaign by 'downing' an Iraqi MiG-29 *Fulcrum* at 0310hr on 17 January. USAF Eagles bore the brunt of air-to-air combat throughout the war, claiming some 31 further enemy aircraft destroyed during *Desert Storm*, with the 33rd TFW being at the forefront of this action.

Over the following days, the F-15E Strike Eagles were particularly heavily-involved in the hunt for Iraqi Scud missile sites. Attacks on airfields continued, particularly by F-111s, with special attention being paid to the destruction of hardened aircraft shelters. During the first 11 days of *Desert Storm*, the efforts of Coalition aircraft were concentrated on gaining air superiority over the Iraqi Air Force. With the upper hand in air combat well and truly gained, more sorties deep into Iraqi territory could

Lockheed C-130Hs – Kuwait

then be executed, making particular use of the dual-role F-16 Fighting Falcon force, as the ground war drew nearer. F-111Fs carried out sorties against bridges on important Iraqi supply routes, as well as continuing attacks against airfields. By the end of January, General Schwarzkopf was able to announce that during the first two weeks of Allied operations some 75% of the Iraqi command, control and communications systems had been hit, of which a third was by now inoperable.

While tactical fighters continued their operations deep into Iraq, there had been a concentrated series of strikes by B-52G Stratofortresses against enemy troop concentrations. Regular operations from Diego Garcia in the Indian Ocean and the B-52s' home bases in the USA were augmented from late January and early February by additional deployments to Moron AB, Spain and RAF Fairford, UK. In total, more than 80 B-52Gs were

assigned to offensive missions. While the 'BUFFs' carried out saturation bombing, A-10A Thunderbolt IIs were at the forefront of attacks on Iraqi tanks and artillery, assisted by F-16Cs. This rate of destruction allowed the final planning to be made for the ground offensive, Operation *Desert Spear*, which commenced on 24 February. While B-52s, F-117As and F-111s attacked strategic positions, F-16s and AC-130 Hercules conducted ground support missions as C-130 Hercules of MAC flew 82nd Airborne Division paratroops to the north of Kuwait City, in preparation for the impending liberation of the country. A-10s continued to operate in the tank-killing role, two from the 23rd TFW destroying a record 23 tanks on 25 February alone. Some 100 hours after the ground war had commenced, at 08.00hr local time on 28 February, Saddam Hussein ordered his troops to observe a ceasefire and agreed to comply with the UN resolutions.

The pages for 1991 generously supported by Evans Halshaw

Lockheed F-117A Night Hawk

January: Fairchild Swearingen received a USAF contract to produce a 53 further C-26A Metros for use by ANG units.

11 January: Two pre-production Boeing E-8A J-STARS aircraft were sent to Riyadh, in preparation for possible operations in the Gulf.

17 January: The Department of Defense authorised the activation of Stage 2 of CRAF, under which 116 commercial aircraft were brought in for logistics supply requirements in Operation *Desert Shield.*

17 January: Operation *Desert Storm* began with a strike by Lockheed F-117As on targets in Baghdad and southern Iraq.

17 January: Captain Kelk of the 33rd TFW, flying F-15C Eagle 85-0125 shot down an Iraqi MiG-29 at 0310hr, making the first 'kill' of the conflict.

31 January: The loss of an AC-130H Hercules (69-6567) in combat in the Persian Gulf, with 14 crew killed, was the costliest aircraft casualty of Operation *Desert Storm.*

24 February: The massive Coalition ground offensive against Iraqi forces in Kuwait and southern Iraq got under way in *Desert Storm.* For four days ground support was given by A-10A Thunderbolt IIs and F-16 Fighting Falcons, while B-52G Stratofortresses and F-111s pounded Iraqi troop concentrations.

28 February: President George Bush ordered a complete halt to all Allied military operations in southern Iraq, after 100 hours of ground war against the forces of Saddam Hussein.

6 March: The 4411th Joint STARS Squadron was withdrawn from the Gulf theatre after flying 49 missions using the two pre-production E-8A J-STARS aircraft.

20 March: An F-15C Eagle on patrol over Iraq attacked and shot down an Iraqi Air Force Sukhoi Su-22 *Fitter* over Tikrit. The Su-22 was flying in violation of the ceasefire agreement that prohibited any Iraqi military air activity.

April: A Department of Defense study into cost-saving base closures was made public. Candidates announced for closure included Bergstrom, TX; Carswell, TX; Castle, CA; Eaker, AR; England, LA; Loring, ME; Lowry, CO; Moody, GA: Myrtle Beach, SC; Richards-Gebour, MO; Rickenbacker, OH; Williams, AZ and Wurtsmith, MI.

April: Operation *Provide Comfort*, to protect the Kurds in northern Iraq, was started.

April: The last RF-4C Phantom II was withdrawn from the 26th Tactical Reconnaissance Wing at Zweibrücken AB, thereby ending Air Force dedicated photo reconnaissance capability in Europe. A limited number of F-4G *Wild Weasels* remained with the 52nd Tactical Fighter Wing at Spangdahlem.

22 April: The first composite Wing was activated at Seymour Johnson AFB, NC, where the 4th Wing operated KC-10A Extenders and F-15E Strike Eagles. This spearheaded a planned switch to multi-mission tactical units in place of organisations.

23 April: The Lockheed/General Dynamics/Boeing YF-22A was selected by the Air Force as its Advanced Tactical Fighter.

May: MAC transport aircraft, including C-5 Galaxies and C-130 Hercules, took part in Operation *Productive Effort* in the aftermath of a disastrous cyclone that struck Bangladesh.

1 May: The last Ground Launched Cruise Missile (GLCM) was destroyed under the provisions of INF treaty.

17 May: In line with announced cut-backs in US defence spending, the USAF announced closure of its facilities at RAF Bentwaters and Woodbridge in England.

June: The improved MC-130H Combat Talon II Hercules entered active service with AF Special Operations Command.

1 July: Deactivation of AF Communications Command.

5 July: The first flight took place of the Beech T-1A Jayhawk, the new twin-jet for service with Air Training Command.

10 July: Final flight of a General Dynamics FB-111A was made when 68-0267 was ferried from Plattsburgh AFB, NY to the storage facility at Davis-Monthan AFB.

31 July: The START Treaty was signed by US and USSR.

12 August: The McDonnell Douglas F-15 'Agile Eagle' STOL and manoeuvre technology demonstrator programme ended after three years of tests at Edwards AFB, CA.

16 August: The first of ten Chrysler/Alenia C-27As (90-0171) was delivered. The aircraft served with the 310th Tactical Airlift Squadron at Howard AFB, Panama from 26 September.

1 September: SAC was reorganised from two to four numbered Air Forces and the allocation of units according to type (8th AF – bombers, 15th AF – tankers, 2nd AF – reconnaissance, and 20th AF – missiles).

15 September: The McDonnell Douglas YC-17 (subsequently named Globemaster III) heavy-lift transport aircraft was flown for the first time.

27 September: SAC Ground Alert was 'stood down' after 30 years, following the diminishing threat of a nuclear war.

1 October: Air Force Intelligence Command was established. It absorbed the Electronic Security Command and other Air Force intelligence functions.

22 November: The 'Open Skies' Treaty was signed. This cleared the way for unrestricted overflight of Soviet airspace for the purpose of arms reduction verification.

26 November: The flag was lowered over Clark AB in the Philippines after 90 years. The resident 13th AF (PACAF) HQ was relocated to Andersen AFB, Guam.

December: The Lockheed TR-1 was re-designated U-2R.

Roger Middlebrook's Gulf War painting illustrates the dramatic rescue of downed F-14 Navy pilot Lieutenant Devon Jones from Iraqi territory on 21 January 1991. The Sikorsky MH-53J Enhanced Pave Low III helicopter hovers inches above the desert as crewmen help Lt Jones aboard. This new painting is reproduced by kind permission of the artist.

Desert Rescue by Roger H Middlebrook GAvA

1992

MAC, SAC and TAC disappeared on 1 June when all three were formally disestablished, with assets previously under their control being redistributed between two newly-created command agencies. These were the Air Combat Command (ACC) and Air Mobility Command (AMC), respectively headquartered at Langley AFB, VA and Scott AFB, IL. Headed by General John M Loh, ACC assumed responsibility for the management of tactical resources that had constituted TAC's 'muscle' as well as strategic bomber, missile and reconnaissance elements previously under SAC control. AMC, led by General H T Johnson, acquired the former MAC airlift assets and most, but by no means all, of SAC's huge fleet of KC-135 and KC-10A tankers. Overseas-based commands also gained direct control over former SAC and MAC elements within their areas of responsibility at this time, this being exemplified by the 435th Airlift Wing at Rhein-Main, which now reported to USAFE rather than MAC as had previously

been the case. Overall the number of Air Force personnel was to be reduced from 570,000 to 400,000. Another new organisation created in 1992 was Air Force Materiel Command (AFMC), responsible for the development, acquisition, delivery and operational support of Air Force weapons systems. This resulted in the merger of Air Force Logistics Command and Air Force Systems Command.

A Strategic Arms Reduction Treaty (START) was signed by Presidents Bush and Yeltsin on 17 June, paving the way for further cuts in arsenals of strategic weapons. For the USA, this would bring about the withdrawal of 50 LGM-118A Peacekeeper missiles assigned to the 90th Missile Wing's 400th Missile Squadron at F E Warren AFB, WY as well as 300 LGM-30F Minuteman IIs, split equally between the 44th Missile Wing at Ellsworth AFB, SD (66th, 67th and 68th MSs) and the 351st Missile Wing at Whiteman AFB, MT (508th, 509th and 510th MSs). Removal of these silo-based weapons will culminate in inactivation of both Missile Wings by 1997.

USAFE's longest-serving aircraft departed in January, when the last Boeing EC-135H (61-0286) of the 10th Airborne Command and Control Squadron left its base at RAF Mildenhall for Offutt AFB, NE. Two weeks previously, the squadron's WC-135B (61-2667) had also departed, having been operated as a crew trainer since early 1989. This marked the end of airborne command post operations from Mildenhall, that had commenced in 1965.

The airlift of food and urgently required medical supplies into Somalia began on 28 August when Operation *Provide Relief* was launched from Mombassa, Kenya. This was, in fact, just one of a number of humanitarian aid efforts undertaken by Air Mobility Command in the closing months of 1992 and initially involved a mix of C-130 Hercules and C-141B StarLifter aircraft, although the latter type was withdrawn from the relief effort on 1 September and replaced by extra C-130s hurriedly deployed to the area by the ANG and AFRes. At the beginning of November, the number of C-130Es involved was 14, eight being regular force machines from the 314th Airlift Wing at Little Rock AFB, AR and the remainder from ANG units at Baltimore, Maryland and Minneapolis, Minnesota plus AFRes units at Peterson AFB, CO and Willow Grove NAS, PA. Operations were not without hazard, with aircraft suffering minor damage after being hit by ground fire on at least two occasions at Belet Huen and Baidoa. The subsequent televised landing of Marine Corps troops near Mogadishu in early December in Operation *Restore Hope* was intended to make life easier for humanitarian agencies involved in relief work.

General Dynamics EF-111A Raven

Two of the many variants of the Boeing KC-135 family used by the US Air Force are the much upgraded and re-engined KC-135R tanker (this example is from the 100th ARW at RAF Mildenhall) and the RC-135U, used primarily for electronic intelligence gathering (ELINT) missions. It operates under the 55th SRW at Offutt AFB, Nebraska. Last Chance to Tank up is reproduced here by kind permission of the artist.

The pages for 1992 generously supported by Kodak Eastman Aerial Systems

Last Chance to Tank up by Ronald Wong BSc(Hons), GAvA, GMA, ASAA

Boeing EC-135H

January: It was announced that the entire fleet of Lockheed F-117A 'Stealth' fighters would transfer to Holloman AFB, NM. Realignment of the F-117As will result in the three existing squadrons coming under the control of the 49th Fighter Wing.

January: USAFE activated the 100th Air Refueling Wing at RAF Mildenhall, Suffolk and began preparations to accept the first of nine permanently resident KC-135R Stratotankers destined for service with the European Tanker Task Force (ETTF).

15 January: The 39th Special Operations Wing headquarters moved from Rhein-Main AB, Germany to RAF Alconbury, Cambridgeshire.

17 January: The USAF's first T-1A Jayhawk tanker/transport trainer was handed over to the Air Force at the Beech factory in Wichita.

21 January: Boeing EC-135H airborne command post operations were concluded at RAF Mildenhall, Suffolk, with the departure of the 10th Airborne Command and Control Squadron's last example (61-0286) to Offutt AFB, NE.

21 February: Re-equipment of the 48th Fighter Wing at Lakenheath began when the first of some 50 F-15E Strike Eagles was delivered to the 492nd Fighter Squadron. It marked the start of the Wing's transition from the F-111F.

28 February: President Bush announced during his State of the Union address to Congress that the Northrop B-2A

would not be developed any further after the completion of 20 airframes.

24 March: Withdrawal of USAF forces from Spain continued with the departure of the last F-16C Fighting Falcons assigned to the 401st Fighter Wing from Torrejon AB, transferring with the co-located 16th AF to Aviano AB, Italy.

1 April: The team of Slingsby Aviation and Northrop Worldwide Aircraft Services beat eleven other contenders to be awarded the Air Force contract for a new EFS (Enhanced Flight Screener) aircraft. The Slingsby T67M-260 Firefly was chosen to replace the Cessna T-41 Mescaleros used by Air Training Command.

23 April: A C-130H Hercules on a counter-narcotics mission in Peru was attacked by a Peruvian Air Force Su-22 *Fitter*, resulting in one crewman being killed and four others wounded.

15 May: The 2,000th Lockheed Hercules, a C-130H, was delivered to the Kentucky ANG.

1 June: Substantial restructuring of the USAF was effected. Strategic Air Command (SAC) and Tactical Air Command (TAC) were replaced by a single Air Combat Command. This also assumed responsibility for tactical tankers and transport aircraft previously operated by Military Airlift Strategic Transport Command (MAC). A new Air Mobility Command replaced MAC in the strategic transport support role, and absorbed a number of air-to-air refuelling tanker aircraft previously operated by SAC.

17 June: A Strategic Arms Reduction Treaty (START) was signed by Presidents Bush and Yeltsin, which paved the way for further cuts in the arsenals of strategic weapons.

1 July: The merger of Air Force Logistics Command and Air Force Systems Command into new Air Force Materiel Command was effected.

1 July: Operation *Provide Promise*, the airlift of relief supplies to Bosnia-Herzegovina, commenced. Lasting until 6 January 1996, it was to become the longest-running air supply effort.

10 July: The Upper Heyford-based 42nd Electronic Combat Squadron was formally inactivated, marking the withdrawal of the EF-111A Raven from Europe.

Beechcraft T-1A Jayhawk

10 July: The General Dynamics FB-111 was withdrawn from service with the new Air Combat Command.

24 August: Homestead AFB was all but flattened when Hurricane *Andrew* swept across southern Florida, causing damage and destruction on an unprecedented scale.

27 August: Operation *Southern Watch* was launched. It established an exclusion zone over that part of Iraq lying to the south of the 32nd Parallel.

28 August: The last regular Air Force RF-4C Phantom II reconnaissance squadron – the 12th RS (formerly TRS) 67th RW, was inactivated at Bergstrom AFB, TX.

28 August: Operation *Provide Relief* was initiated from Mombasa, Kenya for the airlift of food and urgently required medical supplies into Somalia. This involved C-130 Hercules and a C-141B StarLifter aircraft of AMC.

1 October: Air Mobility Command established its first Air Mobility Wing, the 97th (AMW) at Altus AFB, OK.

18 December: The 48th Fighter Wing at Lakenheath disposed of its last General Dynamics F-111F (74-0178), which was ferried to Wright-Patterson AFB, OH.

27 December: One of two Iraqi MiG-23s encountered violating the UN 'No-Fly' zone in southern Iraq was shot down by an F-16C Fighting Falcon (90-0778). This was the first air-to-air combat engagement by a USAF F-16 and the first use in combat of the AIM-120 AMRAAM.

1993

Aircraft of the USAF were in action over Iraq early in the year, after Saddam Hussein once again tested the determination of the United Nations. Despite the shooting-down of an Iraqi MiG-23 at the end of the previous year by a USAF F-16C Fighting Falcon patrolling the 'No-Fly' zone, there were numerous incursions across the Kuwait border by Iraqi troops. Saddam Hussein still refused to comply with the UN's order to remove SA-2 and SA-3 missiles from sites south of the 32nd Parallel, within the exclusion zone. On 13 January, USAF F-117A Night Hawks, F-15E Strike Eagles and F-16Cs, together with US Navy, RAF and French Air Force aircraft, carried out air strikes on command and control centres and SAM sites in the 'No-Fly' area. They were supported by EF-111A Ravens and F-4G *Wild Weasel* Phantoms operating in the defence suppression role. Four days later, on 17 January, there were further attacks on targets that had not been completely put out of action, while a 52nd FW F-16C shot down an Iraqi MiG-29 on the same day. This was the last major action over Iraq for the time being.

In Europe the escalation of the crisis in Bosnia-Herzegovina and the onset of winter resulted in the start of Operation *Provide Promise*. This involved, at first, air-dropping vitally needed relief supplies to isolated parts of the former Yugoslav Republic. The tasks were carried out by C-130E Hercules of the 37th ALS from Rhein Main, Germany, augmented by TDY aircraft from the 317th ARW at Pope AFB, NC. MC-130E Hercules of the 7th Special Operations Squadron had flown leaflet-dropping sorties in order to warn local residents in the areas involved of the airdrops, and to attempt to prevent the warring factions from firing on the C-130s. The first 'deliveries' of food were made to the village of Cerska, the drops being carried out at night to lessen the risk to the aircraft from hostile fire. In spite of a lack of accuracy on this initial mission, the drops were continued successfully. C-130s continued to fly daily relief missions to Sarajevo as well.

With a widening commitment to the crisis in Bosnia,

Slingsby T-3A Firefly

Air Force KC-135s on temporary duty with the European Tanker Task Force at Mildenhall were detached to Italy in support of fighter deployments. The 36th FW despatched 12 F-15C Eagles, as part of Operation *Deny Flight*, based at Aviano AB alongside E-3B/C Sentries, which provided AWACS facilities. In July, the F-15s were replaced by F-16Cs of the 52nd FW, while the expansion by NATO of its operations over Bosnia to include close-support missions protecting UN relief convoys saw the arrival of 12 A-10As, also from the 52nd FW. Command and control facilities were provided by Aviano-based EC-130Es of the 7th ACCS, while Brindisi hosted 16th SOS AC-130Hs that flew night support sorties as well as MH-53Js and HC-130s for search-and-rescue and Special Operations duties. By the end of the autumn, fully-armed USAF combat aircraft were constantly operating *Deny Flight* patrols, protecting humanitarian convoys and UN troops.

There was further offensive action involving the USAF

during June, as Operation *Continue Hope* replaced the previous *Restore Hope* in Somalia. The killing of 23 Pakistani UN troops led to the Security Council calling for the use of force in order to bring those responsible to justice. A deployment of AC-130H Hercules made attacks, using their 105-mm Howitzers, on illegal weapons storage sites and the headquarters in Mogadishu of General Mohammed Farah Aidid, starting on 11 June. After further night raids, daylight operations began on 14 June. However, arguments regarding the exact role of the UN in Somalia led to the announcement in mid-July that the four AC-130Hs would be withdrawn.

There were further significant changes in USAFE's inventory, most notably the inactivation in May, after 42 years of service in the UK alone, of the 81st Tactical Fighter Wing. The unit's last two A-10A Thunderbolt IIs had previously departed from RAF Bentwaters for their new home with the 52nd FW at Spangdahlem AB on 23 March.

The pages for 1993 generously supported by Northrop Grumman

13 January: Air Force Major Susan Helms became the first US military woman in space.

17 January: An Iraqi MiG-29 was shot down by a USAF F-16C Fighting Falcon.

5 February: The Air Force announced that the C-17A would take up the name Globemaster III.

19 February: A Beech T-1A Jayhawk completed the first student training flight at the 64th Flying Training Wing's 52nd Flying Training Squadron at Reese AFB, TX.

28 February: Three C-130E Hercules from the 37th Airlift Squadron at Rhein-Main AB, Germany and aircraft detached from the US undertook the first airdrop of relief supplies to isolated areas in Bosnia-Herzegovina.

March: Another long-term resident left from RAF Mildenhall, as the C-130E Hercules Bravo squadron detachment departed for Little Rock AFB, AR.

23 March: Flight operations by the 81st TFW finally came to an end when the last A-10A Thunderbolt IIs to be based at RAF Bentwaters were ferried out to their new base at Spangdahlem AB, Germany.

1 April: The 509th Bomb Wing was re-established at Whiteman AFB, MO as the first unit to operate the B-2A bomber.

12 April: First participation was made by the Air Force in Operation *Deny Flight*, joining NATO air patrols over Bosnia.

28 April: Restrictions were removed on women aircrews' participation in combat. Of the Air Force's 16,000 pilots, only 295 were women.

11 June: Operation *Continue Hope* replaced *Restore Hope* in Somalia, with the deployment of AC-130H Hercules gunships to carry out offensive missions.

14 June: The first C-17A Globemaster III (89-1192 *Spirit of Charleston*) was delivered to an operational unit, the 437th Airlift Wing's 17th Airlift Squadron at Charleston AFB, SC.

14 June: After completing almost 35 years of service in the VVIP transport role, the first Boeing VC-137B (58-6970) was officially retired at Andrews AFB, MD.

30 June: The 55th Wing at Offutt AFB, NE took delivery of the first of three Boeing OC-135Bs (61-2674, previously a WC-135B) to be modified for 'Open Skies' inspection flights over former Eastern Bloc countries.

1 July: The merger of Air Training Command and Air University into Air Education and Training Command took place.

1 July: The 20th Air Force and all ballistic missile units were transferred to Space Command.

1 October: Air Mobility Command transferred its entire C-130 force to the operational control of Air Combat Command.

November: The first Slingsby T-3A Fireflies were handed over to the Air Force.

15 November: The 48th FW at Lakenheath was expanded when the first of 21 F-15C/D Eagles were delivered from Bitburg, for service with the re-formed 493rd FS.

7 December: The last three General Dynamics F-111s to see service with USAFE at RAF Upper Heyford were ferried back to the USA by the 20th Fighter Wing.

17 December: The first Northrop B-2A was delivered to an operational unit, the 509th Bomb Wing's 393rd Bomb Squadron at Whiteman AFB, MO.

McDonnell Douglas KC-10A Extender and Northrop B-2A

The tranquillity of the Highlands and Islands of Scotland is regularly shattered by the roar of military jets on their low-level exercise flights. By 1993 the new F-15E Strike Eagle had replaced the F-111F at RAF Lakenheath. Thunder over the Western Isles, reproduced here by kind permission of Ronald Wong, shows an F-15E of the 494th FS, 48th FW flying over Eilean Donan Castle late on a summer's evening.

Thunder over the Western Isles by Ronald Wong BSc(Hons), GAvA, GMA, ASAA

The largest operation by Air Mobility Command (AMC) during the year was Operation *Support Hope*, which commenced in July. This provided humanitarian relief supplies to the mass of refugees fleeing from the fierce civil war in Rwanda. Much of AMC's fleet was involved, with tanker support being provided for non-stop flights between the USA and Africa. The 'hub' for USAF operations in Central Africa was established at Entebbe Airport in Uganda, with the war-torn airport at Kigali, the Rwandan capital, being kept open by US forces in order to handle the relief flights. Also involved were some C-130 Hercules units of the Air National Guard, providing in-theatre transport, as well as some of the Civil Reserve Air Fleet. In addition, AMC C-5 Galaxies and C-141B StarLifters assisted the UK government with its support, whereby some 35 sorties were flown from RAF Brize Norton during August.

In Bosnia there was also further military action, which, in February included the first ever occasion that a NATO aircraft had shot down another aircraft. A pair of 86th Fighter Wing F-16Cs, operating out of Aviano, destroyed four Serb-operated Super Galeb G4s, using AIM-120A AMRAAMs and AIM-9M Sidewinder missiles. Further USAF combat aircraft were also sent to Italy during February, including F-15E Strike Eagles of the 48th FW from RAF Lakenheath. The first air strike to protect a UN-designated 'safe haven' occurred during April, when two F-16Cs attacked Serbian forces near Gorazde, while later in the year two A-10s (the Thunderbolt II force then being provided by AFRes and ANG units) attacked an anti-tank gun emplacement. Also joining the *Deny Flight* effort were F-16Cs of the 31st FW, by now a permanent resident at Aviano, and employing the Martin Marietta LANTIRN night navigation and attack system.

Operation *Provide Promise*, the air dropping of vitally needed relief supplies in Bosnia-Herzegovina, was expanded in the New Year, with further Air National Guard and Air Force Reserve C-130 Hercules detachments augmenting

Rockwell B-1B Lancer

the 37th Airlift Squadron aircraft flying from Rhein-Main. However, C-141B StarLifters from the 437th AW took over much of the task from May, the type being able to carry three times the payload of a Hercules and thus allowing a reduction of the airlift's intensity.

Major unit and air base changes in 1994 included the gradual reduction, from October onwards, of the 57th Fighter Squadron's F-15C Eagle operations at Keflavik in Iceland, that had come under the command of the 85th Wing during the summer. The 57th FS was scheduled to disband on 1 March 1995, with rotational detachments of F-15s from the USA providing air defence cover for the region. USAF Sikorsky HH-60Gs of the 56th Rescue Squadron were still to be permanently based at Keflavik.

USAFE saw the end of its F-4 Phantom operations during February, when the last four F-4G *Wild Weasels* departed from the 52nd FW at Spangdahlem for service with the 561st FS at Nellis AFB. This was now the Air Force's sole remaining active service unit operating the F-4. The B-52 force was further re-organised after the last B-52G was retired in May from the 93rd Bomb Wing at Castle AFB, leaving just the B-52H in the inventory. With B-52 operations closed down at Fairchild, K I Sawyer and Griffiss AFBs, this left just Minot AFB (5th Bomb Wing) and Barksdale AFB (2nd BW and the Air Force Reserve's 917th Wing) as the only two remaining 'BUFF' bases.

In the conflict in Bosnia, the UN asked NATO to enforce a No-Fly Zone, and Operation Deny Flight *was started, with round-the-clock combat air patrols (CAP) flown by NATO fighters. In Ronald Wong's painting* The Road to Sarajevo *an A-10A Thunderbolt II of the 81st FS, 52nd FW on a CAP releases protective flares while an UNPROFOR convoy snakes through the valley below. It is included here by courtesy of the artist.*

The pages for 1994 generously supported by Certified Aircraft Parts Inc.

The Road to Sarajevo by Ronald Wong BSc(Hons), GAvA, GMA, ASAA

15 January: The last F-15As of the USAF 32nd Fighter Group left Soesterberg, ending 40 years of USAF fighters at this Dutch air base. Departing aircraft were transferred to the ANG's 102nd FW/101st FS at Otis ANG, MA.

21 January: The entire fleet of C-141B StarLifters was grounded following the discovery that repairs intended to redress fatigue cracks in the wing structure may have resulted in the contamination of fuel tanks.

1 February: The first mission to be flown by an Air Force Reserve (AFRes) bomber crew took place from Barksdale AFB, LA when a B-52H of the 93rd Bomb Squadron, 917th Wing completed a successful sortie.

18 February: The last four F-4G *Wild Weasel* Phantoms, assigned to the 81st Fighter Squadron, departed Spangdahlem AB, Germany. The departure of the F-4Gs made room for 18 F-15C/D Eagles, that were transferred to the 53rd FS from Bitburg AB. The Phantoms returned for continued active duty in the US with the 501st FS at Nellis AFB, NV.

25 February: The first T-3A Fireflies were accepted for service with Air Education and Training Command. Instruction began in the 12th FTW at Hondo, TX in March.

28 February: The first air-to-air combat engagement was made by NATO forces when F-16C Fighting Falcons from the 86th Wing serving on a *Deny Flight* duty at Aviano in Italy, shot down three Serb-operated Super Galeb G4 ground attack aircraft and damaged a fourth.

15 April: Bitburg AB, Germany was closed. It had been the base for the 36th FW, whose F-15C Eagles flew their final mission on 11 February. The 22nd FS transferred to RAF Lakenheath and became the 493rd FS with the 48th FW. The 53rd FS was re-assigned to the 52nd FW at Spangdahlem, Germany.

20 April: The ANG accomplished its first B-1B Lancer mission when a crew of the 184th Fighter Group flew a successful sortie from McConnell AFB, KS.

May: Almost four decades after the first Stratofortress entered service with SAC, the 93rd Bomb Wing at Castle AFB, CA, the last B-52G (58-0240) was flown to Davis-Monthan AFB, AZ.

General Dynamics F-16C Fighting Falcon

21 June: Following the transfer of the resident F-16C Fighting Falcons to Aviano, the 512th Fighter Squadron was formally inactivated, marking the end of fighter operations by units permanently resident at Ramstein AB, Germany.

24 June: After years of being known by various appellations such as the *Black Jet*, *Wobblin' Goblin* and *Senior Trend*, Lockheed's F-117A 'Stealth' fighter was officially named Night Hawk.

1 July: Air Force Special Operations Command took delivery of the first of 13 new AC-130U *Spectre* Hercules gunships. It was assigned to the 16th SOW at Hurlburt Field, FL.

23 July-25 August: Operation *Support Hope*, the airlift of relief supplies to the victims of the civil war in Rwanda was started.

August: F-16C Fighting Falcons successfully launched 12 anti-radar AGM-88 High-speed Anti-radiation missiles in an air-to-ground weapon system evaluation programme conducted at the Utah Test and Training Range.

September: Operation *Uphold Democracy* – action to oust the military junta in Haiti. US air power support was limited to just a few Special Operations Command elements, although

F-15C Eagles were deployed to Puerto Rico for a few days to provide top cover, should it have become necessary.

October: The Pentagon announced plans to station an Air Force squadron of A-10A Thunderbolt IIs permanently in Kuwait.

10 October: Operation *Vigilant Warrior*, a response to Iraqi troop movements south towards Kuwait, prompted the re-deployment of F-15E Strike Eagles, F-16 Fighting Falcons and A-10A Thunderbolt IIs.

28 October: The first re-engined examples of the Lockheed U-2R, re-designated U-2S, were handed back to the USAF at Palmdale, CA.

December: The 419th Fighter Wing from Hill AFB, UT deployed to Incirlik AB, Turkey as part of Operation *Provide Comfort II*, supplying F-16 Fighting Falcons to patrol the northern Iraq security zone and protect Kurdish towns from Iraqi aggression.

22 December: The first of three SR-71 Blackbirds to be restored for Air Force service was flown again from the NASA facility at Edwards AFB.

After many delays, and some four years after the issue of the operational requirements documents, the announcement finally came in June that the Raytheon Beech/Pilatus MkII (a derivative of the proven Pilatus PC-9 turboprop trainer) had been selected to meet the USAF/US Navy's Joint Primary Aircraft Training System (JPATS) requirement. The programme had originally been instituted solely to replace the Cessna T-37B in USAF service, but in 1989 it became a joint-Service requirement to find a successor to the Navy's Beech T-34C as well. This followed the recommendation that the Air Force and Navy should adopt the same primary trainer. Pilatus had entered the 'contest' on 1 May 1990, teaming up with Beech to provide two PC-9s for the American company to develop into JPATS prototypes. The JPATS contract is expected to finally be worth $7 billion, with 711 aircraft to be delivered (372 as USAF T-37 replacements, and 339 to supersede the Navy's T-34s).

The situation in Bosnia worsened during August, when a Bosnian Serb mortar attack on a market in Sarajevo killed 38 civilians. In response to this, air strikes were launched two days later on Serb military targets in the country in Operation *Deliberate Force*. Much of the USAF's contribution to the strike packages came from the 7490th Composite Wing at Aviano, comprising 48th FW F-15E Strike Eagles and F-16C Fighting Falcons of the 31st FW. Between the two types, 450 sorties were flown and some 400 laser-guided bombs dropped with a very high success rate. Many missions employed the LANTIRN system to acquire targets at night, this being the first use of these pods for many Aviano F-16 crews. Suppression of enemy air defences was provided by EF-111A Ravens of the 429th Electronic Combat Squadron, which jammed Serb radars prior to attacks on them by F-16Cs of the 52nd FW, using AGM-88 HARMs. Alongside the Ravens, more than 40 long-range communications jamming missions were flown by EC-130H *Compass Call* Hercules.

Close-air support to UN troops came from A-10As of

Lockheed TR-1B

the 131st FS, which flew more than 180 sorties, often themselves backed-up by the four EC-130E Hercules from the 42nd ACCS, operating as Airborne Battlefield Command and Control Centre (ABCCC) aircraft. This provided the links between the attacking NATO fighter-bombers, forward air controllers and UN Rapid Reaction Corps artillery commanders. Air-to-air refuelling support for *Deliberate Force* strike sorties came primarily from KC-10A Extenders of the 60th Air Mobility Wing detached to Genoa as well as KC-135Rs of the 91st and 99th Air Refueling Squadrons, at Pisa and Istres. These deployments allowed up to ten tankers to be constantly airborne. Also committed to this NATO operation were aircraft of the 9th RW's U-2S detachment at RAF Fairford, that daily photographed enemy installations. Electronic intelligence was gathered by the RC-135s of the 45th RS (55th wing detachment) at RAF Mildenhall.

Special Forces aircraft deployed during *Deliberate Force* included AC-130H Hercules of the 16th SOS, which were in action almost nightly around Sarajevo providing close air support and attack missions. A-10s, the *Spectres* and MH-53Js of the 21st SOS were also very active. Within a week, the heavy NATO air offensive had forced the Serbs to give in to NATO's demands and they withdrew heavy weapons from around Sarajevo. This allowed re-opening land supply routes into the Bosnian capital and, on 15 September, the airport. Operation *Provide Promise* recommenced a day later, with C-130Es of the 37th AS carrying out daily operations from Ancona in Italy. On 20 December, it was announced that the UN had handed over responsibility for peacekeeping in Bosnia to NATO's Implementation Force (IFOR). However, the USAF maintained a major commitment to the efforts to bring an end to the long-running conflict in the region.

The pages for 1995 generously supported by the McDonnell Douglas Corporation

January: As part of the Mission *Hope for the World*, an Air Force Reserve C-130 Hercules, from the 94th Airlift Wing, Dobbins ARB, GA, became the first US aircraft to fly into Albania, to deliver supplies to orphanages in Tirana.

17 January: The C-17A Globemaster III attained Initial Operational Capability with the 437th Airlift Wing's 17th Airlift Squadron at Charleston AFB, SC.

25 January: Flight restrictions on the C-141B StarLifter were lifted following completion of a 12-month project to repair cracks discovered in the lower wing panels.

3 February: Air Force Lieutenant Colonel Eileen Collins, at the helm of *Discovery*, became the first woman to pilot a space shuttle.

14 March: First flight of an EF-111A Raven upgraded by the System Improvement Programme (the first major upgrade for EF-111As since delivery in 1981) took place at Eglin AFB, FL.

15 March: Three Lockheed U-2Rs, with the 9th Reconnaissance Wing's Operating Location – United Kingdom (OL-UK) were transferred from RAF Alconbury to RAF Fairford.

29 March: Operation *Provide Promise* marked its 1,000th day, becoming the longest sustained humanitarian airlift in history – surpassing the length of the Berlin Airlift.

May: The Air Force ordered 50 tilt-rotor CV-22 Ospreys for Air Force Special Operations Command.

2 June: F-16C Fighting Falcon (89-2035) of the 555th FS, 31st FW from Aviano was shot down by Bosnian Serb ground troops. After six days evading capture the pilot was picked up by a Marine Corps Sikorsky CH-53E.

22 June: It was revealed that the successful candidate for the Joint Primary Aircraft Training System (JPATS) order was the Raytheon Beech/Pilatus MkII – a variant of the Swiss designed Pilatus PC-9.

28 June: Lockheed SR-71A NASA 832 (64-17971) was ferried from Edwards AFB to Palmdale for servicing by Lockheed Martin. This was the first step in readying the Blackbird for a return to operational service with the 9th Reconnaissance Wing.

18 July: The first 'Global Power' mission was flown by an Air Force Reserve B-52H Stratofortress crew, from the 93rd Bomb Squadron at Barksdale AFB, LA.

August: After 22 years of flying fighters, the 116th FW at Robins AFB, GA bade farewell to its F-15 Eagles and converted to the B-1B Lancer, becoming the 116th Bomb Wing.

10 August: The last Minuteman II missile was removed from its silo.

30 August: Under Operation *Deliberate Force*, attacks were made on Serb military targets in Bosnia, continuing until 14 September.

22 September: Seventeen years old Eagle 77-0156, the last active F-15B, left Tyndall AFB, FL for its final flight to Sheppard AFB, TX where it became a permanent maintenance trainer for new crew chiefs.

27 September: The last RF-4C Phantom II was retired from the 152nd Reconnaissance Group, Nevada ANG. This marked the end of dedicated tactical recce operations by the USAF.

3 November: The Pentagon approved a further contract for 80 C-17A Globemaster IIIs.

December: The 347th Transportation Squadron's Air Delivery Flight at Moody AFB, GA became the first Air Combat Command flight to air-drop loads from a C-5 Galaxy.

5 December: The 4th Space Launch Squadron at Vandenberg AFB, CA successfully completed its first Titan IV launch for more than two years.

Bell/Boeing V-22A Osprey

After a difficult development period, the McDonnell Douglas C-17 Globemaster III was quickly established in service with the 437th Airlift Wing at Charleston AFB, SC. Robert Smith's painting shows the first aircraft, appropriately named The Spirit of Charleston, *in a majestic setting. The painting is from the Air Force Collection.*

C-17 'The Spirit of Charleston' by Robert G Smith ASAA

Operation *Provide Promise* was officially concluded on 4 January, the last relief flights arriving at Sarajevo five days later. During more than three years, a total of 21 nations involved flew almost 13,000 sorties and airlifted some 160,000 metric tons of food, medicine and other vital supplies to Bosnia-Herzegovina. Not surprisingly, the USAF made a major contribution, being responsible for a total of 4,597 sorties. Approximately 90% of the US effort was provided by USAFE's 37th Airlift Squadron and this unit's C-130E Hercules were in action again on the final day of the airlift. Operation *Joint Endeavour* had been implemented during the winter months and required an enormous airlift effort to move NATO's Implementation Force (IFOR) into the Balkans. The newly-delivered C-17A Globemaster IIIs of the 437th AW became involved, the first major operational use of the new transport. The missions, transporting US military vehicles and palletised cargoes, were mounted from Rhein-Main, flying into Tuzla airport in the former Yugoslavia and Taszar in Hungary – the main 'hub' for *Joint Endeavour* operations. The contribution by C-17s concluded in February, and was declared a great success.

Operational flying in the Persian Gulf area intensified during the year, which was the fifth for Operation *Provide Comfort*. The 366th Wing took over these missions during July, basing its aircraft at Incirlik. F-16Cs of the 389th

Boeing RC-135V

Convair QF-106 Delta Dart drone

Fighter Squadron led the rotation and relieved the 23rd FS from Spangdahlem. Over the next week, they were joined by F-15Cs of the 390th FS and F-15Es of the 391st FS, which respectively replaced the similarly-equipped 493rd and 492nd FSs, allowing the latter units to return home to RAF Lakenheath. By September, Iraqi actions against the Kurds had grown, leading to Operation *Desert Strike*. Two B-52H Stratofortresses of the 2nd Bomb Wing joined Navy warships in launching a cruise missile attack on targets in Iraq. Flying from Andersen AFB, Guam, the B-52s launched 13 AGM-86C Conventional Air-Launched Cruise Missiles (CALCMs) against air defence sites including radars. The 4 September offensive move coincided with an extension of the southern 'No-Fly' zone from the 32nd to the 33rd Parallel. Subsequent to that, the USA also deployed additional forces to the region, with eight F-117A Nighthawks flying direct from Holloman AFB, NM to Kuwait, while a small number of B-52s moved from Andersen to Diego Garcia. In the event, they were not required for offensive operations.

1996 also marked the end of an era for the USAF, when its last F-4G *Wild Weasel* Phantoms were formally retired on 26 March by the 561st Fighter Squadron at Nellis AFB. Eight F-4Gs took part in farewell ceremonies to commemorate the Phantom's 33-year career with the USAF. Little more than three weeks later, the last Air National Guard examples were also retired, when the 190th FS, Idaho ANG at Boise Municipal Airport formally ceased F-4G operations on 18 April. Although no longer a front-line type, the Phantom is set to continue operating in USAF markings for a few more years yet, as QF-4E/G unmanned drone target models are due to progressively replace the QF-106 Delta Dart for live missile-firing exercises and trials. In addition, the 20th FS at Holloman AFB, New Mexico carried on using about 20 examples of the F-4E. These machines were assigned to the 1st German Air Force Training Squadron and scheduled to be replaced by 24 F-4Fs early in 1997.

Steven Moore says of his painting The Dawning *that it "portrays two Lockheed YF-22As slicing through the early morning air of the Mojave Desert, a compelling display of the dawn of American airpower for the 21st Century". It is reproduced by kind permission of the artist and Lockheed Martin Aeronautical Systems.*

The pages for 1996 generously supported by Lockheed Martin Aeronautical Systems

The Dawning by Steven Moore

January: Delivery of the 113th and last Slingsby T-3A Firefly was made to Hondo, Texas, completing procurement of the USAF's flight screening aircraft.

4 January: Operation *Provide Promise* officially ended, although it was not until 9 January that the final humanitarian missions were flown to Sarajevo.

4 January: Lockheed U-2S operations at RAF Fairford ended with the departure of the final two aircraft to Istres-le Tube in France.

10 January: Three decades after completing its first operational tasks, the F-4 Phantom II recorded its final combat-coded sortie when F-4Gs of the 561st Fighter Squadron flew a *Southern Watch* mission from King Abdul Aziz AB, Saudi Arabia. A few days later, they returned to Nellis AFB, NV.

29 January: The 93rd Air Control Wing, assigned to Air Combat Command was formally activated at Robins AFB, GA. At the time it had no aircraft, although it will eventually operate a 20-strong E-8C J-STARS fleet.

February: The Pentagon announced that it would cut some 5,300 Air Force Reserve positions in 1996, a 6% reduction from 1995 levels.

15 March: The Air Force Reserve's 513th Air Control Wing was activated at Tinker AFB, OK, becoming the first AFRes unit to operate the E-3 Sentry.

22 March: Northrop Grumman delivered the first production E-8C J-STARS (92-3289).

26 March: The last front-line F-4 Phantoms in active service with the Air Force, F-4G *Wild Weasels*, were formally retired by the 561st Fighter Squadron at Nellis AFB, NV.

April: Funding was approved to re-engine the Boeing RC-135 fleet operated by the 55th Wing at Offutt AFB, NE with improved CFM 56 turbofans.

6 April: Aircraft from USAFE and Special Operations Command played a key role in the evacuation of 2,100 US citizens and other civilians from Liberia under Operation *Assured Response*. It followed an increase in fighting between various factions intent on seizing control of the country.

24 April: An F-15 Eagle of the ACTIVE programme,

equipped with thrust-vectoring engine nozzles, made its first supersonic 'yaw-vectored flight'.

30 April: *Tacit Blue*, the forerunner of today's stealth technology, was revealed when the aircraft was handed over to the Air Force Museum. Only sparse details were released of the then Northrop Corporation's $165m programme between 1978 and 1985.

May: The ANG fleet of C-26A Metros was declared surplus to requirements and transferred to the US Army.

5 May: Reserve Colonel Betty L. Mullis became the first woman appointed to command a USAF flying wing organisation when she took command of the 940th Air Refueling Wing, AFRes at McClellan AFB, CA.

4 June: The first flight of the USAF's Lockheed Martin C-130J (94-3026) took place at Marietta, GA. This was the second example of the new generation Hercules to fly, having been preceded by the RAF's longer C-130J-30 in April.

8 July: It was revealed that the conventional warfare capability of the B-2A Spirit had taken a big step forward following delivery of the first 17 of an eventual total of 128 Global Positioning System-Aided Munitions (GAMs).

17 July: The first USAF F-16 Fighting Falcon launch of the AGM-154 was successfully completed at Eglin AFB, FL.

27 July: The USAF's last four General Dynamics F-111Fs returned to the Fort Worth, TX, factory where they had been built more than 25 years ago and were officially named 'Aardvark' – the F-111's long-standing nickname.

31 July: USAF deactivated the 17th Air Force at Sembach, Germany leaving only two Europe-based numbered air forces – the 16th (HQ, Aviano) and 3rd (HQ, Mildenhall).

3 September: Operation *Desert Strike* – a cruise missile attack on targets in Iraq – followed action by Saddam Hussein's troops against the Kurds. Two B-52H Stratofortresses of the 2nd Bomb Wing were involved, flying from Andersen AFB, Guam.

4 September: An F-16C Fighting Falcon fired an AGM-88C HARM at an Iraqi SA-8 'Gecko' mobile surface-to-air missile system. Two further HARMs were launched from F-16s on 2 and 4 November against Iraqi radar sites.

McDonnell Douglas C-17A Globemaster III

October: After 15 years in storage, both YC-15As (70-1875 and 70-1876) were returned to service by McDonnell Douglas to act as technology test-beds for the development of future cargo aircraft.

12 November: The Air Force awarded a $1.1 billion contract to Boeing, teamed with Lockheed Martin and TRW, to produce a prototype Airborne Laser (ABL) attack aircraft, designated YAL-1A. The ABL system will be installed in a Boeing 747-400F.

16 November: Development of new equipment for the USAF of the 21st century came a step nearer with the Joint Strike Fighter project decision. One of the three contenders, that by McDonnell Douglas was eliminated leaving submissions from Boeing and from Lockheed Martin to go on to the fly-off stage. Boeing announced that it was taking over McDonnell Douglas in a $13.3 billion deal a month later.

This specially commissioned painting by Wilfred Hardy shows the 'New Breed' of Hercules, the C-130J, that is in production 40 years after the first C-130 first flew. As the title suggests, the 'J' is in fact a very different aircraft, having been upgraded in many ways. The first Hercules II to fly in 1996 was a C-130J-30 for the RAF, closely followed by this standard length version for the USAF.

New Breed by Wilfred Hardy GAvA

The United States Air Force Museum, which is internationally recognised as the world's oldest and largest military aviation museum, is appropriately located at Wright-Patterson Air Force Base, near where the Wright brothers developed the first aeroplane and went on to perfect their flying skills, at Dayton, Ohio.

The Air Force Museum story is a progressive one, starting with the early history of flight and continuing through to the present. Man's first recorded thoughts about flight include Leonardo da Vinci's experiments with helicopters, the use of kites and gliders, ballooning and then to dirigibles - all are displayed for visitors as they first enter the museum. They are soon introduced to the work of the Wright brothers and continue with the early flying machines of World War 1, the exciting record breaking flights of the 1920s and 1930s, leading to the action of World War 2, Korea, followed by Vietnam and then on into the space age and beyond.

As an American national museum of aviation history it does not glorify war or dwell on the destructive aspects of combat but seeks to illustrate, through historic aircraft and authentic displays, the development of aviation and airpower as embodied in the United States Air Force. The museum demonstrates how military aviation has brought major advancements to civil aviation with the knowledge gained from World War 2 playing an important role in developing civil aviation for the next two decades. This same principle was true in later years when, for example, the Boeing 707 jet transport, the backbone of the commercial airline fleets, was developed alongside the Air Force's KC-135 tanker.

The story told in the displays is not static, rather it is one which is constantly changing as exhibits are added to or enlarged, both indoors and out. Of the 46,000 items in the museum's collection over 6,000 are currently on view to the public. Historic aircraft comprise the major displays, however they also include such things as clothing and diaries of flying aces, prisoner of war exhibits, the story of Stumpy the homing pigeon, a German V-1 flying bomb, all side by side with American military chapel displays and the actual capsules from early space exploration. It is not just American aircraft displayed here but also significant examples from Germany, Great Britain, Japan and the Soviet Union. The museum is a paradise for the aviation enthusiast or the photographer of any age, but more importantly it is a place of interest for everyone. This is attested to by the attendance figures of about one million visitors annually.

In addition to the aircraft and other equipment, famous people in world aviation history are depicted at the Air Force Museum. The visitor can find displays honouring such people as Octave Chanute, who built gliders as a first step towards a powered flying machine. The famous Captain Eddie Rickenbacker, the top American World War 1 ace and all the other Air Force recipients of the Medal of Honor. Somewhat unexpected perhaps, is the exhibit honouring musician Glenn Miller who, as a Major, commanded the famous Army Air Forces Band during World War 2. Significantly the Glenn Miller Band was acclaimed as 'the greatest morale builder' in Europe, second only to a letter from home. The Air Force Museum tells the Glenn Miller story in a simple display which includes his original trombone (also used by actor James Stewart in the Glenn Miller film), his 'fifty mission crush' hat, spectacles and music case.

From meagre beginnings in 1923 located in a corner of a hangar, the Air Force Museum has expanded into a $25 million facility on a 400 acre site, that was started in 1970/71 and enlarged in 1975/76, added to in 1985/87 and again in 1989/91. The site lies in the north-west portion of the old Wright Field between a runway and a taxiway and within three miles of Huffman prairie where the Wright brothers developed the art of controlled flight in 1904 and 1905. It was here that they established a flying school and trained many of America's pioneer pilots. Today this area is a portion of Patterson Field which, together with Wright Field, comprises Wright-Patterson Air Force Base. Wright Field is no less historic in its own way and since its dedication in 1927 it has been known as an Air Force centre for research and development. In the two decades before World War 2 numerous aircraft were tested and made ready for Air Force acceptance at this site.

Established in 1923, the first museum was located in Dayton at McCook Field, the Aeronautical Engineering Center. The museum's mission called for the collection of technical intelligence related to American and foreign aircraft and equipment used in previous wars. It was moved to Wright Field in 1927 and occupied 1500 sq ft in a laboratory building. Then in 1935 the museum acquired its first real home, a $235,000 building provided by a federal works project. With a collection of about two thousand items, the new museum at Wright Field was opened to the public in 1936.

With the advent of World War 2, Wright Field was closed to the public and the museum building converted to wartime office use, all museum property went into storage and remained there until long after the war. After the Allied victory over Germany and Japan an engine overhaul building at Patterson Field was designated as the museum's new home. In 1946 the curator Mark Sloan, who retired in 1972, began the search for items both for the Air Force Museum and the Smithsonian Institute. After eight years of acquiring and preparing items for display the Air Force Museum was opened in 1954 at this, its fourth location.

However, the 1954-1971 museum was from the beginning only a temporary home. It was neither fireproof nor air conditioned and it had supporting posts every 16ft in one direction and every 50ft in the other. This made it unsuitable for the proper display and protection of the museum's growing and priceless collection. By the early 1960s the building itself was outgrown and there was little expansion room in the outdoor aircraft display area.

The start of the 1960s saw a group of private citizens under the leadership of Dayton philanthropist Eugene W

Kettering, establish the Air Force Museum Foundation as a non-profit and tax exempt organisation. He brought together individuals from industry, government, education and philanthropic organisations to form a board of directors for the museum foundation. Their objectives were to 'foster and perpetuate the ideal of the Air Force Museum by serving as a philanthropic corporation within which the development and expansion of the museum facilities could take place and would function by receiving, holding and administering gifts from persons, organisations, foundations and philanthropies'.

In 1964 they launched a drive for funds that eventually netted $6 million, largely from Kettering himself, members of his family and from local and national business and industry. Further funds from private citizens and from officers and airmen of the USAF, including those on active duty, reservists, guardsmen and veterans was also forthcoming. Construction of the new museum started in April 1970, the museum was opened to the public in August 1971 and was dedicated by President Nixon the following month. Unfortunately Kettering did not live to see his project completed, he died in 1969. This permanent museum structure is 766ft long and follows the design of two aviation hangars joined by a 'core' administrative section which has a wing like roof.

Each of the hangars, or galleries, has an arched roof that reaches 80ft above the ground and with an interior width of 240ft is exactly twice the distance first flown by Orville Wright on 17 December 1903. This provides more than 230,000 sq ft of space within the structure including a total of 160,000 sq ft of uninterrupted aircraft display space.

Approximately 100 aircraft and missiles are featured inside this 1970 structure. Early aviation history, the Wright aircraft, those flown up to World War 2 and associated memorabilia are displayed in the smaller of the two galleries, now known as the Early Years Gallery. Aircraft, weapons and space vehicles, together with memorabilia of the corresponding period are exhibited in the larger Air Power Gallery. More than 40 aircraft and missiles initially were displayed outdoors but in 1977, to prevent further deterioration, they were moved temporarily across the field to two old hangars – now designated the Museum Annexe. The Convair B-36 Peacemaker bomber was the first aircraft placed in the new quarters but with a wingspan of 230ft had to be moved into position before the museum was completed.

During 1975/76 a two-storey addition was constructed in front of the core building at a cost of slightly more than $900,000, received jointly from the Air Force Museum Foundation for the Air Force and a contribution from the estate of Brig Gen Erik K Nelson, who died in 1970. This was particularly appropriate as in 1924 he had participated in the first flight around the world. This addition contains a reception area on the ground floor, offices on the mezzanine floor and an enlarged restaurant on the top level whilst also affording a view of the outdoor missile park.

Ground was broken in October 1985 for another addition, the Modern Flight Gallery which was completed by December 1987 and officially opened in April 1988. A hangar-like structure measuring 800ft by 200ft, it is located behind and parallel to the main museum building. Half of the $10.8 million cost was voted by the Congress with the remainder being raised by public donation through the foundation. With the Annexe, 10.5 acres of exhibits were under cover making the US Air Force Museum the largest in the world.

A very different addition was completed and dedicated in May 1991 – a giant wide screen theater. Work on this 500 seat IMAX Theater began shortly after the contract was awarded in October 1989. The $8 million project also includes an 80ft high dome glass atrium over a new lobby which serves as the architectural focal point of the entire museum complex.

Although the museum is operated and maintained by the Air Force, the private Air Force Museum Foundation continues its support. Through its office at the museum the foundation raises funds and generally assists wherever and whenever, including operating the museum gift shop, the IMAX Theater and contracts for the operation of the restaurant. In January 1978 the foundation initiated a membership scheme called 'Friends of the United States Air Force Museum' to draw together aviation enthusiasts who are interested in the activities of the museum and in furthering its aims.

One of the objectives of the official museum of the Air Force is to serve as an educational tool for teaching young people about aviation. In 1971 Secretary Seamans perhaps best summarised the goal of the museum in these words: "The new Air Force Museum will serve as a tribute to all Americans who have contributed so much to the field of aviation. It will also serve as an inspiration to future generations of Americans to increase their knowledge and awareness of the United States Air Force and the history of flight".

Now 25 years later, the world's biggest and oldest military aviation museum has outgrown its splendid purpose built accommodation. The aircraft annexe display, housing about 30 aircraft on the old Wright Field flight line, is now full, as is the storage and restoration unit alongside. The Air Force Museum Foundation is actively working with the Museum to develop the Museum 2020 Plan. This aims to have three additional new, parallel buildings to the main complex, two for exhibits and one for aircraft restoration work, together with an outdoor arena for 3,000 people, expansion of the Memorial Park and a new restaurant, all to be completed by 2020.

The Air Force Museum is open to the public seven days a week from 9.00am to 5.00pm and is closed only on Thanksgiving, Christmas and New Years Days. There are no parking or admission charges. For current information telephone (937) 255-3286 or write to the US Air Force Museum, Wright-Patterson AFB, Ohio 45433-6518.

Nick Apple and Gene Gurney

ACKNOWLEDGEMENTS

PHOTOGRAPHS

The Royal Air Force Benevolent Fund is grateful to the following for the use of their photographs, as detailed:

Andrew March on pages 122, 138
Bob Archer on page 52
Daniel March on pages 140, 150
David Menard Collection on pages 14, 22, 28, 34, 36, 40, 46, 54, 119
Don Spering on page 96
Graham Finch on pages 109, 110(2), 132
John Dunnell on pages 118, 157(2), 160
Larry Davis Collection on pages 19, 20, 22, 25(2), 28, 31, 37, 40, 46, 55, 60, 62, 64, 67, 74, 78, 82, 86
Lockheed Martin Aeronautical Systems on pages 102, 140
Lockheed Martin Skunk Works on pages 13, 31, 37, 92, 100, 121

McDonnell Douglas Corporation on page 115
Northrop on page 144
Peter R March on pages 90, 96, 112, 116, 121, 130, 140, 146, 150
PRM Aviation Collection on pages 34, 36, 52, 55, 61, 64, 68, 79, 84, 85, 92, 98, 103, 127, 151, 158, 160
Richard L Ward on pages 43, 80
Tim Ripley on page 156
United States Air Force Museum on pages 30, 126

The remaining photographs are from the United States Air Force via the National Air and Space Museum, the National Archives and the 11th Communications Squadron, courtesy of Maj A Bahler, USAF.

THE CONTRIBUTING ARTISTS

The Royal Air Force Benevolent Fund is grateful to the artists, copyright owners or their estates, together with the USAF Art Collection, for being permitted to reproduce the paintings that so uniquely illustrate the 50 years of the United States Air Force.

George Akimoto: 1968 *RF-4C at Udorn, Thailand*
Charles J Carroll Jnr: 1972 *Landing at Thule*
Anthony RG Cowland GAvA: 1950 *Bolt from the Blue*
Robert E Cunningham ASAA: 1949 *The High and Mighty;* 1952 *Gabby Scores Again;* 1969 *Firefly;* 1973 *Night All-Weather;* 1984 *The Crossover Break*
Lou Drendel: 1987 *Low Level Bomb Run*
Keith Ferris ASAA: 1910 *Gallant Beginning*
Henry Godines ASAA: 1947 *Fueling the Orange Beast*
George Guzzi: 1983 *OV-10A Broncos at Patrick AFB*
Rita Guzzi: 1945 *General Henry 'Hap' Arnold*
Wilfred Hardy GAvA: Cover *Fifty Years Have Flown;* 1960 *The Edge of Space;* 1976 *Black Magic;* 1997 *New Breed*
Chuck Hodgson: 1951 *Lockheed F-80 Shooting Star;* 1959 *Lockheed F-104 Starfighter*
Ralph Iligan: 1958 *Launching an Atlas ICBM*
Craig Kodera: 1988 *Darkness Visible*
Richard Kramer: 1974 *C-5 Galaxy at Dover AFB*
Otto Kuhni: 1962 *Lockheed U-2C*
Mike Machat: 1989 *McDonnell Douglas KC-10 & F-15E*
Robert T McCall ASAA: 1955 *DEW Line Helicopters at Goose Bay;* 1964 *C-133 Transport Mission*

Harold McCormick: 1977 *Talon*
Roger Middlebrook: 1991 *Desert Rescue*
Steven Moore: 1996 *The Dawning*
William S Phillips ASAA: 1966 *Survivor on Board, Heading Home;* 1970 *The Song Begins*
Hugh Polder: 1953 *Mission Inn*
Walter D Richards: 1965 *Cessna 0-1 Bird Dog*
Robert G Smith ASAA: 1948 *Berlin Airlift;* 1995 *C-17 The Spirit of Charleston*
Charles J Thompson GAvA, ASAA, GMA: 1957 *A Real Honey*
Michael Turner: 1979 *Eagles Prey*
Mark Waki: 1981 *McDonnell Douglas F-4G Wild Weasel Phantom*
Andrew Whyte ASAA: 1975 *F-106 New Jersey Air National Guard;* 1980 *On-Spot Delivery*
Ronald Wong BSc(Hons), GAvA, GMA, ASAA: 1963 *Jungle Jim Goes to War;* 1978 *Aeromedic Airlift;* 1982 *Friendly Flight;* 1985 *Soldiering On;* 1986 *First Blood for the Spark Vark;* 1990 *All quiet over the Mojave;* 1992 *Last Chance to Tank Up;* 1993 *Thunder over the Western Isles;* 1994 *The Road to Sarajevo*
Keith Woodcock GAvA: 1967 *Martin B-57B on Interdiction Mission*
Jack Young: 1954 *Northrop F-89D Scorpion*
John Young GAvA, VP ASAA: 1956 *Cold War Warriors;* 1961 *Soon Distant Thunder;* 1971 *Top-up*

ACKNOWLEDGEMENTS

THE AMERICAN SOCIETY OF AVIATION ARTISTS

Founded in 1986 by five renowned American aviation artists – Keith Ferris, Jo Kotula, Robert McCall, Robert G Smith, and Ren Wicks – the ASAA has grown in ten years from a charter membership of 25, to include today 160 Artists and Artist Fellows and 150 Associate members. Artists and Fellows are juried into ASAA by a review panel consisting of the Founding members and other top Artist Fellows. Artist Fellows are those who make significant portions of their income from aviation/aerospace art and have achieved wide public recognition for the high calibre of their work. Many Associates are artists themselves, while others are gallery owners, museum curators, or collectors of aviation art. We are proud to count among our membership a number of artists from other countries, including Canada, Great Britain, Pakistan, Switzerland, South Africa, and Australia.

The ASAA has chosen as its primary objective the raising of standards of aviation art and the promotion of aviation art as a major means of preserving aviation/aerospace history. Our efforts include publication of a quarterly newsletter and other educational documents, an annual Aviation Art Forum, regional meetings, and an annual juried exhibition at a major museum or other appropriate venue, usually in conjunction with our Annual Forum. ASAA also helps in soliciting works for other exhibitions and for publications. The members have one book of ASAA art in print – Aviation, a History Through Art – and are working towards another book representing the Society's best art. A scholarship program helps finance participation of young artists in mentoring programs and in our forums.

Works by ASAA members appear in many museums, corporate offices, military installations, and private collections throughout the world. ASAA members frequently win top honors in aviation art contests sponsored by various corporations.

Enquiries about ASAA may be made to:
Luther Y. Gore, Executive Secretary, ASAA, 1805 Meadowbrook Hts Rd., Charlottesville, VA 22901, USA. Telephone: USA (804) 296 9771.

THE GUILD OF AVIATION ARTISTS

The Guild of Aviation Artists, which was founded in 1971, incorporates The Society of Aviation Artists, which had held its first exhibition in 1954 at London's Guildhall, but by 1958 a number of professional members had become somewhat disenchanted with the new society and turned their attention to a small social club catering for light flying and gliding enthusiasts, called the Kronfeld Club, who were keen to put on an exhibition of aviation art at their Victoria premises. So it was that top professionals like Wootton, Turner and Young hung their work alongside artists who actually flew the aeroplanes.

It is the same today and from these small beginnings the Guild now has over 200 members and a like number of 'friends' who are also mostly artists. An annual open exhibition is entitled 'Aviation Paintings of the Year' and is sponsored, amongst others, by British Aerospace and Rolls-Royce. It attracts a prize of £1,000 for the artist of what is judged to be the best exhibit. Other exhibitions are organised to commemorate many of the important events in our aviation history and members work continues to be sought by historians, publishers and collectors alike. Their paintings are hanging in service messes and clubs, museums, galleries and aviation offices throughout the world.

Enquiries regarding paintings, exhibiting or membership should be made to:
The Secretary, The Guild of Aviation Artists, Unit 418, Bondway Business Centre, 71 Bondway, Vauxhall Cross, London, SW8 1SQ.
Telephone: UK (0)171 735 0634.

SPECIAL THANKS

The Royal Air Force Benevolent Fund wishes to extend its warm and grateful appreciation to the following companies and organisations for their most generous support of the Fund by sponsoring individual pages within this book, covering the first 50 years of the distinguished history of the United States Air Force:

Aeroclub Sanicole
Aerosystems International
AIR & SPACE/Smithsonian Magazine
Airclaims Limited
Arkells Brewery Limited
Boeing Defense and Space Group
Certified Aircraft Parts Inc
Chevron Aerospace Limited
Colebrand Limited
Colonel Mary M Tripp United States Air Force
Colonel William J Ryan's family
Evans Halshaw
Flight International

GEC-Marconi Avionics
Hughes
Inflite Engineering Services Limited
Jeppesen – A Times Mirror Company
Kodak Eastman Aerial Systems
Lockheed Martin Aeronautical Systems
Lockheed Martin Corporation
Lockheed Martin Skunk Works
Lockheed Martin Tactical Aircraft Systems
Lucas Aerospace
Main Event Catering
Messier-Dowty and Dowty Aerospace
Normalair Garrett Limited

Northrop Grumman
Paul Bowen and Tim Prince
Royal Air Force News
Short Brothers plc
The B-52 Stratofortress Association
The Marshall Group of Companies
The McDonnell Douglas Corporation
The Rolls-Royce Aerospace Group
The Royal Air Force
The Royal International Air Tattoo
The Society of British Aerospace Companies
The SSVC Group
The United States Air Force Museum

The Royal Air Force Benevolent Fund would also like to extend its sincere thanks to the following companies for their exceptional support with the production of this book:

INTERFOR LIMITED
of HONG KONG
for kindly donating
some of the paper

JADE PRODUCTIONS of HONG KONG
for overseeing all aspects of production

Finally, to the following personnel and organisations who have provided invaluable assistance with the compilation of this book:

Maj Audrey Bahler, Chief, Public Affairs,
    US Air Force 50th Anniversary Office
James Binnie, Blaze International Productions Inc
Larry Davis, Aviation Historian
Luther Gore, Executive Secretary,
    The American Society of Aviation Artists
Gary S Grigg, Lockheed Martin Skunk Works
Ken Kong, Jade Productions, Hong Kong
Howard and Karen Kotlicky,
    The AvIATion Collection, USA
Robert Limbrick,
    US Air Force History Office – Art Collection
Hogan Loh, Interfor Limited, Hong Kong

David Menard, Research Division,
    The US Air Force Museum
Joseph W Stout, Lockheed Martin
    Tactical Aircraft Systems
Jim Summers, Lockheed Martin
    Aeronautical Systems
Hugo Trotter DFC, Secretary,
    The Guild of Aviation Artists
National Air and Space Museum, Washington, DC
National Archives, College Park, MD
United States Air Force Museum, Dayton, OH
11th Communications Squadron, USAF,
    Andrews AFB, MD